DATE DUE

SEP 0 1 2005	
NOV 1 4 2005	

DEMCO, INC. 38-2931

GOLD!

GOLD!

THE STORY OF THE
1848 GOLD RUSH AND
HOW IT SHAPED A NATION

FRED ROSEN

THUNDER'S MOUTH PRESS
NEW YORK

GOLD!

THE STORY OF THE 1848 GOLD RUSH AND HOW IT SHAPED A NATION

Published by
Thunder's Mouth Press
An Imprint of Avalon Publishing Group Inc.
245 West 17th St., 11th Floor
New York, NY 10011

AVALON
publishing group incorporated

Copyright © 2005 by Fred Rosen

First printing August 2005

Library of Congress Cataloging-in-Publication Data is available.

ISBN 1-56025-680-X

9 8 7 6 5 4 3 2 1

Book design by Maria Elias
Printed in the United States of America
Distributed by Publishers Group West

For Leah, whose soul always glitters

CONTENTS

14.

The Belief Lives On   *237.*

Epilogue   *253.*

Afterword
Coloma, 2005   *255.*

Appendix I
The Treaties   *261.*

Appendix II
Advice to Miners by Samuel McNeil   *291.*

Appendix III
President Polk's 1848 State of the Union Address   *293.*

Bibliography   *309.*

Index   *311.*

ACKNOWLEDGMENTS

The opportunity to write about history is as chance an occurrence as history itself. That is rather appropriate, considering this book itself is about a chance occurrence.

It was John Oakes who came up with the idea and gave me the vision. He saw first that the Gold Rush affected everybody, and I thank him for the opportunity to prove him right. Catheline Jean-François's editing and suggestions made it even better.

Lori Perkins *is* George Tobias, the great Hollywood character actor who always played the sympathetic agent. I thank her for her ideas and support and thank God she looks nothing like George Tobias.

The librarians and others at the Library of Congress in Washington, D.C., made my research easy. As did the California state rangers in Sacramento and Coloma. They are wonderful custodians of our nation's history.

Most of all, thanks to my wife, Leah, and my daughter, Sara, for their support.

AUTHOR'S NOTE

This book is a work of nonfiction, though many of its elements have been heavily fictionalized in the past. If there is any doubt about that, just glance at the story of Joaquin Murietta; it has been fictionalized so many times, it is almost impossible to tell fiction from fact.

To try to present as accurate a record as possible of the time in question, I have treated the Gold Rush as a story of investigative journalism. I have gone to the primary sources. Through research at the Library of Congress, the California Historical Society, and other databases, this book relies on firsthand accounts of the participants in the period of California's change into a state and America into a postindustrialized society. On-site research at Sutter's Fort, Coloma, Hangtown, and other towns in gold country helped to understand things first-hand.

I retain the journalistic prerogative to evaluate the information from these sources, and when two or more accounts compete, I have made a concerted judgment on which is the most truthful.

California is a neck of the woods everyone is fascinated with. It was El Dorado. I don't know anyone who was holding his breath over Prince Georges County, Maryland.

—James M. Cain,
The Baby in the Icebox and Other Short Fiction

PREFACE

I finally made it to Sutter's Fort long after my father set out for California.

In 1961, like so many young men before him, Murray had trekked to California in the hope of finding a better life for his family. I was eight years old then. I listened from the next room to the breathless, late-night phone calls in hushed tones between my mother and father about moving *"out there."*

Murray was a furrier, and the fur trade in New York was going downhill. Moving west wasn't a decision made lightly, something we had in common with every family who in the 150 years since the Gold Rush began have had to make the same difficult decision. Even in 1961, a coast-to-coast plane ticket was expensive, not to mention you might have a propeller-driven plane instead of a jet on many routes.

Murray's brother, my Uncle Harry, had prospered "out there." Harry had gone on *The $64,000 Question* and won a lot of money. And he had four fingers missing on his right hand. He took the money, opened a cigarette business, and bought a house in a place with the exotic-sounding name—to a Brooklyn native—of Montebello.

Montebello, California! It sounded so exciting! Those late-night phone calls did it. I knew that California was a place I just *had* to go to. It didn't happen early, though. My mother, Ruthie, didn't want to leave her family. They had all their digits except my Uncle Izzie, who was missing a few in the head. Her family is so close, they still all live within a mile of each other. And, as it turned out, the fur trade was no better in L.A. than it was in New York—it sucked.

My father came home; we never moved west. The illusion my father had that California could be the new El Dorado—the legendary lost city of gold—was the same one that has been inspiring people around the world since the middle of the nineteenth century. Between the Louisiana Purchase in 1806 and the beginning of the Civil War in 1861, the one event that most influenced Americans then, and now, was the California Gold Rush, which began in 1848.

People left their homes and families behind for the California Gold Rush. From all over the world they came, by land and by sea; there was no air. One in four never made it back. Hundreds of thousands of people, both here and abroad, lost relatives to the lure of the precious yellow metal.

To everyone, American and immigrant alike, who went to what became known as "the diggings," it was the absolute belief that they would get rich that fueled them. Even after the truth was known, that few of the gold seekers became rich, that you were lucky to escape the gold fields with any money let alone your life, still, they came.

On December 31, 1850, almost two years into the Gold Rush, gold sold on the world market for $20.67 per ounce. One hundred and fifty-four years later, on December 31, 2004, the price of gold was $455.75 per ounce, more than twenty times as much. With that kind of money involved, it was no wonder that the Gold Rush was a history-changing event.

The America that had existed since Colonial times, characterized by a strong work ethic and belief in a righteous God that, if he did not reward you in this life would reward you in the next, was replaced instead by a belief in the power of wealth to redeem a life without privilege. Overnight.

Yes, I'll say it again, overnight. Not *almost* overnight; I mean *overnight.*

The people who crowded into the foothills of the Sierra Nevada were the "have-nots" looking to be redeemed as the "haves." What those who survived found was the real expression of wealth.

As I looked out at the white oak tree behind the west wall of Sutter's Fort, which Sutter himself had written about, I realized that the history of those events, and how it touches us to the present day, is still being written.

Sacramento, California,
October 17, 2004

PROLOGUE

Missouri, 1847

R obert James was a very discontented man. Nothing seemed to satisfy him.

Born a Kentuckian, James grew up to become one of Missouri's most charismatic preachers. He won lasting, legitimate acclaim on February 27, 1849, when, as one of the three founders of William Jewell College in Liberty, Missouri, he helped open the doors to that private Baptist institution.

James didn't stick around Liberty long enough to see the place grow. Instead, he moved to Clay County, Missouri. There, he bought a hundred-acre farm that brought in about $70 annually for its hemp crop alone. State and county taxes totaled $10.58 yearly. That left him $59.42. And that was just one crop of many. He also rented out eighty acres, on which he received a monthly stipend.

James's assets also included thirty sheep whose wool he sold, and the hogs coveted by his neighbors. Among his prized possessions were the slaves he brought with him from his home in Kentucky when he moved to Liberty and then to Clay County. In the latter, Robert had accumulated even more wealth, enough to have a library of books that included works by Josephus, a Jewish historian of the ancient world; Charles Dickens; Aristotle in Greek; and Latin books on theology and astronomy.

These books had formed the foundation of his education, as he hoped they would of his sons, Franklin and the baby Jesse. His wife, Zerelda, had given birth to baby Jesse on September 5, 1847. Coming as it did a short time after Robert Jr. died in childbirth, James acknowledged this gift from God. And yet Robert was melancholy, depressed by his life, wishing there was something else out there to give it new meaning.

He kept looking for God, for him to show him the way to his life's purpose. He cared not for temporal things when in service to the Lord—or at least it seemed that way to his neighbors. Robert thought he would do whatever it was he felt God wanted him to do. Robert James always figured he would work in the service of the Lord. He never figured to worship any other god.

If Robert James knew that his blasphemy would lead to his family name being forever impressed into the American consciousness as synonymous with killing and evil, he probably would have tried to stop himself.

And failed.

Ohio had been Indian territory, unsafe for settlers, until the defeat of the hostiles at the Battle of Fallen Timbers in 1794, and the Treaty of Greenville in 1796. With the natives pacified, settlement within Ohio's interior became safe from the "savages," and for the first time, legal. Like all great dreamers, Colonel Ebenezer Zane of Wheeling saw an opportunity and acted on it.

Merchant, trailblazer, pioneer, soldier, Zane figured that Ohio would quickly fill with settlers. If he owned land in Ohio, he might make a pretty penny. Acting on that intuition, he petitioned Congress, which, in 1795, gave him a contract to open a road through Ohio from Wheeling to Limestone, Kentucky, a distance of 266 miles.

What became known as "Zane's Trace" was blazed into Ohio in 1797. In return, Congress granted Zane three-square-mile tracts of land at the crossings of the Muskingum, the Hocking, and the Scioto Rivers. In early 1798, the first settlers came over the Zane Trace. Two years later, in 1800, Zane decided to make his killing.

Enough settlers had arrived in the Hocking Valley. He dispatched sons Noah and John, as his attorneys, to lay out the town and sell lots. Chestnut Street, Main Street, Wheeling Street, and Mulberry Street were laid out from Pearl Street on the east to Front Street on the west. Because so many of the early settlers were Germans from the vicinity of Lancaster, Pennsylvania, the town was named "New Lancaster," and shortened to "Lancaster" in 1805.

Samuel O'Neil was born there in 1819, William Tecumseh Sherman in 1820. Though their paths would later cross, at least figuratively, they did not know each other growing up. What neither man knew was that each would play an essential role in the Gold Rush—one to a present generation, the other to a future one.

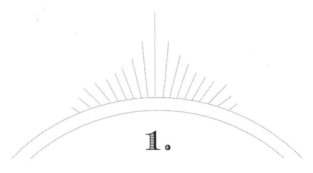

1.

NEW HELVETIA

L ooking out over the far western wall of his fort at
a newly planted white oak tree, Colonel John
Sutter felt very, very good. Before him lay the culmina-
tion of his life's work, the fort he named after himself.

It was a rectangular compound that had been built on
a hill with a sweeping view of the surrounding countryside. In the eastern yard of the fort were built into the
walls, one after the other and stretching around, the
stable, bakery stores rooms, weaving room, immigrant
room, storeroom, and cooper's shop. In the far end of
the rectangle were the beehive oven and the fire pit, next
to a small grove of birch trees.

On the west side, that yard consisted of the same con-
figuration of rooms built into the walls. There was a carpenter's shop, trade store, guest quarters, a gunsmith

shop, blacksmith shop, storage rooms, and the guard-room. On the far western side of the western yard were two covered work areas and a fire pit. In the middle of the yard was the well, and next to it, the fort's bell. The western and eastern yards met at the south gate, twenty feet high and made of rough hewn logs. If that didn't look imposing enough, there were two gun platforms on either side of the gate, each containing a two-thousand-pound cannon. Directly in front of the gates stood Sutter's headquarters.

As Sutter continued to look over his domain, beyond the fort, about five miles south, he could see Sacramento Harbor, unobstructed by anything but trees. Tents had sprung up along the banks of the Sacramento River. It was likely that in the very near future, a real town might be established. If it was, Sutter's Fort, the only bastion of civilization in the northern California wilderness, would likely get the credit . . . and the settlers money.

John Sutter would tell anyone he knew in California that he had been a member of the Swiss Guard, the elite group of Swiss mercenaries that was charged by the Vatican centuries ago with the responsibility of protecting the pope. During the middle of the French Revolution, for example, when the mob stormed the palace looking for Louis XVI, it was the Swiss Guard who mounted a valiant though vain defense of the monarchy. It was of that long and proud tradition that John Sutter claimed to be a part.

That he lied completely about being a member of this honorable group should shame him. Instead, it informs his modesty in believing that the public would not accept the real truth, nor that it would do his businesses any good. It was hard to tell where the real John Sutter stopped and the exaggerated one began.

In truth, John Sutter was not born a captain and he wasn't born in Switzerland. He was born in Germany in 1803, in the town of Baden. His birth took place during the first year of the Lewis and Clark Expedition, which would later play such a profound role in his life. Sutter's father was Swiss-born. That made John Sutter a citizen of the Swiss village of Runbenberg, where his daddy and great-granddaddy before him had been born.

When he was about twelve years old, Sutter became a publisher's apprentice in a book publishing house in Basel, on the Rhine. Sutter noticed how people could be judged by what was printed about them. It was there that he learned the value of the printed word, including the effect of manipulating it. He never forgot that.

Seeking a better financial future, he left publishing and became a store clerk. In 1826, the twenty-three-year-old Sutter married Anna Dubeld. The next day, his first son was born. Once again wasting no time, two years later in 1828, he started his own dry goods business. Sutter had an ear for language and spoke and wrote four—English, French, German, and Spanish. It was of invaluable use in his business because he could talk, in their own language, to just about anyone except Asians.

But despite his gifts, for the first time in his young life, a business venture didn't prosper; his debts grew. Even so, he spent lavishly for clothing, books, and entertainment. During those years, he trained in the Swiss militia, *not* the Swiss Guard. He rose to the rank of underlieutenant, *not* captain.

John Sutter was charming and handsome. He looked dashing in a self-designed uniform that made him look like some form of Prussian nobility. He had a gift for conversation and making friends. These were all fine attributes, he knew. He also knew that despite all that, his life on the Continent was over.

There was no way to avoid his business debts; there was only one way for him to survive financially. He was thirty-one years old and bogged down. So in 1834, John Sutter left Switzerland for good. He took his clothes and his books but left behind his wife and five children. He would send for them when his fortunes had improved. It was a not uncommon arrangement for any immigrant male at the time.

It meant that the husband would go ahead, to America. Handbills circulating on the Continent said that fortunes could be made there. Sutter had noticed advertising that particularly highlighted the opportunities in the western territories of the United States. Sutter was on deck when the ship he had sailed on from Europe came into New York Harbor. The hustle and bustle on the Wall Street wharves must have energized his entrepreneur's spirit. Seizing immediately on the opportunities to be made on the frontier, Sutter headed West and settled in the slave state of Missouri. From there, in 1835 and 1836, he joined trading caravans headed for Santa Fe.

Sutter thought he could make money by investing in real estate. He bought a hotel and dry goods business in

Westport, Kansas (now part of Kansas City). Neither proved profitable. Sutter tried selling whiskey and tobacco to the Indians. He soon found that sales of the former did not sit too well with the settlers, who had to reap the "benefits" of Sutter's liquor when the Indians got drunk and started "acting up."

Not staying around to lick his wounds or deal with his creditors—again—Sutter got a job with the American Fur Company that took him to the Hudson Bay Company's Pacific headquarters at Fort Vancouver (now in Washington State). Always on the lookout for a little adventure with his profiteering, Sutter booked passage on the company's ship *Columbia*, then embarking for Honolulu, Hawaii.

When Sutter got to Honolulu, he decided to look for a connecting passage to the town of Yerba Buena in the Gulf of San Francisco, off the California coast. Unfortunately, Sutter couldn't find any ships going there. He was stranded in Honolulu for three months before he could get one. That time, though, proved much to his liking. He enjoyed the climate and the people, finding the latter particularly industrious. Sutter began formulating an idea to exploit this.

John Sutter finally boarded the trading ship *Clementine*, bound for Sitka, a small Russian town on the Alaskan coast. This time, Sutter was not alone. He was accompanied by eight Hawaiian workers in his employ. Once in Alaska, Sutter lost no time in booking them all passage on to Yerba Buena, where they arrived on July 1, 1839. Sutter was now under the law of the Mexican government.

Taking stock of where he found himself, Sutter realized that Yerba Buena was nothing more than a tent city, with an occasional clapboard structure. Horse dung and mud blended with other foul-smelling detritus to make the streets a squishy obstacle course. There was no sewer system. It clearly was not to his liking. Yet there was something in this odoriferous metropolis that made John Sutter's genius take form.

Sutter immediately noticed that without four walls, there could be no protection. In this section of the country, there were few if any permanent structures. Worse, this was not land under the control of the U.S. government, which could then dispatch troops to protect it. This land was under the control of the Mexican government, which was as corrupt as they come.

What Sutter saw was a place desperately in need of a refuge, a fort, to protect against marauding Indians or vaqueros. It would be a place that people could seek out for refuge, protection, sustenance, fortitude—and, of course, services that John Sutter would gladly supply at a fair price. He conceived of this place as a self-sufficient entity that he would christen New Helvetia (New Switzerland), in honor of his mother country.

It was John Sutter, underlieutenant of the Swiss militia, who landed that day in Yerba Buena. But it was Captain John Sutter of the Swiss Guard who sailed out of Yerba Buena Harbor in mid-August as a visionary, an entrepreneur, and an explorer all rolled into one. What he intended when they got to where they were going was to literally carve a trading empire out of the wilderness.

That meant, of course, getting a lot of people who were already there quite angry at him.

Indians, Mormons, Californios—the native vaqueros—all of them had more right to the land than Sutter could ever have. But Sutter also knew from his experience as a debtor that it helped to have the law, whatever it was, on your side in any dispute. Plus, Sutter was cognizant enough to know that on a day-to-day basis, there was no rule of law except who had the bigger army.

Accompanying Sutter were his Hawaiian laborers and Indians he had decided to employ as well. They sailed on the schooner *Isabella*, with two other ships carrying their supplies, up the Sacramento River, to its confluence with the America River, and docked. Setting foot on the dock, Sutter saw that the place was no better in terms of permanent structures than Yerba Buena was. Sutter and his companions called the place Sacramento.

Sutter had no intention of settling in such a dump. He preferred going inland; he needed higher ground, which would be easier to defend. Sutter had his laborers build some makeshift grass structures for shelter. They would take the winter to get ready to implement his vision. To make that vision a reality, in the summer of 1840, John Sutter became a Mexican citizen, thus protecting his future property rights.

Next, followed by his Hawaiians and a growing workforce of Indians—he employed hundreds of Indians as field hands, weavers, cooks, and drivers, and paid them in clothing, food, and shelter—Sutter moved inland, about five miles from the Sacramento docks. Sutter decided to situate his fort on a high, dry patch of ground that offered a commanding view of the surrounding countryside, lush with maple, oak, birch, and aspen fir.

Sutter's design called for walls 2½ feet thick and 15 to 18 feet high. The interior was 320 feet long. Sutter began building an adobe fort in the fall of 1840. When completed in 1841, Sutter's Fort was larger than the U.S. Army's Fort Laramie.

Inside the compound, the central building of Sutter's headquarters was in the middle, directly in front of the gates. The building was three stories high and made of strong oak timbers; its top floor gave Sutter a platform from which to view his own private, burgeoning empire. Sutter had constructed quarters for some of the workers, a bakery, blanket factory, blacksmith shop, carpenter shop, and other shops dotted around the fort, fitting snuggly within the walls. On the nearby American River he located a tannery.

Sutter's concept was for his domain to be self-sufficient. He had his workforce plant acres of barley, peas, and beans. He hired vaqueros to run cattle. And then he did something that was absolutely brilliant: he advertised in the eastern papers that his fort was the place the stop, the haven, for pioneers going West.

To further protect his investment, Sutter put his Swiss militia training to good use, training his own private army of Indians. Sutter maintained an Indian guard of fifteen mounted cavalry and twenty-five infantry. He did not hesitate to punish any tribes he suspected of raiding his property. Sutter's Indian guard was so respected on the frontier that no one ever attacked his fortress.

The business that Sutter the entrepreneur knew would come, came. Russia had a problem supplying its colony in Alaska, which stretched out across the territory down the western coast of the continent. Sitka, for example, was actually easier to supply from California than Russia. Seeing this, the Russians made a deal with John Sutter to begin exporting wheat to Sitka and other Russian towns in Alaska.

Sutter established a successful trading business with pioneers and Indians alike, specializing in everything from furs and cotton to whiskey and even brandy from his own personal distillery, on the eastern side of the fort. Unfortunately, the land on which he had his fort was still owned by the Mexican government. Despite the improvements he had made, the Mexicans still owned the land.

Sutter applied to Mexican governor Juan Alvarado for a land grant. Only a Mexican citizen could be granted one, and since Sutter had taken care of that in 1840, that legal hurdle had been surmounted. Seeing an opportunity for the Mexican government to make money through Sutter's prosperity, Governor Alvarado officially deeded Sutter eleven leagues of land, or 47,827 acres! Alvarado made it clear in the grant that Sutter was to maintain order among the Indians and "secure the land for Mexico in return."

Returning to his fort with the grant in hand, Sutter carried something else in his other. Handing the Mexican flag to one of his men, he ordered that it be raised above the fort. Anyone who came to Sutter's Fort would know instantly that they were on Mexican land. Sutter began to see a flow of settlers into his fort, who came for respite, supplies, and shelter.

They partook of the goods and services he offered. Business was good, good enough for Sutter to buy Fort Ross, in nearby Alta. To Sutter it was just another deal; he bought the fort on $30,000 credit, which he agreed to pay off in four years with a combination of produce and coin. In return, Sutter got Fort Ross's supply stores, lumber, cannon, hardware, and livestock.

For the U.S. government, the deal was even better. The Russians owned Fort Ross and were the next-to-last foreigners to get out of the United States and its contiguous territories. Mexico was to be next—that had to happen eventually. For the country to expand, they needed all foreign powers off of it. Russia was now one less country to worry about.

He made regular trips to the territorial capital in Monterey, where he established himself as a political presence. In 1844 he met William Maxwell Wood, a ship's surgeon, on one of his regular visits there.

"Captain Sutter was a man of medium or rather low stature, but with a marked military air," Wood later wrote. "He wore a cap and a plain blue frockcoat; a mustache covered his lips. His head was of a very singular formation, being flat and well shaped behind and rising high over the crown, with a lofty and expanded forehead. His manners were courteous."

For the first time since leaving Switzerland, Sutter was

beginning to enjoy life. Part of that was his love of waffles. Sutter liked them made from wild duck eggs and coarse grain flour from his own mill, cooked on an open fire in a rectangular iron pan that had been divvied up into numerous small, square indentations that gave the waffle its unique shape.

By 1845, Captain John Sutter of the Swiss Guard was prospering. He owned 4,000 head of cattle, 1,700 horses and mules, and 3,000 sheep. He was doing well. While no more than 50 people stayed inside the fort at any one time, a maximum of 200 could use the fort during daylight hours.

Sutter even got to help out his adopted country of Mexico in a military capacity. That happened in February 1845, when the governor needed military assistance against a revolt. He appointed John Sutter "Captain of Sacramento troops" and gave him a land grant of 33 leagues, which superseded his previous one.

With his businesses going well, Sutter finally sent for his wife and children. They joined him from Europe. Everything was looking up. His control of the frontier trade through his fort was unrivaled. His agricultural and cattle interests were extensive. He had plans for a new sawmill to help supply the lumber needs of settlers. There was no reason to assume anything would change that. With his businesses flourishing, Sutter was now poised to become the multimillionaire he had always wanted to be.

A long way from the plains of Lambertsville, New Jersey, where he'd grown up, a middle-aged James Marshall, thirty-three years old, rode his horse through the soaring Sierra Nevadas. In one way or another, he had been traveling for the past decade.

Marshall had drifted west after his parents died in the 1830s. He settled in Missouri on a nice piece of property on the banks of the Missouri River. There he began farming. He was just about to make a go of it when he caught malaria. His treatment was exactly the same as it had been for General Washington's troops in 1775: massive doses of quinine. It worked. Marshall's fever abated, but the Missouri doctors told him he needed a drier, more hospitable climate if he were survive even six more months. Marshall took that as a mandate to do what most people did in 1840s when times were bad: continue to go west. There was still a mythic quality to the West.

To be sure, Lewis and Clark and their Corps of Discovery had been there first, back in the early part of the century. Since that time, the West had not been fully settled by white men. In 1844, when Marshall took the Oregon Trail west, it had been only *one year* since the first wagon train had departed Missouri for Oregon.

Watching Marshall's wagon train depart was preacher Robert James of Clay County, who stayed behind.

There was his family to consider, which now consisted of his wife, Zerelda, and their young son, Franklin. That plus his hemp crop and his slaves made him a fairly contented man by Southern standards, for while Missouri was a border state, Clay County was controlled by slave-holding families. No, it would take a lot more than simply settling in a new land for Robert James to leave his family, his home, and his God.

And so, while pioneers flowed west, and his family was firmly ensconced at their farm and his slaves in the field, James left home and hearth on a spiritual journey back to his Kentucky roots to decide what to do about his future.

While Robert James was visiting Kentucky, James Marshall arrived in Oregon in 1845 and for some reason didn't like the place. Taking to horse again, Marshall wound up in July of that year mounting a rise just south of Port Sacramento. Looking down, there in the middle of no place was a huge adobe fort set in a perfect rectangle. It was ideally situated on a hilltop, with a view of the Sacramento River harbor. Marshall rode his horse up to the fort and faced the giant gates. They were open, and the first thing that hit Marshall was the activity. He saw the shops that Sutter had set up all around the interior perimeter, and the open areas. The place was full of people, a veritable shopping plaza.

James Marshall was a very clever man, but he did not know that he was the only wheelwright in all of northern California. Combining the talents of both a carpenter and a blacksmith, Marshall specialized in producing wheels for carriages, stagecoaches, whatever was needed to keep people and freight going. It was a very important talent to have in an outpost of civilization where such skills were heavily valued.

Realizing this, Sutter hired him immediately. Plying his trade in the fort's blacksmith shop, Marshall soon made enough to buy a ranch outside the fort, on Butte Creek. He was excited at the prospect of farming again.

Marshall was perfectly content to continue and perhaps end his life as a farmer. It gave him peace and contentment and quelled the desire to have a drink. Marshall was an inveterate drinker of alcohol, so anything that stopped him from drinking was inherently, in his opinion, a good thing. Sutter, meanwhile, had taken special pains to become a Mexican citizen so he'd own vast tracts of land on his march to entrepreneurial independence.

Neither man expected what happened next. History always has a way of biting its participants in the ass.

2.

MARSHALL ON THE MOVE

I t had been a long time coming. Ever since Texas declared independence from Mexico in 1836, the final showdown with Mexico was inevitable. While the United States, Britain, and France all acknowledged the Republic of Texas as a free and independent state, Mexico reneged on its promise and did not.

What's more, Texans fixed their southernmost boundary at the Rio Grande. The Mexicans felt it should be a hundred miles farther north, encompassing millions of fertile acres. The Texans also wanted to be annexed by the United States and had unsuccessfully petitioned the U.S. Congress to do exactly that. The Mexicans, in turn, were outraged that the United States was trying to cheat them out of what was rightfully their property.

By 1844, this border dispute led to calls for war in both countries. Before President John Tyler could act, he lost the election to James K. Polk, who favored annexation. Polk's inauguration was in March 1845, but Tyler thought that too long too wait. To hasten things along, the lame duck president suggested a joint resolution of Congress offering Texas statehood.

The new state would have to meet certain preset conditions to become an official member of the Union. Accordingly, the U.S. Congress passed the Texas annexation resolution on February 28, 1845. All that was left was for envoy Andrew Jackson Donelson to get to Texas and get the Texans to sign on the dotted line.

The United States sent government agents to Texas to lobby the citizens to accept annexation as the only viable option for the state's future. Texas public opinion, already in support of annexation, skewed the pendulum even farther. Now it was all up to two bodies: the Texas Congress and a specially convened state constitutional election.

Anson Jones, president of the Texas Republic, called the Texas Congress to order on June 16, 1845. He did the same with the state delegates on July 4. Each body was given a choice: annexation to the United States, or independence recognized by Mexico. Seeing little future with the latter solution, both voted for the former. Quickly, the state delegates drew up a state constitution. Ratified by popular vote in October 1845, it was accepted by the U.S. Congress on December 29, 1845. On that date, Texas entered the Union as a state that allowed slavery within its borders.

In leaving his post as the last president of the Republic of Texas, Anson Jones said, "The final act in this great drama is now performed; the Republic of Texas is no more." Not only was Jones wrong, his counterpart, General Santa Anna, the same Santa Anna who had butchered Davy Crockett, Jim Bowie, and the Alamo defenders, *that* Santa Anna was still alive and well as Mexico's dictator.

"The new state had come into the Union claiming the Rio Grande as her southern and western boundary. By the terms of annexation all boundary disputes with Mexico were referred by Texas to the government of the United States. President Polk sent John Slidell of Louisiana to Mexico in the autumn of 1845 to adjust any differences over the Texan claims. But though Slidell labored for months to get a hearing . . . Mexico refused to recognize him, and he was dismissed from the country in August 1846," explains David Saville Muzzey in his popular 1911 text, *American History*.

President Polk ordered General Zachary Taylor to the southern U.S./Texas border, which had been previously established in the annexation ratification as the Rio Grande. When Taylor got there, he saw that Mexican troops had already fortified the southern bank of the river. The Mexicans ordered Taylor to retreat; he refused. The Mexican commander then crossed the Rio Grande, ambushing a scouting force of sixty-three Americans. The killed and wounded Americans added up to sixteen. As soon as President Polk received word of the attack in early May, he sent a special message to Congress that concluded:

"We have tried every effort at reconciliation. . . . But now, after reiterated menaces, Mexico has passed the boundary of the United States [the Rio Grande], has invaded our territory and shed American blood upon the American soil. She has proclaimed that hostilities have commenced, and that the two nations are at war. As war exists, and, notwithstanding all our efforts to avoid it, exists by the act of Mexico herself, we are called upon by every consideration of duty and patriotism to vindicate with decision the honor, the rights, and the interests of our country."

By a vote of 174 to 4, the House approved a measure to go to war with Mexico. The Senate followed with an even more impressive 40 to 2 vote. Back in Texas, Taylor was not waiting for orders. He had engaged the Mexicans in the Battles of Palo Alto and Resaca de la Palma and pushed them back into Mexico.

Six days after Congress voted to sanction the war, Taylor crossed the Rio Grande and occupied the Mexican frontier town of Matamoros. Making the town his base, during the summer and autumn of 1846 he captured the capitals of three of the Mexican provinces. But as with most wars, the government had more in mind than the Republic of Texas, which had become the biggest state in the Union in land size.

No; the United States had other matters in mind, especially the last two parts of the continental United States still under Mexican control: New Mexico and California. New Mexico and Texas were big but California was the real prize. Its fertile lands, a vibrant, Spanish-influenced character, and most importantly, its border on the Pacific Ocean and the attendant trade made California the greatest prize of all. It was no surprise, then, when Lieutenant Colonel John C. Frémont arrived in Upper California in early 1846. He had been there the previous year, when looking out upon the entrance to San Francisco Bay, he called it Chrysoplylae (Golden Gate). The name stuck. Already famous as an explorer of the Far West, Frémont was there to search out "a new and shorter route from the western base of the Rocky Mountains to the mouth of the Columbia River." That was the official government story given out by Secretary of State William L. Marcy.

The possibility that the handsome and dashing Frémont could be working as a government operative in foreign territory the United States prized was never mentioned publically. Nor, for that matter, was Frémont's close relationship with his father-in-law, Missouri's expansionist senator, Thomas Hart Benton.

Frémont next showed up in Monterey in the spring of 1846, in command of an all-civilian party of "explorers." The only one in uniform, Frémont petitioned General José Castro, the Mexican government's commander of Upper California's military forces, for permission to quarter his men securely in the San Joaquin Valley. At first Castro granted permission, but then reneged. There was a good possibility that Frémont, well known and respected, could easily incite American settlers to revolt against Mexico.

Frémont wasted no time in responding to his censure. He went to the top of a mountain adjacent to Monterey.

There, Frémont had his men build a makeshift fort, which, he told anyone who would listen, he would defend in a "fight to extremity . . . trusting to our country to avenge our death."

Rhetoric aside, Frémont was a practical man. Whoever the men he commanded really were—explorers, soldiers, or a combination of both—he had little or no confidence in their fighting prowess. It only took Frémont a few days of siege warfare by the Mexicans to decide to retreat. He managed to spirit his men out and away from the Mexican lines before the Mexicans realized what was going on.

A messenger from Washington, D.C., Lieutenant Archibald Gillespie, caught up with Frémont, who was in camp at Klamath Lake, Oregon. Gillespie carried a dispatch from Frémont's military superiors. Frémont read his secret orders, then mounted his men up and headed them south. Frémont turned up at Sutter's Fort, where he demanded that Sutter replenish his supplies. While Frémont was with Sutter, settlers outside the fort revolted against the Mexicans.

On June 6, 1846, the California rebels took over the Mexican garrison at Sonoma. Instead of hoisting a U.S. flag, the rebels instead put up a crudely made piece of cloth that bore the rough likeness of a grizzly bear. Thus was born "the Bear Flag Revolt," in which California was declared by the rebels as a separate republic, much like Texas had been a decade earlier. This time, Washington's response was swift.

President Polk ordered Commodore John D. Sloat to sail from Mazatlán to the territorial governor's office in

Monterey. The rebels gave up without a fight. On July 5, 1846, sailors from Sloat's flagship *Savannah* raised the American flag over the Mexican customs house. Sloat also brought California the news that America had been officially at war with Mexico since the past May.

Unlike Texas and New Mexico, acquiring California did not engender any gunplay. The Mexicans surrendered without firing a shot at Yerba Buena, Sonoma, and Los Angeles. In honor of their victory, the Americans renamed Yerba Buena, San Francisco. There was one other place in California left for Frémont to conquer: Sutter's Fort.

John Sutter had chosen to ally himself for monetary gain with the government of Mexico. Never mind that Sutter did more business with American settlers than with any other group of people, or that he could never in his wildest dreams imagine himself firing on an American soldier. Sutter was a Mexican citizen, and his fort was, technically, Mexican property. Frémont promptly took it over and raised the American flag.

It was a crowning moment as one king began the process of usurping another. Like Sutter, Frémont knew that part of that process was accumulating real estate. The land, itself, would prove to be invaluable. Frémont purchased large tracts of land fifty miles outside of Sacramento, along the American River.

While he was at Sutter's Fort, Frémont made James Marshall's acquaintance. Marshall became one of the volunteers whom Frémont recruited for the next part of his drive to have all of California securely under U.S. control. Sutter may have been thinking that his luck had run out with the detested Frémont's annexation of his fort and the loss of his wheelwright to Frémont's blandishments.

As luck would have it, the winter of 1846 was settling in hard. The passes through the northern mountains had cut off a wagon train full of settlers. They were stranded in the northern snows. That natural disaster was about to give Sutter's Fort reams of free publicity in Eastern newspapers, the same ones he advertised in.

The California Star newspaper was the first to report on the incident:

Distressing News

by Capt. J. A. Sutter's launch which arrived here a few days since from Fort Sacramento—we received a letter from a friend at that place, containing a most distressing account of the situation of the emigrants in the mountains, who were prevented from crossing them by the snow,—and of a party of eleven who attempted to come into the valley on foot. The writer, who is well qualified to judge, is of the opinion that the whole party might have reached the California valley before the first fall of snow, if the men had exerted themselves as they should have done. Nothing but a contrary and contentious disposition on the part of some of the men belonging to the party prevented them from getting in as soon as any of the first companies.

The following particulars we extracted from the letter:

"The company is composed of twenty three waggons [sic], and is a part of Col. Russell's company that left the rendezvous on Indian Creek near the Missouri line on the 13th day of May last. They arrived at Fort Bridger in good time, some two weeks earlier than the last company on the road. From that point they took the new road by the south end of the Great Salt Lake, which was then being marked out by some seventy five waggons [sic] with Messrs. Hastings and Headspath as pilots.

"They followed on in the train until they were near the Weber River canion [sic], and within some 4 or 5 days travel of the leading waggons [sic], when they stopped and sent on three men (Messrs. Reed, Stanton and Pike) to the first company to request Mr. Hastings to go back and show them the pack trail from the Red Fork of Weber River to the Lake. Mr. H. went back and showed them the trail, and then returned to our company, all of which time we remained in camp, waiting for Mr. Hastings to show us the rout.

"They then commenced making the new road over the Lake on the pack trail, so as to avoid the Weber river canion [sic], and Mr. Reed and others, who left the company, and came in for assistance, informed me that they were sixteen days making the road, as the men would not work one quarter of their time. Had they gone on the road that we had made for them, they would have easily overtaken us before we reached the old road on Mary's river.

"They were then but some 4 of 5 days travel behind the first waggons [sic], which were travelling [sic] slow, on account of being obliged to make an entire new rout for several hundred miles through heavy sage and over mountains, and delayed four days by the guides hunting out passes in the mountains, and these waggons [sic] arrived at the settlement about the first of October. Had they gone around the old road, the north end of the Great Salt Lake, they would have been in the first of September.

"After crossing the long drive of 75 miles without water or grass, and suffering much from loss of oxen, they sent on two men (Messrs. Stanton and McCutcher). They left the company recruiting on the second long drive of 35 miles, and came in to Capt. J. A. Sutter's Fort, and asked for assistance.

"Capt. Sutter in his usual prompt and generous manner, furnished them with 7 of his best mules and two of his favorite Indian vaqueros, and all of the flour and beef that they wanted. Mr. C. S. Stanton, a young gentlemen from Syracuse, New York, took charge of the vaqueros and provisions, and returned to the company. Afterwards, Mr. Reed came in almost exhausted from starvation; he was supplied with a still larger number of horses and mules and all the provisions he could take. He returned as far as the Bear River valley, and found snow so deep, that he could not get to the company. He cached the provisions at that place and returned.

"Since that time (the middle of November), we heard nothing of the company, until last week, when a messenger was sent down from Capt. Wm. Johnson's settlement, with the astounding information that five women and two men had arrived at that point entirely naked, their feet frost bitten— and informed them that the company arrived within three miles of the small log cabin near Trucky's Lake on the east side of the mountains, and found the snow so deep that they could not travel, and fearing starvation, sixteen of the strongest (11 males and 5 females) agreed to start for the settlement on foot. Scantily clothed and provided with provisions they commenced that horrid journey over the mountains that Napoleon's fete on the Alps was child's play compared with.

"After wandering about a number of days bewildered in the snow, their provisions gave out, and long hunger made it necessary to resort to that horrid recourse casting lots to see who should give up life, that their bodies might be used for food for the remainder. But at this time the weaker began to die which rendered it unnecessary to take life, and as they died the company went into camp and *made meat of the dead bodies of their companions.*

Nine of the men died and seven of them were eaten by their companions—The first person that died was Mr. C. S. Stanton, the young man who so generously returned to the company with Capt. Sutter's two Indian vaqueros and provisions; his body was left on the snow. The last two that died was Capt. Sutter's two Indian vaqueros and their bodies were used as food by the seven that came in. The company left behind, numbers sixty odd souls; ten men, the balance women and children. They are in camp about 100 miles from Johnson's, the first house after leaving the mountains, or 150 from fort Sacramento. They say that Capt. Sutter's seven mules were stolen by the Indians a few days after they reached the company, which had provisions sufficient to last them until the middle of February.

The party that came in were at one time 36 hours in a snow storm without fire; they had but three quilts in the company. I could state several most horrid circumstances connected with this affair such as one of the women being obliged to eat part of the body of her father and brother, another saw her husband's heart cooked & eaten, which would be more suitable for a hangman's journal than the columns of a family newspaper.

I have not had the satisfaction of seeing any one of the party that has arrived; but when I do, I will get more of the particulars and send them to you."

As soon as we received the information we drew up the appeal of which I enclose you a copy, calling a meeting in the armory of the Fort, explained the object of the meeting and solicited the names of all that would go. *We were only able to raise seven here,*—they started this morning for Johnson's to join the party raised there.

Capt. J. A. Sutter in his usual generous manner ordered his overseer to give this brave band of men all the provisions they could carry. They took as much beef, bread, and sugar as they thought they could carry and started in good spirits on their long and perilous trip. Capt. Kern the commander of the Sacramento District, will go up as far as Johnson's to-morrow to assist in starting the party, and may go as far as the Bear River Valley.

It's interesting how no place in the story is the name "Donner" mentioned, though this is the first public report of what became known as the "Donner Party." That was the name bestowed by sensationalistic frontier newspapers to that party of westward-traveling migrants who included the families of brothers George and Jacob Donner. During the winter of 1846–1847 they became trapped in the Sierra Nevada by the early winter.

Most lived in makeshift cabins; others in canvas huts that did little to keep out the elements. One by one the would-be settlers died, until finally survivors resorted to cannibalism to stay alive. As the above account makes clear, even Sutter's rescuers were not immune to the weather and that most basic of survival instincts.

Even as outside help was trying to come to their assistance, the Donner Party did its best to endure in subzero temperatures. Patrick Breen, who was born in Ireland and came to the United States in 1828, was one member of the Donner Party. Eight of the others were his wife and seven children, with whom he began the overland trek from Iowa on April 5, 1846, to California. Even as conditions deteriorated with the weather, Breen continued to keep a diary.

Frid 26th Froze hard last night today clear & warm Wind S: E: blowing briskly Marthas jaw swelled with the toothache; hungry times in camp, plenty hides but the folks will not eat them we eat them with a tolerable good apetite. Thanks be to Almighty God.
Amen Mrs Murphy said here yesterday that thought she would commence on Milt. & eat him. I dont that she has done so yet, it is distressing.
The Donnos [Donners] told the California folks that they commence to eat the dead people 4 days ago, if they did not succeed that day or next in finding their cattle then under ten or twelve feet of snow & did not know the spot or near it, I suppose they have done so ere this time.

Of the eighty-three members of the Donner Party who were trapped in the High Sierra, only forty-five survived to reach California. Breen and his entire family were fortunate enough to be among the survivors who staggered into Sutter's Fort after they were rescued.

But even as this story was breaking in northern California, in the southern part of the newly liberated Mexican province, the Mexican-American War was still going on. In October 1846, insurrectionists attempted to besiege the U.S. garrison in the old pueblo of Los Angeles. It seemed that the United States had neglected, as it had almost since its inception, its intelligence services. Admiral Stockton did not know that the southern Californians still held a Spanish/Mexican identity.

There in Los Angeles, the Mexican militia handed the U.S. military an embarrassing defeat. Not only did they kick the Americans out of the pueblo, they also kept them out despite repeated attempts to reenter. In addition to regular soldiers, the Mexican militia numbered cultured, well-educated, well-trained *caballeros* from families of "good blood." These were the Californios, who went back generations on California soil and who had much to lose if the Americans won.

Since 1769, Californios had lived in California. They were Spanish-speaking California natives who dated their ancestry back to the Spanish Franciscan priests, the *freys*, who built missions or churches up and down the coast. Their herculean efforts were in the service of God; they hoped to convert all the Indians to Christianity to save their souls.

The Californios had been granted their land rights by the Spanish king himself, and were later acknowledged by their Mexican conquerors. They had carved out of the virgin country huge ranchos, or cattle ranches, up and down the coast. Besides raising cattle, the ranchos also had a terrific cattle hide and tallow trade. Some of the ranchos made excellent wines; others grew citrus oranges and lemons that attracted an international trade.

By 1849, two hundred Californio families owned approximately fourteen million acres of prime California land. But there was no guarantee that the Americans, despite protestations to the contrary, would continue to honor the Spanish land grants, which took in millions of miles of California's prime lands.

Frémont and the California volunteers, including wheelwright James Marshall, were on the move. Riding south to Los Angeles, they were to be one of the cavalry units that, along with infantry, artillery, and naval forces, would combine to assault the Los Angeles pueblo where the Mexican militia was still holding out.

By January 8, 1847, Frémont had not yet arrived. The commanding officers, Admiral Stockton and General Kearney, decided they had staged their forces long enough; they would attack without Frémont. The American forces met the Californios on January 8 and 9 at the Battles of Rio San Gabriel and La Mesa. Both times, the Californios, under the command of General José Maria Flores, failed to beat back the American advance. On January 10, just as Frémont and his volunteers finally showed up, the Americans retook Los Angeles.

The beaten militia retreated into the shadow of the San Fernando Valley, near a little settlement later named Pasadena. As they did, Frémont marched his men farther west and occupied Mission San Fernando. Frémont knew he had him, so he sent a messenger, Jesus Pico, to General Flores's camp. Frémont wanted to see if he could negotiate surrender without further bloodshed.

Realizing the hopelessness of the situation, General Flores decided to save himself. He turned over command to his executive officer, and rode south. The Mexican officers who were left decided to sue for peace. On January 14, 1847, Pico, the new commander in chief of Mexican forces in California, met Frémont at the adobe house of Tomas Feliz outside the pueblo. Signed and countersigned on Feliz's kitchen table, the treaty ended the uprising in California.

Afterward, Frémont gave Sutter back his fort. Sutter hated his guts for the rest of his life. Still, he had more important matters to deal with now that he had his fort back under his personal control. Sutter hadn't stopped making money just because a war was on. He had run his businesses all along like nothing special was going on, even when Frémont was in control. It had become obvious that he didn't have enough lumber to help businesses and settlers build outside the fort. What he needed was a sawmill.

A sawmill set up on a river needed a waterwheel that powered the operation. He needed someone to strike out from the fort and find a path to a river that had enough force to power a paddlewheel and had enough timber to give the sawmill a regular supply. Of course, at the heart of the operation was the waterwheel. Without that, there was no power. And, as Sutter well knew, there were few men who were wheelwrights.

As luck would have it, in mid-1847, Marshall's volunteer enlistment with Frémont ran out. Like many of the other volunteers, they went home. When he returned to Sutter's Fort in 1847, Marshall found his ranch in ruins, his livestock missing, probably rustled. With no other means of supporting himself, Marshall went back to work as a wheelwright for Sutter, who put him to work immediately on the problem of where to situate and construct his sawmill.

Back in Clay County, Missouri, preacher Robert James watched as the county's men lined up to enlist in the First Regiment of Missouri Mounted Volunteers, commanded by Colonel Alexander Doniphan. Doniphan's brother-in-law, O. O. Moss, was busy, too. In nearby Liberty, Moss put together a company of more than a hundred men.

Instead of going to war with the Mexicans, Robert James had refreshed himself in the wellspring of his childhood. James returned home from Kentucky, passing recruit after recruit on the open road. When he got home, he could think of nothing except saving more souls for Christ and being with his family. And then God bestowed on his family the greatest blessing he could imagine.

Zerelda got pregnant again, and this time everything went well. She gave birth to a healthy baby boy on September 5, 1847. Now Robert could imagine nothing that would ever take him away from the bosom of his family, and his new son. Christened by Robert himself, the baby was named Jesse Woodson James.

3.

MARSHALL IN THE RACE,
JANUARY 24, 1848

James Marshall tramped along the banks of the southern fork of the American River. He would later remember the morning as cold, dark, and rainy. The wheelwright's keen intellect was on the problem at hand.

Building the tailrace had required damming up and redirecting some of the river's water. The tailrace, which carried water away from the mill, was much too shallow; the water kept backing up, which meant the millwheel had difficulty turning. That meant no wood being cut up. If the waterwheel didn't run, his and Sutter's investment would be ruined. Marshall knew that the solution was to deepen the tailrace. And the way to do that, Marshall also knew, was to have his Indian laborers loosen the rock by day. At night, they would allow the dammed-up water to flow through, washing away all the loose stones too small for the Indians to pull out.

That work had been going on for a while. It had become Marshall's habit to inspect the tailrace early in the morning before the laborers began their day's work. The weed-strewn path he traveled on went a few hundred yards downstream from the mill. The path had been blazed by the workmen during the summer months, when the mill had been built with the big timbers cut from the hardwood trees that were abundant on the south fork.

The sawmill project had actually started the previous year—in May 1847.

"With my rifle, blanket, and a few crackers to eat with the venison (for the deer then were awful plenty), I ascended the American River, according to Mr. Sutter's wish, as he wanted to find a good site for a saw-mill, where we could have plenty of timber, and where wagons would be able to ascend and descend the river hills," Marshall later wrote. "Many fellows had been out before me, but they could not find any place to suit; so when I left I told Mr. Sutter I would go along the river to its very head and find the place, if such a place existed, anywhere upon the river or any of its forks.

"I traveled along the river the whole way. Many places would suit very well for the erection of the tile mill, with plenty of timber everywhere, but then nothing but a mule could climb the hills; and when I would find a spot where the hills were not steep, there was no timber to be had; and so it was until I had been out several days and reached this place, which, after first sight, looked like the exact spot we were hunting."

Marshall was thinking forward to the transporting of the sawmill's timbers to Sutter's Fort. Without a well-blazed trail, the project wouldn't work. He spent the next couple of days scouting the area until he found a place where the ground was level enough that the wagons could negotiate those foothills relatively easily. Then, on his return to the fort, Marshall went out through the country examining the canyons and gulches, picking out the easiest places for crossing them with loaded wagons.

When he finally arrived back at the fort, "Mr. Sutter was pleased when I reported my success. We entered into partnership; I was to build the mill, and he was to find provisions, teams, tools, and to pay a portion of the men's wages. I believe I was at that time the only wheelwright in the whole country.

"In August, everything being ready, we freighted two wagons with tools and provisions, and accompanied by six men I left the fort, and after a good deal of difficulty reached this place one beautiful afternoon and formed our camp on yon little rises of ground."

The first thing Marshall needed to do was put up some "long houses, as we intended remaining here all winter. This was done in less than no time, for my men were great with the ax. We then cut timber, and fell to work hewing it for the framework of the mill. The Indians gathered about us in great numbers. I employed about forty of them to assist us with the dam [building]."

A low dam was built across the river by the Indians and

a labor force formed from members of the U.S. Army's Mormon Battalion. Central to the plan's success was the ability of the Indians to work side by side with the whites. They did, forming within Marshall a lifelong respect for Indians. When it was finished, in only four weeks, the dam funneled part of the stream into a diversion channel that carried it through the mill.

"In digging the foundation of the mill we cut some distance into the soft granite; we opened the fore bay and then I left for the fort, giving orders to Mr. Weimar to have a ditch cut through the bar in the rear of the mill, and after quitting work in the evening to raise the gate and let the water run all night, as it would assist us very much in deepening and widening the tail-race."

When Marshall returned a few days later, he found work proceeding well, with all the men at work in the ditch. By January 1848 the mill was ready to be tested.

"When the channel was opened it was my custom every evening to raise the gate and let the water wash out as much sand and gravel through the night as possible; and in the morning, while the men were getting breakfast, I would walk down, and, shutting off the water, look along the race and see what was to be done, so that I might tell Mr. Weimar, who had charge of the Indians, at what particular point to set them to work for the day. As I was the only wheelwright present, all of my time was employed upon the framework and machinery."

The January rain beat down on Marshall's slouch hat with a wide band. Despite the greatcoat he wore, the chill, wet mountain air from the Sierra Nevada penetrated his coat; he felt it in his bones. Marshall had a bit of a nip every now and then to keep warm. He was near the bank of the race, about two hundred feet from the western end of the mill, when "My eye was caught with the glimpse of something shining in the bottom of the ditch.

"There was about a foot of water running then. I reached my hand down and picked it up; it made my heart thump, for I was certain it was gold. The piece was about half the size and of the shape of a pea.

"Then, I saw another piece in the water! After taking it out, I sat down and began to think right hard. I thought it was gold, and yet it did not seem to be of the right color: all the gold coin I had seen was of a reddish tinge; this looked more like brass. I recalled to mind all the metals I had ever seen or heard of, but I could find none that resembled this.

"Suddenly the idea flashed across my mind that it might be iron pyrites. I trembled to think of it. This question could soon be determined. Putting one of the pieces on a hard river stone, I took another and commenced hammering it. It was soft, and didn't break: It therefore must be gold, but largely mixed with some other metal, very likely silver; for pure gold, I thought, would certainly have a brighter color."

Marshall was used to thinking on his feet. It just made sense that if there was one chunk, there might be another, washed down from the mountains in the rain. Marshall turned and headed out on the race toward the river. He hadn't gone far before he dipped his hand down in the brackish water and snatched up one . . . two . . . three . . .

four more golden rocks, all in less than half an hour. Similar to the first one except of different sizes, these, too, he put into the depressed crown of his hat.

It was enough for now, enough to at least test if he had really made a find. Soon, Marshall made his way back upstream to the mill. Coming on it, all of a sudden, without knowing it was there, it made quite a sight. It rose out of the primordial forest like a strange, surreal harbinger of the future. It was industrialization brought to the wilderness and the wilderness didn't have any choice.

There, soaring fifty feet into the air over the riverbank was Marshall and Sutter's sawmill. A latticework of broodingly large oak timbers, it was dominated by the magnificent waterwheel that powered it. It was Marshall's wheelwright talent that produced a paddlewheel that, when operated correctly, would power the mill's saw to cut the wood for sales at as quick a rate as any machine on the planet.

Most of the millworkers who hustled about as they began their morning labors were the same Mormon and Indian labor who had helped to build the mill that summer. Marshall respected his men and cared nothing of their backgrounds. The men looked up when they saw their boss coming.

"Boys, I believe I have found a gold mine!" Marshall announced.

There is some elemental connection to gold on the cellular level. It makes human beings turn into happy, raving lunatics when they discover it. Henry W. Bigler, one of the Mormon workers, was the first to drop his tools and crowd in when he saw Marshall take off his hat and take the glittering chunks out of his hatband.

"It appeared to be gold," Bigler later said. "They ranged in size from the tiniest fleck to a grain of wheat."

Still, they couldn't be sure. They were carpenters and laborers, not geology experts. Neither was Marshall. Alan Scott, a carpenter who worked at the mill, disagreed with Marshall. He felt sure it was not that most valuable of elements.

"I know it to be nothing else," Marshall replied with great confidence.

Marshall took his find, and in front of the assembled throng, beat it on an anvil to show how malleable it was. It was also bitten. The cook, Jenny Wimmer, was making up a vat of lye soap. If the stuff really was gold, it would drop to the bottom of the barrel and resist the lye's corrosive qualities. Rising to the challenge, Marshall dropped all of the gold in the corrosive vat.

It sunk into the brackish mixture; the color faded from gold to nothing. When the mixture was subsequently poured out, that unmistakable golden hue began to shine through from the bottom of the barrel until finally, with the lye soap mixture emptied, it was clear that all of the gold had indeed not only survived its bath, but had indeed fallen to the bottom of the barrel, where Marshall recovered his find. Marshall took special note of the emotion of the men around him.

"They were all a good deal excited, and had they not thought that the gold only existed in small quantities they would have abandoned everything and left me to finish my job alone. However, to satisfy them, I told them that as soon as we had the mill finished we would devote a week or two to gold hunting and see what we could make out of it."

That night, Bigler wrote in his diary, "Thus was first received, James W. Marshall discovering of gold at Sutter's sawmill, Coloma, California, Monday, January 24, 1848."

For the next week or so, while they worked in the race after this discovery, Marshall and his men always kept a sharp lookout. "Men searched in the race excitedly," said Marshall. "They'd spy a flash of gold, in the early morning sunlight and pick up the pieces with their fingers. Sometimes, they had to use the blade of a knife to pry [the gold] loose [from the rock]."

In the course of three or four days, he and his men had picked up a total of what Marshall estimated was about three ounces of gold. They kept the work up, encouraged at their labors. But none of them, not Marshall or his men, ever dreamed that they were standing right then and there on a mother lode of gold. In fact, some still doubted the validity of the find.

Millworker Azariqah Smith wrote in his January 30 journal entry, "This week Mr. Marshall found some peace [sic] of (as well suppose) gold, and he has gone to the fort for the purpose of finding out.

"In about a week's time after the discovery, I had to take another trip to the fort; and, to gain what information I could respecting the real value of the metal, took all that we had collected with me." Marshall set out by himself for Sutter's Fort.

*   *   *

Beginning in May 1847, the U.S. government opened peace talks with Mexico. President Polk sent Nicholas Trist, a veteran diplomat who spoke fluent Spanish, to Mexico to negotiate a settlement. Immediately he ran into problems.

Despite the fact that they were losing, the Mexicans didn't want to admit it. A second problem was that Trist had words with General Winfield Scott, the overall commander of the American troops attacking Mexico within her borders. It took a while, but they managed to iron out their personality difficulties just in time for the Battles of Contreras and Churubusco, both of which the Americas won decisively. By August 1847 Scott's men were a few miles from the gates of Mexico City. At that point, the Mexicans were ready to talk.

Trist met with the commissioners representing the Mexican government: José Herrera, Bernardo Couto, Ignacio Mora y Villamil, and Miguel Atristan. They settled on terms that *el presidente*, General Santa Anna, rejected. *El presidente* then resumed hostilities. It was probably the greatest mistake he had ever made.

Twice Santa Anna had gotten the Americans angry. The first time was when he slaughtered the Alamo defenders, which led to the enraged American battle cry "Remember the Alamo!" in the subsequent Battle of San Jacinto that Santa Anna lost. The second time was not agreeing to the agreement his peace commissioners had negotiated and going to war against the United States.

It didn't take long for Scott and his men to conquer Mexico City. Santa Anna was removed from power by the Mexicans themselves and sent into exile. With Mexico's former foreign minister Manuel Peña y Peña assuming the role of president, a new Mexican government was formed in Queretaro in November 1847, willing to seriously consider the American peace terms. But this time negotiations were interrupted by a dispatch that recalled Trist to Washington. President Polk was impatient with the lack of movement on the issues and wanted Trist to close down negotiations and come to Washington for further instructions.

Trist knew that, if he went, the opportunity for negotiating peace could be lost. There was no telling; if some other insurgent like Santa Anna came along, there would be more war. Encouraged by General Scott as well as the Mexicans and British to stay in Mexico City, to ignore his recall, and to finish the job, Trist openly ignored the president and stayed. The president had sent him south to negotiate a peace, and by God, he would do it.

In December, negotiations began again in the town of Guadalupe Hidalgo. Across the table from Trist, the lone American negotiator, was a trio of Mexican commissioners who included, once again, Bernardo Couto and Miguel Atristan. They were joined by another former foreign minister whom Trist knew, Luis Cuevas.

Trist demanded that Mexico relinquish all claims to Texas; New Mexico; and, of course, California. The Mexican commissioners were disposed to agree, except they insisted that they retain Lower California, the Baja

Peninsula. They also demanded that there be a separate strip of land between Sonoma and Baja with unrestricted access to Mexican citizens.

At first, Trist hesitated. Who knew how valuable the Baja might be? Still, it was in the southern part, and it was an arid place. The rest of the former colony had much more in the way of natural resources, especially northern California. Even acquired without Baja, California would be a considerable prize for the Union. Trist agreed to the Baja concession.

The only other roadblock was whether San Diego was part of Lower California (Baja) or Upper California, which would make it American. The Stars and Stripes won; San Diego became American and was included in the territory ceded to the United States. By January 27, 1848, the same day Marshall discovered gold, Trist was satisfied that he had gotten everything President Polk had demanded he get. Now it was just a matter of fixing up some fine points and having the treaty signed. On February 2, 1848, Trist, along with Couto, Atristan, and Cuevas, put their signature on the document. That same day, California became a state.

At almost the exact moment Trist put pen to parchment, James Marshall rode into Sutter's Fort to consult with his partner over his discovery. The rain, which had dogged him for days, had not let up. He walked through the compound, ascended the stairs of the central building, and went into Sutter's office without noticing anything else or thinking of anything else but finding out the exact nature of his discovery.

Marshall had been down to the fort only a week before for provisioning, so Sutter was surprised to see him.

"I have some important and interesting news," Marshall told Sutter. "I wish to communicate it secretly to you."

Marshall suggested they go together to a place where they would not be disturbed, where no listeners could overhear their conversation. Curious now, Sutter led the way to his private rooms.

"Lock the door."

Sutter did as requested. He assured Marshall that no one else was around except one of his clerks. Marshall asked for something, which the servants brought. After the servants left the room, Sutter forgot to lock the door. Marshall took a rag from his pocket and carefully opened it. Sutter had just a glance at the precious yellow metal when the door suddenly opened again; it was the clerk. Marshall quickly stashed the handkerchief and its contents back in his jacket pocket.

The clerk had come in on some sort of business and excused himself for interrupting. He and Sutter exchanged a few private comments before the clerk left.

"Now lock the door; didn't I tell you that we might have listeners?" Marshall asked nervously.

"Fear nothing about that," Sutter reassured him, "as it is not the habit of this gentleman."

Once again, Marshall took out his handkerchief and opened it for Sutter to fully see his discovery. The metal was in small pieces of varying sizes.

"I expressed my opinion to the laborers at the mill, that this might be gold; but some of them were laughing at me and called me a crazy man, and could not believe such a thing."

It looked like gold to Sutter, but he couldn't be sure until he tested it. He took a bottle of aqua fortis (nitric acid) from his apothecary shop and applied a few drops to the metal. If it was gold, nothing would happen, except to any impurities. The more impure the gold was—that is, containing other elements—the more it would react to the acid by forming nitrate salts.

Marshall watched Sutter apply the liquid. Nothing happened. All the gold appeared to be pure! Looking around his rustic office with the exposed timbers, Sutter's eye stopped on his extensive bookshelves. Then he saw the book he wanted.

"[He] at last stumbled on an old American cyclopedia [sic], where we saw the specific gravity of all the metals, and rules given to find the quantity of each in a given bulk. After hunting over the whole fort and borrowing from some of the men, we got three dollars and a half in silver, and with a small pair of scales we soon ciphered it out that there was neither silver nor copper in the gold, but that it was entirely pure."

When Sutter was finished, he looked up at Marshall.

"I declare this to be gold of the finest quality, of at least twenty-three carats," Sutter announced.

Marshall was excited. He had been right and now scientifically he had been proven correct. He asked Sutter to start with him immediately for Coloma.

"I cannot leave, as it is late in the evening and nearly suppertime. It would be better for you to remain with me till the next morning, and I will travel with you then," said Sutter.

Marshall shook his head, dissatisfied.

"Will you come tomorrow morning?" asked Marshall, looking for Sutter's word.

"Yes," Sutter promised. When assured of his presence, Marshall took his leave.

This wasn't the first time in history that gold had been discovered in the United States. There was a gold rush when the ore was discovered in North Carolina and Georgia in the 1820s and 1830s, respectively. But now the question was what exactly the construction at Sutter's Mill had brought to shining light. A significant discovery, or a flash in the pan?

"We thought it best to keep it as quiet as possible till we should have finished our mill. But there was a great number of disbanded Mormon soldiers in and about the fort, and when they came to hear of it, why it just spread like wildfire! Soon, the whole country was in a bustle," said Marshall.

Sutter thought a great deal during the night about the consequences that might follow such a discovery. Yet all he wrote in diary entry for the day was, "Mr. Marshall arrived from the mountains on very important business." No one had ever accused Sutter of understatement, but that charge could certainly be leveled at him now. Or more likely, he was so scared of the secret coming out prematurely; he didn't even want to refer to it by name in writing. Sutter ruminated on the matter.

The next morning, Sutter gave the necessary orders to

his laborers and left at seven o'clock, accompanied by an Indian soldier and a vaquero, in a heavy rain, for Coloma. Halfway down the road, Sutter saw at a distance a human being crawling out from the brush.

"Who is that?" Sutter asked the Indian.

"The same man who was with you last evening," the Indian replied.

When they came abreast, they found that the man was indeed a very wet and disheveled Marshall.

"You would have done better to remain with me at the fort than to pass such an ugly night here," said Sutter dryly.

Marshall explained that he had ridden the 54 miles back to Coloma, took his other horse, and came halfway back to meet them. Together, they all rode up to Coloma, which they reached in the afternoon, by which time the weather was clearing up. The next morning, Sutter accompanied Marshall to the tailrace of the mill. Like before, water had been running during the night to clean out the gravel that had been made loose to widen the race. After the water level went down, they waded out.

"Small pieces of gold could be seen remaining on the bottom of the clean washed bed rock," Sutter later wrote. "I went in the race and picked up several pieces of this gold, several of the laborers gave me some which they had picked up, and from Marshall I received a part. I told them that I would get a ring made of this gold as soon as it could be done in California."

Sutter later did. He had a heavy ring made, with his family's coat of arms engraved on the outside, and on the inside of the ring was engraved, "The first gold, discovered in January, 1848."

The next day, Marshall and Sutter went on a prospecting tour in the Coloma vicinity. The following morning, Sutter was scheduled to go back to his fort. Before his departure, "I had a conversation with all hands. I told them that I would consider it as a great favor if they would keep this discovery secret only for six weeks, so that I could finish my large flour mill at Brighton, which had cost me already about from 24 to 25,000 dollars."

Everyone promised to keep the secret. But on his way home, Sutter did not feel happy and contented. Rather, he was surprised to find that he felt uneasy, and the more he thought about it, the more his emotions made sense. In his heart of hearts, he knew that such a secret, despite his men's best efforts, would not remain secret for long.

Two weeks after his return to his fort, he sent up "several teams in charge of a white man, as the teamsters were Indian boys. This man was acquainted with all hands up there, and Mrs. Wimmer (the cook) told him the whole secret; likewise the young sons of Mr. Wimmer told him that they had gold and that they would let him have some too; and so he obtained a few dollars' worth of it as a present.

"As soon as this man arrived at the fort, he went to a small store in one of my outside buildings, kept by Jed Smith, a partner of Sam Brannan, a Mormon merchant in Francisco, and asked for a bottle of brandy, for which he would pay the cash; after having the bottle, he paid [instead] with these small pieces of gold.

"Smith was astonished and asked him if he intended to insult him. The teamster told him to go and ask me about it, Smith came in great haste to see me. I told him at once the truth.

"What could I do? I had to tell him all about it."

4.

"ALL I HAD HEARD . . ."

J oseph Smith was about to take a hand in the next
major event of the Gold Rush. That he was long
dead made it that much more of an achievement.

Smith had been born in 1805 in Sharon, Vermont.
He was one of ten children, and the family moved frequently during his youth. The most significant years
of Smith's early childhood were spent in Palmyra, New
York, where Protestant tent "revivals" were frequent and
well attended. The family eventually moved to Illinois.

There, on the family farm, the man who would later be
called the Prophet claimed to have received his first divine
revelation when he was fourteen years old. God came to
Smith with the revelation that all religions since the death
of the disciples of Christ had turned away from the true
church of Christ. His job was to restore that church.

Receiving subsequent visions of instruction that he obeyed, Smith claimed to have discovered, on a hillside, gold tablets written by ancient Indian inhabitants. A modern-day Moses, his translations of the tablets were published in 1830 as the Book of Mormon. Combined with the Old and New Testaments, plus some of Smith's later revelations, the Book of Mormon became the foundation for a new religion, Mormonism.

Smith's new religion was empowering. His zealots believed in their heart and soul in God and Jesus Christ as real corporeal beings who actively intervened in human affairs. To a Mormon, human beings are innately filled with the divine essence. They can become Godlike through strict conduct. The Mormon Church, under Smith's leadership as the divinely ordained Prophet, would provide the physical and emotional structures through which human beings could make this ascendancy.

The Formal Church of Mormon was established by Smith in 1830 in New York. Friends and family comprised his first converts. He had such a charismatic personality, he had so much of what appeared to be a divine presence, that Mormonism quickly saw thousands of converts to its fold. Even sworn enemies of Mormonism from other religions were left stunned by the power of his presence and the authority with which he spoke.

Feeling hostility to his growing power, Smith moved his people west, to Kirtland Mills, Ohio. There, he hoped the Mormons could thrive and erect their Kingdom of God on earth. The "saints," as Smith's converts referred to themselves, soon found themselves in

1837 in the middle of a nightmare. The banking collapse that year caused their settlement in Kirtland Mills to falter. Rumors had spread that all Mormons endorsed polygamy; some did. Once again, the endemic hostility of outsiders to what was different—and the saints were— forced Smith to move his flock westward yet again.

This time they settled in Missouri for all of one year before Missouri's governor, fearful of what he perceived as the saints' barbarous religious and marital practices, condemned them by executive order to leave the state. At first, the Mormons hesitated but changed their minds rather hastily after armed men surrounded the Mormon stronghold in Far West, Missouri, and "demanded" they leave.

The Mormons fled east and established the city of Nauvoo on the Mississippi River near Quincy, Illinois, in 1839. Five years later, in 1844, the city had grown to ten thousand inhabitants. Mormon missionaries had been sent out by Smith around the world, and they had made another twenty-five thousand converts.

All this explosive growth in the religion was threatening to the Mormons' Gentile neighbors. The latter, aware of the polygamy among the saints, detested them. It didn't help when Smith announced that he was running for the presidency of the United States.

In response, a newspaper in Carthage, Illinois, ran an exposé of the Mormons' practice of polygamy. Incensed at the article, Smith attempted to destroy the newspaper's office but was arrested and charged with incitement to riot. Before he could be tried, a mob overpowered his jailers, broke into his cell, and murdered him.

Suddenly, the saints were at a crossroads. Should they stay, or flee once again?

Most of them followed the banner of Brigham Young. As president of the church's Quorum of the Twelve Apostles, he claimed he was Smith's successor. He became leader just in time to face the ire of the president of the United States, James Polk. Polk thought the Mormons aberrant and a threat to the westward expansion of the United States. If they tried to cross the Rocky Mountains, he intended to intercept them by force.

Young was a much better politician than Smith. He sent letters to Senator Stephen A. Douglas—who would later lock up in a series of debates with an Illinois barrister named Lincoln—and other influential members of Congress. He tried to persuade them that the Mormons were peaceable, that they were not a threat in any way to the United States, and that they were good citizens. In fact, Young had already made the decision for the Mormons to journey farther west, beyond the Rockies, but he now knew he needed government sanction to do it.

When the United States entered the Mexican-American War in 1846, President Polk made plans for an invasion of California. The overtures of Young with Douglas and the others now paid off. Ever mindful that his Army of the West was too undermanned to attempt an invasion of California, Polk chose to put his prejudices aside. He issued an executive order establishing that a military battalion of the U.S. Army be raised from the Mormons. Young saw this as a practical opportunity to expand west with the sanction of the U.S. government.

"The enlistment of the Mormon Battalion in the service of the United States, though looked upon by many with astonishment and some with fear, has proved a great blessing to this community. It was indeed the temporal salvation of our camp," he said.

Thus was born the Mormon Battalion: five hundred men, thirty-four women, and fifty-one children. To assist General Stephen Watts Kearney in California's conquest from the Mexicans, the Mormons' job was to march through New Mexico, Arizona, and California, following the route taken by sixteenth-century explorers across the Chihuahuan, Sonoran, and California deserts. The intent was to rendezvous with General Kearney in San Diego.

Before they left, Brigham Young told the Mormon Battalion:

"Brethren, you will be blessed, if you will live for those blessings which you have been taught to live for. The Mormon Battalion will be held in honorable remembrance to the latest generation; and I will prophesy that the children of those who have been in the army, in defense of their country, will grow up and bless their fathers for what they did at that time. And men and nations will rise up and bless the men who went in that Battalion.

"These are my feelings in brief respecting the company of men known as the Mormon Battalion. When you consider the blessings that are laid upon you, will you not live for them? As the Lord lives, if you will but live up to your privileges, you will never be forgotten, without end, but you will be held in honorable remembrance, for ever and ever."

Among the battalion that day listening to Young's speech were many men destined to build Sutter's Mill. The Mormon trek west began in July 1846 in Council Bluffs, Iowa, with twenty-five army wagons and twelve privately owned wagons. They literally blazed the southern trail that many of the subsequent argonauts bound for northern California's gold fields would take.

Six months later they reached San Diego, thus becoming the first group in American history to take wagons west across the desert. Melissa Burton Couray, a member of the Mormon Battalion, later described the battalion's arrival at Palm Spring, just southeast of Vallecito in the Anza-Borrego region:

"January 18, 1847. The men were so used up from thirst, fatigue, and hunger [after crossing the desert from the Colorado River at present-day Yuma] there was no talking. Some could not speak at all; tongues were swollen and dark. Sixteen more mules gave out.

"Each man was down to his last four ounces of flour; there had been no sugar or coffee for weeks. Only five government wagons and three private wagons remained. . . . When they arrived at Vallecito Creek, they rested and washed clothes and cleaned their guns. An Indian from a nearby village brought a letter from the Alcalde in San Diego welcoming the Battalion to California. In the early evening there was singing and fiddling with a little dancing."

On January 29, 1847, the Mormon Battalion reached San Diego.

"Traveling in sight of the ocean, the clear bright

sunshine, with the mildness of the atmosphere, combined to increase the enjoyment of the scene before us.
. . . The birds sang sweetly and all nature seemed to
smile and join in praise to the Giver of all good; but
the crowning satisfaction of all to us was that we had
succeeded in making the great national highway across
the American desert, nearly filled our mission, and
hoped soon to join our families and the Saints, for
whom, as well as our country, we were living martyrs,"
wrote Daniel Tyler, a battalion member.

Almost a year to the day before gold was discovered,
Mormons discovered their El Dorado there on the California coast. Some members of the battalion were
assigned to garrison duty in San Diego, San Luis Rey, and
Los Angeles, but only temporarily. The members of the
Mormon Battalion, who had enlisted for exactly one year,
were mustered out of the U.S. Army on July 16, 1847.
Eighty-one men reenlisted and served an additional eight
months of military duty under Captain Daniel C. Davis
in Company A of the Mormon Volunteers.

The majority of the soldiers migrated to the Salt Lake
Valley and were reunited with their pioneering families.
Some of those who didn't, found work in Sutter's Fort.
Marshall subsequently hired them to help him set up the
sawmill. After his gold find, when Marshall traveled to
Sutter's Fort in late January 1847, the mill was still not
in full operation. It wouldn't be until the tailrace was
deepened. With Marshall gone, the workers continued to
work on the race, but still found time to do a little
prospecting of their own.

Since the tailrace was where Marshall had made his discovery, the workers concentrated their efforts in that vicinity. Pocketknives and butcher knives were used to extract the gold particles and separate them. During the first week after the discovery, Marshall's men succeeded in picking up approximately $100 worth of gold.

If gold was only limited to that one spot where Marshall had made his discovery, it really wouldn't be much of a discovery at all. For there to be a "gold rush," gold needed to be discovered in another location. The more the locations of the discovery of the precious metal, the more the opportunity to get rich. On Sunday, February 6, only thirteen days after Marshall's discovery, his men Bigler and Barger decided to strike out to the other side of the river.

Searching for gold in the seams and cracks of the granite outcrops that lined the riverbanks, they found what looked like a gold nugget. They jury-rigged a pair of wooden scales to assist them in estimating the value of their find. Using a 12-cent piece of silver as a counterweight, equal to $2.00 in gold, they estimated they had found $10 worth.

An enterprising individual, Bigler had a hunch. Believing that gold might also be discovered farther downstream, he borrowed a gun and said he was going hunting for ducks. About half a mile below the mill and out of sight of his fellows, he noticed an outcropping on the other side of the river, similar to what had been found in the bottom of the tailrace. Wading across the rushing, cold water, he got to the outcropping and began scraping at a particularly bright yellow spot. What he took out was later estimated to be worth $1.50.

So far, the actual yield of the "discoveries" was not even worth mentioning monetarily, except *it was happening.* Gold was being discovered by eye—that is how plentiful it appeared to be. Who knew what lay below the surface, what fortunes there were to be mined out of the rock and earth and water?

Bigler returned without telling anyone what he was doing. On February 22, Washington's birthday and a national holiday, Bigler, using his hunting excuse again, began his trip downstream to his "digs." This time, though, the water level was up and with it the rapids; he had difficulty struggling against the current to cross. But he made it, barely, to the other side, and collapsed, exhausted.

As night settled in, Bigler tried to build a fire to keep warm. He figured to use his gun's primer to spark the fire to life. But the primer had gotten wet. He tried flint and steel to start the fire but that didn't work either, because his hands were shaking so much from the cold, he couldn't get a good strike of the steel on the flint.

"Jumping up and down and dancing over rocks in my misery," Bigler would later write, "I saw every now and then a yellow piece staring me in the face, but was too cold to stop and pick them up." When he felt warmer, he went to work on the rocks with his pocketknife.

Searching closely in the sand near the river, Bigler found a round nugget shaped like a bullet, which was worth about $6.00. This excited him so much that he crouched for several hours looking for more. He picked up several smaller pieces, but when he arose to his full length, he cried out from the pain caused by his cramped muscles, which made him feel as if his back were broken.

After a few minutes of standing and stretching, the agony wore off. Night descended quickly and Bigler made his way back upriver to the dam, where the water was diverted to the sawmill. He called for Brown, who soon crossed the river on a log raft and thus ferried him across to the far bank. At Bigler's cabin that night, his friends questioned him about his hunting and the "reason for his lateness."

He had been acting suspiciously, and they wanted to know what was up. Bigler's answer was to ask for the wooden scales. Pulling up one corner of his shirt, which he had used to tie up his gold, he weighed his findings before the fixed stare of the others. In all, Bigler's gold amounted to $33 worth. He had found it in a few hours. Bigler's usual rate of pay was about one dollar per day. In one day he had found his month's pay!

Marshall's workers knew that they had signed to do a job. They couldn't just desert Marshall; first they needed to finish construction of the sawmill. They decided to finish their millwork during their six-day-a-week work schedule and keep the prospecting to their free day on Sunday.

On February 27, Bigler took his Mormon brethren to his ledge down the river, where, because of the high water, only $33 worth of gold could be found that day. Once again, all swore to secrecy and once again, the secret got out. This time is was Sutter's Swiss teamster, Jacob Wittmer.

On February 9, Sutter had sent his brethren with two wagons to the sawmill. When he got there, Wittmer heard of the discovery from the children of one of the mill-workers. At first Wittmer didn't believe it, but he later proved the story true by his wife, the cook, who showed him some of the gold in the bottom of her vat of soap.

On February 14 in his diary, Sutter recorded:

"Wittmer returned with the two wagons from the mountains, and told every body of the Gold mines there and brought a few samples with him."

George Smith, who ran a general store at Sutter's Fort, was the first one Wittmer told. He bought a bottle of brandy from him. When Smith refused to accept gold dust as payment, Wittmer told him to ask Sutter whether it was really gold. Smith did. Sutter had no choice but to confirm the discovery of gold. Smith wrote to his partner Sam Brannan in San Francisco telling of the find. That was how San Francisco initially found out about the discovery of gold at Sutter's sawmill. Even Sutter himself finally, had to give in to the gold excitement and send an emissary to the territorial governor in Monterey, reporting the discovery. But now the stakes had gone up considerably.

Sutter knew that a great rush of humanity was about to rush to California in search of gold. There was no way to hold back the tide. What he hoped was that he could retain title to his lands on the basis of his land grants from the Mexican government being recognized by the conqueror, the United States of America. Would the conqueror recognize his hereditary rights, what was just and due to as fine a gentleman as he, late of the Swiss Guard? Sutter sent his man Bennett to carry the word of the discovery and Sutter's request to the governor. Sutter's empire, and the freedom for the prospectors to go where they wanted in pursuit of gold and the ultimate expansion of the United States, rested with the decision of the military governor, Colonel Richard Barnes Mason, in Monterey. Mason's adjutant was William Tecumseh Sherman. His family called him "Cump." Take a look at any daguerreotype of Cump and you come away with the impression that he must have been one rough, tough son of a bitch, and you'd be right. Born in Lancaster, Ohio, in 1820. His father gave him the middle name of Tecumseh in honor of the Shawnee chief Tecumseh, who had tried in the first decade of the nineteenth century to unite the tribes of the Ohio River Valley against the white usurpers, and failed.

Cump's father died when he was young. Unable to care for her family, Cump's widowed mother made a painful decision. She sent Cump's brother Thomas to be raised by an aunt. Then she turned to Cump's father's best friend, diplomat Thomas Ewing. A wealthy man, Ewing took Cump in as his own. Cump became a foster child to Thomas. His new brother was Boyd Ewing.

A smart, resourceful child, Cump grew up to graduate from West Point as a second lieutenant in 1840. In 1848, at age twenty-eight, he was posted to California as adjutant to Governor Mason. He quickly gained Mason's confidence and became extremely influential in his correspondence and therefore how government worked in California.

In early March 1848, Cump looked up from his desk in the anteroom of the governor's office in Monterey to see a lanky American. He introduced himself as "Bennett," and said he had just come down from Captain Sutter's on special business. He wanted to see Governor Mason *in person.*

Looking the man over, Cump could see that he meant business; something was going on. Cump escorted him in to see the colonel and left them together. After some time the colonel came to the door and called to Cump.

"Lieutenant, come in."

Cump did as ordered.

"Look at that."

Cump's attention was directed to a series of papers unfolded on the colonel's table, in which lay what looked to Cump like half an ounce or so of placer-gold.

"What is that?" Mason asked.

Cump touched it and examined one or two of the larger pieces.

"Is it gold?"

"You ever see native gold, Lieutenant?"

"In 1844 I was in Upper Georgia, and there saw some native gold, but it was much finer than this, and it was in phials, or in transparent quills. If this is gold, it could be easily tested, first, by its malleability, and next by acids."

Cump took a piece in his teeth, and the metallic luster was perfect.

"Baden, bring an ax!" Cump yelled out to a military clerk. "Also a hatchet and ax from the backyard."

When they were brought in, Cump took the largest piece and beat it flat. Beyond doubt it was metal, and a pure metal. Still, neither Mason nor Sherman at first attached much significance to the discovery. Gold was known to exist at San Fernando, to the south, and yet was not considered of much value there. Colonel Mason then handed Cump a letter from Captain Sutter, addressed to the governor.

In the letter Sutter said, "I am engaged in erecting a saw-mill at Coloma, about forty miles up the American Fork, above my fort at New Helvetia, for the general benefit of the settlers in that vicinity. I have incurred considerable expense, and wanted a 'preëmption' to the quarter-section of land on which the mill is located, embracing the tail-race in which this particular gold has been found." He also wanted Mason to acknowledge the land grants he had previously received from the Mexican government.

"Lieutenant, prepare a letter, in answer, for my signature," Mason instructed his protégé.

Immediately Cump wrote a letter reciting that California was yet a Mexican province, simply held by the United States as a conquest; that no laws of the United States yet applied to it, much less the land laws or preemption laws, which could only apply after a public survey. Therefore it was impossible for the governor to promise him (Sutter) a title to the land; yet, as there were no settlements within forty miles, he was not likely to be disturbed by trespassers. Colonel Mason signed the letter and handed it to Bennett, who immediately departed.

Writing in his memoirs later, Sherman said ruefully, "That gold was the *first* discovered in the Sierra Nevada, which soon revolutionized the whole country, and actually moved the whole civilized world."

On March 13, Bennett returned to the fort from Monterey, bringing word that Colonel Mason, the interim governor, had refused to confirm Sutter's title to the land at the sawmill, because a treaty had not yet been signed with Mexico to end the war. The discovery of gold in California was finally reported publically when Brannan's *Californian* newspaper ran a story about the find in its March 15 edition. That was followed on March 18 with E. C. Kemble's article about the discovery in the *California Star*. Other California newspapers picked up on the story. As for the rest for the nation, they would have to wait.

While the telegraph united sections of the country, there was no way to send a telegram from coast-to-coast simply because a transcontinental telegraph line had not yet been laid. There also was no coast-to-coast railroad. There had never really been any need for one. For the moment, Marshall's gold discovery was just California news.

Meanwhile, by March 19, the millrace had been deepened enough that the mill was working at 100 percent capacity. Work was going well. And every Sunday, the Mormons went out to pan for gold and came back to camp at dusk with gold dust. With the sawmill completed, there was nothing to keep the Mormons, the Indians, or any of the other workers in Marshall's employ when they could just as easily pan for the gold all around them.

As California was writing its history almost every day, the Mexican-American War was coming, after two years of protracted conflict, to an end. A copy of the Treaty of Guadalupe-Hidalgo was sent to President Polk in Washington via James Freaner, a correspondent for the *New Orleans Delta.* He hand-delivered the document to Polk on February 19, 1848.

Angered that Trist had not returned when he demanded, Polk was smart enough to put his feelings aside in favor of recommending the treaty to the Senate for ratification; on March 10, 1848, with two amendments, it was approved. Six days later, Polk signed it into law.

Under the Treaty of Guadalupe-Hidalgo, Mexico ceded California and New Mexico to the United States, and recognized the Rio Grande as the southern and western boundary of Texas. For that land, the United States paid Mexico $15 million in cash, also assuming $3.25 million more in American claims on the Mexican government.

Were it not for the discovery of gold in California—which Mexico would, of course, control if they had owned the land—the deal might actually have been a good one for Santa Anna's country. California might have been a Mexican province, but under minimal control by the "mother" country. It was not inconceivable that colonial powers, including Russia, England, or France, might have moved to take the burgeoning colony at any moment. As for Texas, it had already been lost when that confounded Tennessean with the coonskin cap showed up at the Alamo.

And New Mexico? The Mexicans didn't really care about the place. They had done little to settle the land, nor would they have been successful had they tried. The fierce Apache tribe would have risen to stop them; Comanches would raid Mexican settlements; conquest would have come at great cost in human life. Proving themselves an enlightened country, Mexico could not stomach such slaughter and instead chose a graceful exit.

It was the United States that was the real beneficiary of the Treaty of Guadalupe-Hidalgo. For the first time since the Louisiana Purchase in 1806, the country had expanded by buying its continental land from a foreign government. This was just as good a bargain as last time. For a little over $18 million, the Union expanded into the southwestern and western parts of the American continent.

Washington acquired two new states, California and Texas, and one new territory, New Mexico. The United States was clearly on a roll. Yet, as Sutter and Marshall suspected, history was about to bite them right on the ass. By April, men were staking out their claims on the American River, while others were opting to mine in and around Coloma. One by one, Marshall began to lose his workers to the lure of gold. On April 8, the Mormons Bigler, Stevens, and Brown settled their accounts with Sutter at his fort and went back to the sawmill. This time they weren't millworkers; they were gold miners. After prospecting a little downstream from the mill, they headed over to what became known as Mormon Island in they middle of the river. Seven other Mormons were already there, prospecting. They had $250 worth of gold combined.

For the first time, someone was "mining" gold at the site of the California Gold Rush without using a knife as the principal mining implement. Instead, the Mormons used a contraption made of two closely woven Indian baskets. The idea was to dredge up sand and gravel from the riverbed and put it into the contraption, where gravity and rotating the basket back and forth produced a settling of the heaviest element—gold—to the bottom of the barrel. Only this time, the bottom of the barrel was more valuable than anything toward the top. The Mormons estimated that they could do $2.50 worth of gold for every basket.

By May 1, most of the white men were gone from the mill. The bulk of the work was being done by the Indians. Marshall was worried about the dearth of qualified help, plus the fact that it was difficult to run a business when you had prospectors coming around at all hours.

"I had scarcely arrived at the mill again till several persons appeared with pans, shovels, and hoes, and those that had not iron picks had wooden ones, all anxious to fall to work and dig up our mill, but this we would not permit. As fast as one party disappeared another would arrive. Sometimes, I had the greatest kind of trouble to get rid of them. I sent them all off in different directions, telling them about such and such places, where I was certain there was plenty of gold if they would only take the trouble of looking for it."

What Marshall never imagined was "that the gold was so abundant. I told them to go to such and such places, because it appeared that they would dig nowhere but in such places as I pointed out, and I believe such was their confidence in me that they would have dug on the very top of yon mountain if I had told them to do so." Invariably, the newly minted miners would strike gold.

A May 16 entry in Sutter's diary shows that he was momentarily optimistic with the mill he was constructing at Natamo. But that was just false optimism. Sutter seemed to have a talent for staying too late in a place where things weren't working. Rather than sell his interests right then, he soldiered on as he had been taught in the Swiss militia.

After cutting only a few thousand feet of lumber, the sawmill was forced to close. There was no one to run it, and Marshall couldn't do the whole thing by himself; it just wasn't physically possible. Sutter was worn out. May 25 is the last date recorded in his diary:

"A number of people continue traveling to the Mountains," he wrote simply. In his own backyard, things were literally falling down around him.

The business on the docks was going better than well; it was booming. There was money to be made off this trade if a merchant were situated closer to the docks. Unfortunately, it was a good five miles to travel from the harbor to Sutter's. Why make a customer do that when the store could come to him?

The storeowners in Sutter's Fort owned the adobe brick of the fort that housed their businesses in the fort's interior perimeter. Brick by brick, Sutter's merchants dismantled their part of the fort and carted it down the hill to the shores of the Sacramento River. There, the merchants simply used the brick to rebuild their shops. Sutter's loss was Sacramento's gain.

Back East, the federal government in Washington was concerned. They had heard the rumors of gold discovery coming from California. President Polk wanted a first-hand account of what was going on "out there."

He turned to Thomas Larkin.

5.

THE CONFIDENTIAL AGENT

T homas Larkin was born in Charlestown, Massachusetts, in 1802. When he came of age, Larkin began to travel, first to North Carolina, then migrating across the country to California, where he arrived as a merchant in 1831 and set up a store in Monterey. The store proved profitable; his primary trade was with Mexico and the Hawaiian Islands.

Larkin also was an architect. He invented what would come to be known as the Monterey style of architecture. Combining local adobe walls and the balconies of a southern plantation home with a Massachusetts Yankee's ornamental taste, his Monterey home was the first two-story adobe in California and still stands.

In 1838 he was chosen to be the first—and only—American consul to the Mexican government. He looked more the part of a prosperous merchant. He had a hawk-like nose; a high, intelligent forehead; and deep, penetrating dark eyes, but an unprepossessing physical presence. That suited Secretary of State (and future president) James Buchanan just fine, considering that Larkin's value to the U.S. government went way beyond his consular abilities.

Larkin was a confidential agent for the U.S. government from 1846 to 1848, whose job it was to bring about the U.S. conquest of California with minimal loss of life. The federal government figured that having an intelligence agent in the Mexican province to note the comings and goings was as potentially profitable as a fomenter of revolution, but with half the cost.

Prone to careful observation and ceaseless documentation, possessed of an excellent memory for everything from figures to geography, Larkin was the best choice for a California spy in the government's employ. Besides that, Thomas Larkin was a damn good writer.

Polk needed his agent to authenticate the rumors of gold and give the president an idea of the extent of the find. The president could then craft his official announcement of the gold discovery to support and encourage expansion of the Union. The government had been on a track of westward expansion; everyone knew that. It wasn't "manifest destiny," as it would later be called, that drove that expansion, but rather a distinct aspect of the American character that had yet to come to the fore.

It wasn't that Americans, whether naturalized or not, had a rootlessness in their character. For generations they had been satisfied to stay on their farms, till the soil, and pass on whatever they could to the next generation. Reward for this life was in the next. It was as secure a belief as the clasp of the strongest locket and held as dear to the heart.

The idea of gold would change that, and someplace in *his* heart, James Polk knew it.

Once Americans knew there was gold to be taken from California dirt, that anyone could come and do it, thousands would come streaming to the state. Maybe even hundreds of thousands. It was hard to know what effect that would have on the future, but in the present, such a boom would be a boon to the economy.

Miners would have to buy what they needed somewhere, and they would need transportation to get to California. The idea of a transcontinental railroad had been bandied about by one railroad magnate or another, but supplying transport to men and cargo to California from the East Coast could turn into a profitable situation for the companies that had the vision to expand.

It all relied on Thomas Larkin's observations. His vivid prose provided Secretary Buchanan, and later President Polk, with the first authoritative report of Marshall's discovery and what it would mean to the United States in the future. In the process, Larkin gave an up-to-date account of what it was like to pan for gold at the beginning of the California Gold Rush:

San Francisco (Upper California), June 1, 1848.

Sir: I have to report to the State Department one of the most astonishing excitements and state of affairs now existing in this country, that, perhaps, has ever been brought to the notice of the Government.

On the American fork of the Sacramento and Feather River, another branch of the same, and the adjoining lands, there has been within the present year discovered a placer, a vast tract of land containing gold in small particles. This gold, thus far, has been taken on the bank of the river, from the surface to eighteen inches in depth, and is supposed deeper and to extend over the country.

On account of the inconvenience of washing, the people have up to this time, only gathered the metal on the banks, which is done simply with a shovel, filling a shallow dish, bowl, basket, or tin pan, with a quantity of black sand, similar to the class used on paper, and washing out the sand by movement of the vessel.

It is now two or three weeks since the men employed in those washings have appeared in this town with gold, to exchange for merchandise and provisions. Nearly 20,000 dollars of this gold has as yet been so exchanged. Some 200 or 300 men have remained up the river, or are gone to their homes, for the purpose of returning to the Placer, and washing immediately with shovels, picks, and baskets; many of them, for the first few weeks, depending on borrowing from others.

I have seen the written statement of the work of one man for sixteen days, which averaged 25 dollars per day; others have, with a shovel and pan, or wooden bowl, washed out 10 dollars to even 50 dollars in a day. There are now some men yet washing who have 500 dollars to 1,000 dollars. As they have to stand two feet deep in the river, they work but a few hours in the day, and not every day in the week.

A few men have been down in boats to this port, spending twenty to thirty ounces of gold each— about 300 dollars. I am confident that this town (San Francisco) has one-half of its tenements empty, locked up with the furniture. The owners— storekeepers, lawyers, mechanics, and labourers— all gone to the Sacramento with their families.

Small parties, of five to fifteen men, have sent to this town and offered cooks ten to fifteen dollars per day for a few weeks. Mechanics and teamsters, earning the year past five to eight dollars per day, have struck and gone. Several U.S. volunteers have deserted. The U.S. barque *Anita,* belonging to the Army, now at anchor here, has but six men. One Sandwich Island vessel in port lost all her men; and was obliged to engage another crew at 50 dollars for the run of fifteen days to the Islands.

One American captain having his men shipped

on this coast in such a manner that they could leave at any time, had them all on the eve of quitting, when he agreed to continue their pay and food; leaving one on board, he took a boat and carried them to the gold regions—furnishing tools and giving his men one-third. They have been gone a week.

Common spades and shovels, one month ago worth 1 dollar, will now bring 10 dollars, at the gold regions. I am informed 50 dollars has been offered for one. Should this gold continue as represented, this town and others would be depopulated. Clerks' wages have risen from 600 dollars to 1000 per annum, and board; cooks, 25 dollars to 30 dollars per month. This sum will not be any inducement a month longer, unless the fever and ague appears among the washers.

The Californian, printed here, stopped this week. *The Star* newspaper office, where the new laws of Governor Mason for this country are printing, has but one man left. A merchant, lately from China, has even lost his China servants. Should the excitement continue through the year, and the whale-ships visit San Francisco, I think they will lose most all their crews. How Col. Mason can retain his men, unless he puts a force on the spot, I know not.

I have seen several pounds of this gold, and consider it very pure, worth in New York 17 dollars to 18 dollars per ounce; 14 dollars to 16 dollars in merchandise is paid for it here. What good or bad effect this gold mania will have on California, I cannot fore tell. It may end this year; but I am informed that it will continue many years.

Mechanics now in this town are only waiting to finish some rude machinery, to enable them to obtain the gold more expeditiously, and free from working in the river. Up to this time but few Californians have gone to the mines, being afraid the Americans will soon have trouble among themselves, and cause disturbance to all around.

I have seen some of the black sand, as taken from the bottom of the river (I should think in the States it would bring 25 to 50 cents per pound), containing many pieces of gold; they are from the size of the head of a pin to the weight of the eighth of an ounce. I have seen some weighing one-quarter of an ounce (4 dollars). Although my statements are almost incredible, I believe I am within the statements believed by every one here. Ten days back, the excitement had not reached Monterey. I shall, within a few days, visit this gold mine, and will make another report to you. In closed you will have a specimen.

I have the honour to be, very respectfully,
(Signed.) THOMAS O. LARKIN.

P.S. This placer, or gold region, is situated on public land.

Larkin's letter is an astonishing historical document. In one fell swoop, Larkin describes how an agriculturally based economy, which the United States had been since its inception seventy-two years before, had changed overnight into an industrial one. The gold discovery was prompting science and technology to come up with new ways to extract the ore from the ground.

Equally clear is the value the discovery could have if the United States chose to enforce its title to the very land on which the prospectors were prospecting. The confidential agent shows a distinct lack of bigotry, rare in the nineteenth century, but for a man of Larkin's breeding, not uncommon. He sees the gold fever seizing everyone regardless of race—Chinese, white makes no difference; regardless of profession, from sailors to merchants, all of them united in one common goal: the pursuit of gold.

At first glance, it looked like Marshall's discovery had brought out the greed in people's character. But looked at more closely, and Larkin saw this, the gold and the possibility of getting it offered hope and redemption to literally anyone. There was an egalitarian aspect to the gold fields that was distinctly American that Larkin refers to, specifically that anyone with a pan could find the stuff; there was no magic to it. Placer gold was so plentiful, all you had to do was literally dip your pan in the black sand, sift through it, and just about every time, you were going to find some shiny flecks in the bottom of your pan.

During the next four weeks, Larkin rode out from San Francisco and went to Sacramento and on to the gold fields. When he got back to his base in Monterey, he sat on his veranda and wrote his next letter to Secretary Buchanan, which would be delivered to the president:

Monterey, California, June 28, 1848.

Sir: My last dispatch to the State Department was written in San Francisco, the 1st of this Month. In that I had the honour to give some information respecting the new "placer," or gold regions lately discovered on the branches of the Sacramento River. Since the writing of that dispatch I have visited a part of the gold region, and found it all I had heard, and much more than I anticipated. The part that I visited was upon a fork of the American River, a branch of the Sacramento, joining the main river at Sutter's Fort. The place in which I found the people digging was about twenty-five miles from the fort by land.

I have reason to believe that gold will be found on many branches of the Sacramento and the San Joaquin rivers. People are already scattered over one hundred miles of land, and it is supposed that the "placer" extends from river to river. At present, the workmen are employed within ten or twenty yards of the river, that they may be convenient to water. On Feather River, there are several branches upon which the people are digging for gold. This is two or three days' ride from the place I visited.

At my camping place I found, on a surface of two

or three miles on the banks of the river, some fifty tents, mostly owned by Americans. These had their families. There are no Californians who have taken their families as yet to the gold regions; but few or none will ever do it; some from New Mexico may do so next year, but no Californians.

I was two nights at a tent occupied by eight Americans, viz., two sailors, one clerk, two carpenters, and three daily workmen. These men were in company; had two machines, each made from one hundred feet of boards (worth there 150 dollars, in Monterey 15 dollars—being one day's work), made similar to a child's cradle, ten feet long, with out the ends.

The two evenings I saw these eight men bring to their tents the labour of the day. I suppose they made each 50 dollars per day; their own calculation was two pounds of gold a-day—four ounces to a man—64 dollars. I saw two brothers that worked together, and only worked by washing the dirt in a tin pan, weigh the gold they obtained in one day; the result was 7 dollars to one, 82 dollars to the other. There were two reasons for this difference; one man worked less hours than the other, and by chance had ground less impregnated with gold. I give this statement as an extreme case.

During my visit I was an interpreter for a native of Monterey, who was purchasing a machine or canoe. I first tried to purchase boards and hire a carpenter for him. There were but a few hundred feet of boards to be had; for these the owner asked me 50 dollars per hundred (500 dollars per thousand), and a carpenter washing gold dust demanded 50 dollars per day for working.

I at last purchased a log dug out, with a riddle and sieve made of willow boughs on it, for 120 dollars, payable in gold dust at 14 dollars per ounce. The owner excused himself for the price, by saying he was two days making it, and even then demanded the use of it until sunset. My Californian has told me since that himself, partner, and two Indians, obtained with this canoe eight ounces the first and five ounces the second day.

I am of the opinion that on the American fork, Feather River, and Consumnes River, there are near two thousand people, nine-tenths of them foreigners. Perhaps there are one hundred families, who have their teams, wagons, and tents. Many persons are waiting to see whether the months of July and August will be sickly, before they leave their present business to go to the "Placer."

The discovery of this gold was made by some Mormons, in January or February, who for a time kept it a secret; the majority of those who are working there began in May. In most every instance the men, after digging a few days, have been compelled to leave for the purpose of returning home to see their families, arrange their business, and purchase provisions.

I feel confident in saying there are fifty men in

this "Placer" who have on an average 1,000 dollars each, obtained in May and June. I have not met with any person who had been fully employed in washing gold one month; most, however, appear to have averaged an ounce per day. I think there must, by this time, be over 1,000 men at work upon the different branches of the Sacramento; putting their gains at 10,000 dollars per day, for six days in the week, appears to me not overrated.

Should this news reach the emigrants to California and Oregon now on the road, we should have a large addition to our population. Should the richness of the gold region continue, our emigration in 1849 will be many thousands and in 1850 still more.

If our countrymen in California as clerks, mechanics, and workmen, will forsake employment at from 2 dollars to 6 dollars per day, how many more of the same class in the Atlantic States, earning much less, will leave for this country under such prospects?

It is the opinion of many who have visited the gold regions the past and present months that the ground will afford gold for many years, perhaps for a century. From my own examination of the rivers and their banks, I am of opinion that, at least for a few years, the golden products will equal the present year. However, as neither men of science, nor the labourers now at work, have made any explorations of consequence, it is a matter of impossibility to give any opinion as to the extent and richness of this part of California. Every Mexican who has seen the place says throughout their Republic there has never been any "placer like this one."

Could Mr. Polk and yourself see California as we now see it, you would think that a few thousand people, on 100 miles square of the Sacramento valley, would yearly turn out of this river the whole price our country pays for the acquired territory. When I finished my first letter I doubted my own writing, and, to be better satisfied, showed it to one of the principal merchants of San Francisco, and to Captain Folsom, of the Quartermaster's Department, who decided at once I was far below the reality.

You certainly will suppose, from my two letters, that I am, like others, led away by the excitement of the day. I think I am not. In my last I inclosed [sic] a small sample of the gold dust, and I find my only error was in putting a value to the sand. At that time I was not aware how the gold was found; I now can describe the mode of collecting it.

A person without a machine, after digging off one or two feet of the upper ground, near the water (in some cases they take the top earth), throws into a tin pan or wooden bowl a shovel full of loose dirt and stones; then placing the basin an inch or two under water, continues to stir up the dirt with his hand in such a manner that the running water will carry off the light earths, occasionally, with his hand, throwing out the stones; after an operation of this kind for twenty or thirty minutes, a spoonful of small black sand remains; this is on a handkerchief or cloth dried in the sun, the emerge is blown off, leaving the pure gold. I have the pleasure of inclosing a paper of this sand and gold, which I from a bucket of dirt and stones, in half-an-hour, standing at the edge of the water, washed out myself. The value of it may be 2 dollars or 3 dollars.

The size of the gold depends in some measure upon the river from which it is taken; the banks of one river having larger grains of gold than another. I presume more than one half of the gold put into pans or machines is washed out and goes down the stream; this is of no consequence to the washers, who care only for the present time.

Some have formed companies of four or five men, and have a rough-made machine put together in a day, which worked to much advantage, yet many prefer to work alone, with a wooden bowl or tin pan, worth fifteen or twenty cents in the States, but eight to sixteen dollars at the gold region. As the workmen continue, and materials can be obtained, improvements will take place in the mode of obtaining gold.

How long this gathering of gold by the handful will continue here, or the future effect it will have on California, I cannot say. Three-fourths of the houses in the town on the bay of San Francisco are deserted. Houses are sold at the price of the ground lots. The effects are this week showing themselves in Monterey. Almost every house I had hired out is given up. Every blacksmith, carpenter, and lawyer is leaving; brick-yards, saw-mills and ranches are left perfectly alone.

A large number of the volunteers at San Francisco and Sonoma have deserted; some have been retaken and brought back; public and private vessels are losing their crews; my clerks have had 100 per cent advance offered them on their wages to accept employment. A complete revolution in the ordinary state of affairs is taking place; both of our newspapers are discontinued from want of workmen and the loss of their agencies; the Alcaldes have left San Francisco, and I believe Sonoma likewise; the former place has not a Justice of the Peace left.

The second Alcalde of Monterey to-day joins the keepers of our principal hotel, who have closed their office and house, and will leave to-morrow for the golden rivers. I saw on the ground a lawyer who was last year Attorney-General of the King of the Sandwich Islands, digging and washing out his ounce and a half per day; near him can be found most all his brethren of the long robe, working in the same occupation.

To conclude, my letter is long, but I could not well describe what I have seen in less words. If the affair proves a bubble, a mere excitement, I know not how we can all be deceived, as we are situated. Most of the land, where gold has been discovered, is

public land; there are on different rivers some private grants. I have three such purchased in 1846 and 1847, but have not learned that any private lands have produced gold, though they may hereafter do so. I have the honour, dear sir, to be, very respectfully, your obedient servant,
(Signed.)THOMAS O. LARKIN.

In his second letter, Larkin goes out of his way to downplay his observations. But they are right on the money. The gold fields were not only yielding huge amounts of placer gold, but also the real stuff, in the veins below the surface, had yet to be mined. And yet the state was suffering in some ways.

With everyone going to the gold fields, there was no one left to assume the regular jobs of blacksmith or merchant, for example. And law and order had broken down, too. All the police in San Francisco and other towns close to Coloma, had gone to the gold fields. It would be the rule of the gun and the knife and the noose for some time to come.

Yet Larkin was optimistic. He foresaw a huge population shift, a veritable migration from east to west, of Americans hunting for gold in the California gold fields. He saw the good that could come out of a "gold rush." The state and the nation would profit from the influx of new blood, new ideas.

Twelve days after Larkin wrote his second letter, the *California Star* newspaper published this article:

The excitement and enthusiasm of Gold Washing still continues—increases.

Many of our countrymen are not disposed to do us justice as regards the opinion we have at different times expressed of the employment in which over two thirds of the white population of the country are engaged. There appears to have gone abroad a belief that we should raise our voices against what some one has denominated an "infatuation." We are very far from it, and would invite a calm recapitulation of our articles touching the matter, as in themselves amply satisfactory. We shall continue to report the progress of the work, to speak within bounds, and to approve, admonish, or openly censure whatever, in our opinion, may require it at our hands.

It is quite unnecessary to remind our readers of the "prospects of California" at this time, as the effects of this gold washing enthusiasm, upon the country, through every branch of business are unmistakably apparent to every one. Suffice it that there is no abatement, and that active measures will probably be taken to prevent really serious and alarming consequences.

Every seaport as far south as San Diego, and every interior town, and nearly every rancho from the base of the mountains in which the gold has been found, to the Mission of San Luis, south, has become suddenly drained of human beings. Americans, Californians,

Indians and Sandwich Islanders, men, women and children, indiscriminately.

Should there be that success which has repaid the efforts of those employed for the last month, during the present and next, as many are sanguine in their expectations, and we confess to unhesitatingly believe probably, not only will witness the depopulation of every town, the desertion of every rancho, and the desolation of the once promising crops of the country, but it will also draw largely upon adjacent territories—awake Sonora, and call down upon us, despite her Indian battles, a great many of the good people of Oregon. There are at this time over one thousand souls busied in washing gold, and the yield per diem may be safely estimated at from fifteen to twenty dollars, each individual.—

We have by every launch from the embarcadera of New Helvetia, returns of enthusiastic gold seekers—heads of families, to effect transportation of their households to the scene of their successful labors, or others, merely returned to more fully equip themselves for a protracted, or perhaps permanent stay.

Spades, shovels, picks, wooden bowls, Indian baskets (for washing), etc., find ready purchase, and are very frequently disposed of at extortionate prices.

The gold region, so called, thus far explored, is about one hundred miles in length and twenty in width. These imperfect explorations contribute to establish the certainty of the placer extending much further south, probably three or four hundred miles, as we have before stated, while it is believed to terminate about a league north of the point at which first discovered. The probable amount taken from these mountains since the first of May last, we are informed is $100,000, and which is at this time principally in the hands of the mechanical, agricultural and laboring classes.

There is an area explored, within which a body of 50,000 men can advantageously labor. Without maliciously interfering with each other, then, there need be no cause for contention and discord, where as yet, we are gratified to know, there is harmony and good feeling existing. We really hope no unpleasant occurrences will grow out of this enthusiasm, and that our apprehensions may be quieted by continued patience and good will among the washers.

California Star
Saturday, July 10, 1848

Four days later, on July 14, the *California Star* ceased operations. There was no one left to publish the paper because all of its employees had migrated to the gold fields. In San Francisco, people had heard of the discovery and some had already started for the gold fields. Yet most had hung back out of careful reconnaissance; they would wait until people they knew had gone and confirmed before they, too, left their lives for the lure.

Sam Brannan, the San Francisco merchant who was

partners with Jed Smith at Sutter's Fort, decided to rid San Francisco of that indecisiveness. Certain to profit if the rush to the gold fields included the residents of the clapboard and tent town, on May 12, 1848, Brannan did the "pitch" of his life: he arrived in San Francisco with gold samples and ran through the town brandishing them and shouting of the discovery of gold in Coloma.

"Gold, gold on the American River!" Brannan shouted, waving a bottle of the yellow particles.

Brannan claimed to have just come from the gold fields. He had seen unimaginable wealth there accumulated in just days! Anyone could get wealthy, anyone, just by scooping up the ground. What Brannan didn't know was the scope of the gold discovery. No one did; it could only be suspected. Brannon was only looking to drum up interest for his business. Instead, he ignited a rush to the gold fields. As for San Francisco, the city became a ghost town overnight as everyone, every able bodied man, fled for the gold fields.

Sutter wasn't a fool. He knew he would be one if he didn't at least try his hand in the gold fields, when it appeared to be so plentiful and all around him. Maybe the governor wouldn't give him his sawmill, but he could file a claim like anyone else. He had been unable to stop the gold seekers from pursuing their dreams at the expense of his own. He therefore decided to try his hand at the mines.

In the summer of 1848, he set out from his fort with Indians and other hired labor. He went south of

Coloma, following a creek, until he found a likely-looking spot and began panning for gold. Eventually word got out that Captain Sutter of the Swiss Guard was himself mining. Figuring the captain was enriching himself, men flocked around him to do the same.

A town grew up around a muslin tent where the miners gathered on rainy Sundays. Looking for a name, someone proposed using the name of its most famous citizen. That seemed like a good idea, and the town was dubbed "Sutter's Creek." Unfortunately, John Sutter wasn't a miner. He had brought his hired help with him to do the hard work, and that did not stand well with the other prospectors. If a man did the work, he should get the spoils. It wasn't right for others to profit on another man's labor.

It made no difference. Sutter's workers weren't good miners either. None of them ever hit pay dirt. Sutter returned to his fort, never to mine again. But the town named after him stayed. By 1850, the placer gold had petered out and Sutter's Creek was in danger of becoming a ghost town. Then in 1851, quartz, another valuable mineral, was found in the vicinity. Quartz mining began and saved the town, though Sutter never set foot there again.

❋ ❋ ❋

Sutter's Fort
November 11, 1848

Friend . . .

Have contrived to borrow a sheet of paper from an officer attached to Colonel Mason's command.

I embrace this opportunity of communicating to you some idea of the excitement at present pervading in this district.

About the discovery of such great quantity of the precious ore gold, when I wrote last to my father's at home, I was a quiet and painstaking merchant of San Francisco, my stock in trade consisting of everything and anything that I might come across in the way of domestic utensils.

No sooner, however, had the news reached us of the discoveries at Marshall's that I was instantly deserted by my clerks and even my French Canadian cook, who boasts of having made all imaginable dishes to suit the dainty palate of one or the other of the Iturbide family of Mexico, cut, stick and run, leaving me "alone in my glory."

What in this emergency was I to do? Nobody would serve me, in my brief hour of need. I therefore followed the example of my neighbors and there I am, up to my "flanks" in mud, water and c. with a curiously shaped trowel in one hand and a "cradle" in the other, scraping and hawling [sic] up lumps of gold at each endeavor.

I have, so far, got together 2500 dollars worth of gold and have only been at work a month. My "partners," however, Hackett and Carr, have made a still better thing of it, having struck a richer spot than that yon whoever I am at work. I assure you, I often think of the pleasant hours were have passed at that restaurant on NY and wish that I could find an opportunity of spending some of my hold there, as "once upon a time" I did.

There are a number of U.S. deserters staying about and I should not be at all surprised if the entire regiment followed soot [sic]. As for apprehending all deserters, that would be a difficult matter. In fact, it is a dangerous matter to send out other soldiers to apprehend them, as they also would desert, and Col. Mason would have no effective body left to enforce obedience to his orders.

As there will doubtless be many among you who will be impregnated to visit this fortune-favored region, as soon as the news of the late discovery shall have reached you, I have judged it not malapropos to furnish you with some information respecting the climate, produces of the country, etc. etc. for there will I dare say be many who will locate permanently in the country. You would be astonished to see how rapidly town and villages (of rough material, it is true) are beginning to spring up around the concentrating points on the gold district.

During the summer and greater part of the fall, the winds on the coast about San Francisco blow from the west and never from the ocean. The mornings are pleasant and clear, the temperature of the atmosphere during the major part of the data is about then same. There is little really cold weather during the winter here; in fact you would be astonished and delighted, should you come out there yourself at the change between the climate at gore and that here.

Grapes are raised here in an abundance of a flavor unequalled by those of any country in the face of the globe they are a favorite of diet with everybody, high and low. The soil is in most places fertile beyond description and what water we lack during the dry months is supposed by irrigation. The season for sowing wheat commences early in November and continues until early sprung.

When I have made my fortune, I will perhaps revisit you.

Unknown

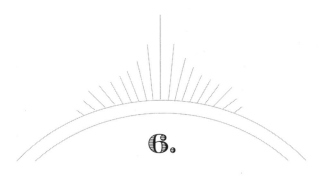

6.

TRAVELING TO
THE GOLD FIELDS

By the end of 1848, the discovery of gold had brought thousands to the gold fields. They camped up and down the American and Feather Rivers, in every hollow and valley, using the most primitive of equipment to try to extract gold from earth and water and dust. Most of those prospectors were Californios, Mormons, and other "miners," such as the Jack Tars from Australia, who were ex-convicts. The started to arrive on ships in San Francisco Harbor, as did Chinese and Mexicans.

Back east, the stories of gold had been well publicized in all the major newspapers. The *New York Times* and the *New York Herald* carried accounts. But whether the public believed them is a different manner. It was just too good to be true. A man born into poverty could, just like that,

overnight strike it rich and enter the upper class by discovering gold in California?

It couldn't be. Yet . . . if the stories were true, the
country was not physically ready for the population
movement that would occur as people struck for the gold
fields. There were few roads west of St. Louis, and none
were safe from the perils of the western frontier. The
eastern publishing industry saw that.

Book and pamphlet publishers were always on the
lookout for something to make money. To date, they had
survived, but the industry was not firmly established.
Books had to be able to give the reader something they
couldn't get anywhere else, such as in newspapers and
pamphlets. And no story to date had been able to do
that—until Marshall's discovery.

By the end of 1848, New York's publishers were vying
to put out books and pamphlets on the California gold
fields and their infinite possibilities. Pamphlets also
were published that brought together letters of Thomas
Larkin and John Frémont describing the California
landscape and the gold fields.

Suddenly, California guidebooks began to appear in
stores. Sometimes they came from firsthand reporting—
the first consistent example of travel writing in U.S. history. They promoted travel to California and the state's
beauty and possibilities.

In 1848, Henry Simpson published his best seller *The
Emigrant's Guide to the Gold Mines.* On page 27 Simpson offers
advice to emigrants on how to get to the California gold
fields. There are five routes to choose from:

1. The Isthmus route, across the Isthmus of Panama from the Atlantic to the Pacific.
2. The Cape Horn route, around the tip of South America and up the Pacific Coast.
3. The Rocky Mountains route—that is, climbing the Rocky Mountains after crossing the Great Plains and eventually arriving in the gold fields of California.
4. The Nicaraguan route, around the Isthmus of Nicaragua and once again up the Pacific coast.
5. The Mazatlán route, which required crossing northern Mexico to the Mexican coast city and then taking a ship north, to San Francisco.

"Only two [are] feasible," Simpson writes, "with any degree of comfort or economy and we may add safety." Simpson preferred the southern routes. "The Chagres steamer leaves New York monthly as also the British West Indian Mail Steamers and they reach Chagres on the Atlantic side in two days, where they will get a steamer or sailing vessel for San Francisco. The distance by this conveyance from New York to San Francisco is about 17,000 miles and will occupy 150 days or five months. Passengers should provide themselves with the means to guard against contingencies as they may arise from the no arrival of the steamers at Panama."

If you chose the Isthmus of Panama route and your steamer to California didn't show up on time, you'd better have enough cash to get by on until the steamer finally docked. The shipping schedules were erratic and not to be relied on. Going the isthmus route was rough going from one side of the North American continent to the other. To go through the isthmus took ten days.

"Canoes are here employed and passengers carried thirty miles up, when they are transferred to the backs of mules, and in this way reach Panama in two days where they will take another steamer or sailing vessel for San Francisco."

"The safest route," Simpson asserts, "is doubtless via Cape Horn. 25 to 30 days to get there. The price of passage first class is $400."

If the choice was the Rocky Mountains route, the prospector would find himself going "across the Rockies, and the Great Desert, a route which by no means we can recommend." The jumping-off point for such a trek was Independence, Missouri, from which wagon trains bound west, usually on the Oregon Trail, were every day plowing a highway across the country. "[Across the Rockies] the distance is very great; there are deserts to be crossed, mountains to be scaled and hostile Indians to be encountered."

The overland route was the most dangerous. Even armed settlers were at a disadvantage with firearms. Many contemporary revolvers were no more accurate than a thrown knife. They were accurate only at very close range, and even then, misfires occurred frequently. Rifles were good for firing over longer distances, but again, they were none too accurate.

Even as firearms advances came along, west of the Mississippi you couldn't count on buying anything new unless it had been imported. Everything had to be carried with you during that long, lonely trek across the mountains.

The least known, the "Nicaraguan route, is one which offers to travellers . . . as many inducements as now known. This we allude to is the Isthmus of Nicaragua, about 150 miles from the Atlantic to the Pacific. The greatest advice we see in the Nicaragua route is the ease with which it may be traveled and the certainty of proceeding with comfort and safety. The terrain is passable in all seasons."

There was also a little-known route, the Acapulco route, which involved going from Acapulco, "which the American Mails steamers sailed. The passage is $1225 and the distance about 2000 miles. The cost total is $280 and takes about 40 days."

There was one event that year that threatened to eclipse the gold discovery: the presidential election of 1848.

That summer, as the campaign got into full swing, slavery came back into the news as a campaign issue. The Mexican-American War had obscured the country's split on the issue of slavery, which threatened the very ties of the Union. There was concern by antislavery opponents that California and the new Western territories might align themselves with the South; this possibility needed to be avoided at all costs.

Massachusetts senator Daniel Webster, the man Stephen Vincent Benét would later claim argued a case in hell as a defense lawyer in his novel "The Devil and Daniel Webster," excoriated Polk for the useless, arid land he had acquired for Yankee dollars in the Treaty of Guadalupe-Hidalgo. The war itself had taken longer than Polk had anticipated, so long that he had lost the support of his party. The Democrats instead nominated Lewis Cass, who fashioned a self-serving slavery compromise platform.

Breakaway, rebellious Democrats supported former president Martin Van Buren under the Free Soil third-party banner. Once again, the Democrats had shot themselves in the foot, failing to unite early behind one candidate. The Whigs, who had been out of power for twenty years, saw their chance. They no longer had to beat an incumbent.

The Whigs nominated the one candidate guaranteed not to lose. In the tradition of Washington and Jackson, the Whigs put forth the most celebrated military leader of his time, none other than old Rough and Ready himself, Zachary Taylor. Taylor had gotten the nickname because he was a slob and always showed up looking half dressed, with crumbs all over himself. But he was a popular general and an honest man, if a trifle eccentric in his appearance.

By September, all evidence indicated that Taylor's popularity was so high he was going to be elected by a vast majority. Then, on September 15, the *New York Herald* carried this item:

INTERESTING FROM CALIFORNIA—We have received some late and interesting intelligence from California. It is to the 1st of July. Owing to the crowded state of our columns, we are obliged to omit our correspondence. It relates to the important discovery of a very valuable gold mine. We have received a specimen of the gold.

Two days later, September 17, the *Herald* gave the larger part of an inside column to a dispatch from its California correspondent, who called himself "Paisano." Dated July 1, in the dispatch Paisano told *Herald* publisher James Gordon Bennett, "[You] had better fill his paper with, at least, probable tales and stories and not such outrageous fictions as rivers, flowing with gold."

Everyone in California had gone to the mines, Paisano reported. Many came home quickly with many hundreds of dollars in gold dust and nuggets in their pockets. Prices for mining equipment had soared. Spades and shovels were $10 apiece. Blacksmiths made $240 a week. Comparing California to El Dorado and the *Arabian Nights*, the *Herald* correspondent said that "the famous El Dorado was but a sand bank, the *Arabian Nights* were tales of simplicity."

On September 18, the paper carried another dispatch from Paisano, on page 3, the prize inside page that the eye goes to immediately upon turning the first or headline page. That day, page 3 also contained stories on France's election and a cholera outbreak in London. Two days later, the paper reprinted an article from the *Washington Union* in which the gold discovery was confirmed by official letters, including one signed by American counsel Thomas Larkin.

The article went on to say that "the danger in California is from want of food for the residents, and still more for the stream of immigrants. Would not some of our merchants find it a profitable speculation to send cargoes of biscuit, flour, &c., 'round to the Pacific Coast."

It was a good point. If people were going to leave home and hearth for the gold fields, what other place other than Sutter's Fort existed then in the wilderness to supply their wants? The *Herald* made sure to mention that the U.S. steam packet *California* would sail from New York on October 2 for California laden with a rich cache of supplies to provide for the needs and wants of aspiring gold seekers.

For the rest of the month, the *New York Herald* had continuous coverage of the California gold fields through Paisano's dispatches. The presidential campaign and the troubles in Europe still dominated the front pages, but you could count on Paisano to be in the paper someplace toward the front. Not surprisingly, the coverage was helping to sell advertising.

Outfitters' advertisements were coming in. So were notices by groups preparing for the trip to El Dorado. No one was rushing yet, for it would still take an official edict to make the easterner finally believe en masse and act on that belief. The same thought was going through the head of the editor of the *Times of London*.

He had been scanning the overseas dispatches from the United States and come across a short story regarding gold discoveries in California. Not only did the *Times of London* editor chooses to bury it on page four, he also doubted its validity, concluding with this paragraph:

The placer sand is said to be so rich, that if exported to England or the United States, it would be very valuable. Consequent upon this excitement, the price of provisions has increased enormously. We need hardly observe that it is necessary to view these statements with great caution.

The British government knew that if the gold discovery proved to be real, Britain could benefit quickly. If the discovery were confirmed, California could act as a relief valve, siphoning off the overpopulation of Britain's cities. In November, the *Times* of London printed a notice that the gold fields had been denounced as a delusion. The accuser said he had prospected in California for years, to no avail.

By late in the month, Britain had momentarily lost interest in gold. A cholera epidemic had broken out throughout the British Isles. More than nineteen hundred were already dead, with many thousands more infected, and the disease showed no sign of letting up.

In the nineteenth century, cholera was a deadly disease. First given prominence by the medical community during an outbreak in India in 1817, ironically it was forward-thinking technology in the form of transportation improvements, especially the steam engine, that brought cholera to Britain's shores. It then spread from town to town by horse and cart. Cholera swept through London in 1832, causing the death of seven thousand people in a most horrible way.

Cholera causes extreme stomach upset, nausea, and

dizziness, which lead to violent vomiting and diarrhea. Stools turn into a gray liquid that includes fragments of intestinal membrane. Muscular cramps and an insatiable thirst follow. Then, finally, the pulse drops and the final lethargy begins. Dehydrated, near death, the victim's face shows the classic cholera look of puckered blue lips in a cadaverous face.

What no one knew, because epidemiology was in its infancy, was that cholera was caused by the bacterium *Vibrio cholerae*. The bacterium released deadly toxins into the intestine, increasing secretions of water and chloride ions (salts) into the body. That resulted in the diarrhea, severe dehydration, and death of the victim. Luckily, only 25 percent exposed to the bacterium develop the disease, which was why in the same household, one parent or child might be sick and the others not.

Most importantly, what was not known was that the filthy sanitary conditions that existed in England during the nineteenth century, and many parts of America as well, contributed to the growth of the cholera bacterium and therefore the disease. Bathing, defecating, urinating, and drinking from the same stream or water source without regard to health consequences was common nineteenth-century practice. Cholera spread rapidly, especially in smaller settlements, where dung, filth, and refuse quickly commingled on streets and in ditches.

While a cholera epidemic was nothing to be ignored, Americans had a tough time understanding how something happening abroad could affect them at home. They pushed that health crisis out of their minds and went to the polls. This time they elected a new president, General Zachary Taylor of the Whig Party, by a narrower margin than previously anticipated. Nevertheless, in the wake of the election, there was a feeling in the country that business was about to boom. As for the Democratic presidential nominee Lewis Cass, he stayed Lewis Cass.

In Washington, the lame duck president James K. Polk was watching all the speculation about gold and could not believe his good fortune. He was a no-nonsense Tennessee lawyer, and his war with Mexico had just paid off in a way one could only dream about. Reading Thomas Larkin's letters to Secretary Buchanan, Polk realized that in light of all the dispatches he was receiving from California, especially the ones from his confidential agent, it was time to officially confirm the discovery. His State of the Union address on December 5, 1848, was the perfect time to make the public announcement verifying the gold discovery.

Everyone had been waiting for it. No matter the political party, everyone trusted Polk's word implicitly because he was the president, and the president didn't lie. Hearing enough of the rumors of California gold, the nation waited to see what he would say about California in his address. And no one waited on his the edge of his seat more than Polk's political enemy Daniel Webster.

"It is known that mines of the precious metals existed to a considerable extent in California at the time of her acquisition. Recent discoveries render it probable that these mines are more extensive and valuable than anticipated," the president told the Congress and Supreme

Court assembled in the House chamber to hear his address. "The accounts of the abundance of gold in that territory are of such an extraordinary character as would scarcely command belief were they not corroborated by the authentic reports of officers in the public service, who have visited the mineral district, and derived the facts which they detail from personal observation."

The most trusted man in the Union, the president of the United States, had finally proclaimed the discovery of gold in California real! People *were* getting rich. Daniel Webster suddenly shut his famous mouth. It looked like Polk's treaty was a bargain. In St. Louis, an invisible gate that stood at the boundaries of civilization opened.

No matter there were no highways, instead rutted trails west. People would now line up at that gate, they wouldn't wait for their mark. Instead, over the line in a flash, hightailing it for the gold fields as fast as their legs, their horses' legs, their kids' legs, their dogs' legs, *any* legs could carry them.

Thus on December 5, 1848, when President Polk confirmed Marshall's find, the American character changed. At the moment when Polk's lips uttered the magic word "gold!," Americans began their phantom pursuit of wealth.

From its beginnings at Jamestown and Plymouth Rock in the seventeenth century, the American character had not matured all that much by the middle of the nineteenth century. America was still primarily an agrarian society with a belief that good work leads to a good life, which then leads to a good afterlife. But Polk's announcement let loose something primordial that had been lurking in the American character since John Adams had been a boy.

What had Marshall wrought?

Farmers in stony New England fields that yielded little, shoemakers in Ohio, preachers in Missouri, it made no difference who you were; what was certain was that whatever economic class you were born into was the one you were condemned to inhabit for the rest of your life. Only the truly lucky ones got financial success. But Marshall's discovery offered the opportunity of a lifetime, of a generation, of an *age*, to redeem the quintessentially American character: the ability to reinvent yourself regardless of your past. Marshall's gold offered hope not just for the present, but also for the future, for if enough gold could be found in California, your children and your children's children would benefit, too.

Legitimate, confirmed accounts began to appear in Eastern newspapers of individuals who struck it rich by the banks of the American River. It became clear: Americans could, literally, through a few weeks in California's gold fields, go from poverty to riches. Advertisements in newspapers and magazines continued to display the wares of enterprising merchants looking to make a buck off the backs of the miners. They offered everything from camp hampers to Spanish lessons, even portable houses made of galvanized iron.

Guides sought out readily obtainable appointments to take settlers and miners west to the new El Dorado.

Suddenly there was a boom in the transportation business, with the steamer coming into popular vogue over the more traditional sailing ship as a quick and efficient method of carrying passengers.

Steamer lines sprung up to take miners to California who wanted to get rich quick. Smart easterners, men such as John Armour and John Studebaker, determined to get rich not by mining but by plying their fortunes through trade with the miners. Armour was a butcher and Studebaker a carriage-maker.

People began organizing into travel groups that promoted safety. In New Orleans, a group met at the St. Charles Hotel to organize an expedition to California. In Boston, hundreds put up $500 apiece for a ship and cargo, and were counting on selling their goods to pay for passage around Cape Horn. Philadelphia was sending tremendous amounts of flour, while the price of Baltimore clothing, bound for the Pacific Coast, skyrocketed.

By the end of 1848, not only San Francisco had been emptied of its inhabitants, but also the city pueblos down the coast—San Jose, Santa Barbara, and Los Angeles. And now the rest of the country, and the world, were coming, too. Upon reading Polk's statement, the British people were just as excited as the Americans at the prospect of instant wealth. There was nothing to stop them from coming to America immediately to prospect. The borders of the United States were wide open to gold speculators.

Still, the British press, perhaps jealous of their former colony's sudden wealth, refused to acknowledge the true depth of the find. The *Journal of Commerce* stated in an article that the minute quantity of gold discovered in California wouldn't affect the world price of the ore. In fact, the *Journal* stated, placer gold usually indicated not much more below the ground.

They were wrong. There was much more below the ground. But having the machinery to mine it was another matter.

How could he make a dollar off the argonauts bound for the gold fields? That's what John Sutter was wondering as the year wore on.

It had become evident that his dream of a self-sustained community, of becoming a multimillionaire through his fort and other nearby interests, was going down the river. There were men all over the place now, and more coming in every day. The Americans refused to recognize his Spanish land grant. Already there were men prospecting on Sutter's land, including the area in and around the now-abandoned Coloma sawmill, and there was nothing he could do about it except try to make some money while the demand lasted.

The entrepreneurial Sutter came up with the idea of taking his headquarters building in the fort and turning the second and third floors into a hotel. He established a small bowling alley on the lower floor for recreational purposes. And he allowed merchants to rent out space in his fort, making it the first shopping "mall" in state history. Sutter, the entrepreneur, Sutter of the Swiss Guard, would carry on.

7.

MCNEIL'S TRAVELS

When gold was discovered on January 24, 1848, by James Marshall, shoemaker Samuel McNeil was in Lancaster Ohio, thousands of miles from Coloma. The distance didn't make a difference. By the end of the year, everyone in Lancaster knew about the gold discovery. Just like in every small town in every one of the states, in every nook and cranny of the territories, gold fever took hold.

It really was a fever, or perhaps using another medical metaphor, an epidemic. Men by the thousands decided to leave home and strike for the gold fields to change not only their luck, but their family and family's family luck as well. To strike it rich meant that unless such fortune was squandered, generations in the future might have its benefit.

Samuel McNeil heard the siren song of gold. It was long, sweet, as alluring as the turn of a woman's ankle. One of Lancaster's citizens, McNeil was an articulate, driven man who wanted to rise above his station. Quickly. The discovery of gold excited his fancy and hopes. McNeil believed that the celebrated Golden Age had arrived at last.

"I am sure the critics will have mercy on my writing when I inform 'the public' that I am a shoemaker, not ashamed of the occupation by which I have earned my bread for twenty years. Therefore, I am not as well skilled in writing as a [James Fennimore] Cooper or a Washington Irving; but, what I have, I freely give unto you. In shoemaker style, I will bestow my *awl* of literature, feeling that at the *last* they will find I have done my best to amuse and instruct them, while the critics will not *strap* me for doing my duty!" McNeil later wrote in his memoirs.

In 1850, Scott & Bascom, printers in Columbus, Ohio, printed less than one hundred copies of his eponymous title, *McNeil's Travels in 1849 to, through and from the gold regions, in California*. Over the years, it became shortened to *McNeil's Travels*. It stands as the best contemporary account of an individual joining the Gold Rush, what was later known as a "49er."

While Marshall's discovery had taken place in 1848, primarily local Californians and Mexicans had flocked to the gold fields. It wasn't until 1849 that the California Gold Rush became a true national and international phenomenon. Those who came in that first, "official" year of the Gold Rush would forever more be labeled affectionately as 49ers. The fact that the gold was actually discovered in 1848 was lost in popular history.

Samuel McNeil was about to become a "49er."

"Counting the cost and measuring the difficulties, I joined a respectable company going to the Promised Land. The company consisted of Boyd Ewing, a son of the Hon. Thomas Ewing, Secretary of the Interior; James Myers, a capable and honest constable; Rankin, State Attorney; Jesse B. Hart, a shrewd lawyer; Benjamin Fennifrock, a farmer; Samuel Stambaugh, a merchant; Samuel Stambaugh, a druggist; Edward Strode, a potter, from Perry county; John McLaughlin, from the same county; Denman, nephew of the Hon. Thomas Ewing; William F. Legg, from Columbus, and Leverett, from the same."

Boyd intended to look up his foster brother, Cump Sherman, Colonel Mason's adjutant, when he got out West. For his part, McNeil was aware of Ewing's lineage and connections, but did not know, nor did anyone else except those close to Governor Mason, that it had been his letter to Sutter, authored by Sherman, that had allowed the gold prospectors to converge on Sutter's sawmill and vicinity, "Captain" Sutter's Mexican property rights be damned.

While political connections were always good, McNeil realized, more importantly there was strength in numbers against the deprivations the miners would face—arid desert, boggy lands, insurmountable mountains, infesting disease, murders and killers and robbers of all sorts, as well as sandstorms, hail the size of rocks, rocks the size of mountains, and torrential rains. If half of what had been printed about the transcontinental trek in current books could be believed, it would be a long and dangerous haul to the gold fields.

No less of a danger were the hostiles, Indian nations that had refused to sign treaties with the U.S. government, thus ceding their lands for a reservation life. Depending on what route was taken across the continent, the argonauts would have to face the Sioux, the Cheyenne, the Comanche, and the Apache, all proud Indian nations that would not give up or allow trespassing on their lands. The answer to invasion would be butchery of any white men who dared invade.

And yet with all that, the Mormon Battalion had made it. The Mormons had shown how effective a group working together could travel to the West, especially when the goal on the other side was gold. Religion aside, the Mormons wanted to get rich, too. Suddenly the continent was mobile; it could be traversed by the common person, not just some dime novel mountain man. All you needed was what the Mexicans called *cojones.*

Sometimes prospectors would go straight across the continent and all that entailed. Sometimes they would travel from their homes in the interior to a river that could take them south to a port where they could pick up a ship for South America and thereby make their way around and up the Pacific Coast.

Regardless of which route you took, it took a lot of time to go from Wherever, U.S.A., to California.

"February 7, 1849, we started by coach, from Lancaster,

Ohio, passing through Columbus, to Cincinnati," McNeil wrote, "remaining a week at the latter place, where we obtained the necessary outfit, consisting of two years' provisions and the appropriate weapons of defence. The articles were sea biscuit, side pork, packed in kegs; six tents, knives, forks, and plates; each man a good rifle, a pair of revolvers, a bowie knife, two blankets, and crucibles, supposing that we would be obliged to melt the ore, not knowing that nature had already melted it to our hands.

"On February 15, we started in the steamer *South America*, commanded by Capt. Logan, for New Orleans, 1600 miles, costing each $10 in the cabin." The journey required traveling on the Ohio River, into the Mississippi, thence down to New Orleans, where a ship could be engaged for the South American route to the gold fields.

"I cannot omit saying that we found Capt. Logan a perfect gentleman, fit for a higher station, and his boat one of the best in the western waters. The trip was made in six days."

Even McNeil the humble shoemaker was capable of making a judgment based on the popular perception of class. To him, a steamboat pilot was capable of "a higher station."

"While passing around the Falls at Louisville, Kentucky, we saw Porter, the Kentucky Giant, who is keeping tavern at the locks. He is more than eight feet in height, and he looked down upon us little mortals with the feelings of a Goliath when he gazed on David of old. If he is not a temperance man he cannot flourish in his establishment, for his huge corporocity

[size] would speedily oblivionize whole oceans of porter, ale, and brandy."

Born in 1810, Jim Porter was something of a freak in Kentucky. While the average man's height was five-six, he rose a full seven-eight. The best-known and most easily recognizable character in early Louisville history, Porter was so famous that Charles Dickens said of him, "He was a lighthouse among lamp posts." He ran the Big Gun Tavern, which is where McNeil saw him in 1849. But he wasn't 8 feet tall, as McNeil reported.

Porter lied to everyone about his height. He was really seven-eight; eight feet just sounded better. It made him that much more spectacular as a freak. The idea was that while people gazed at him, he made money selling them liquor. Porter, whatever his height, was soon left behind as the steamer continued downriver.

"We found a crowd of gamblers on the steamer, who, like the Devil, are going to and fro on the earth seeking whom they may devour. Considering them turkey buzzards, which is a grade lower than eagles, we avoided them with some difficulty, as they tried hard to get us into their clutches, judging correctly that we had plenty of the silver rocks and gold paving stones at the commencement of our journey.

"We observed one of them fleece a lieutenant in the army out of $50, the latter rising calmly from the table observing that he had paid a big sum for a little amusement, when he ought to have had sense enough to know that he had been cheated, and courage enough to have chastised the gambling robber.

"At Paducah, in Kentucky, a gentleman came on board to see the adventurers who were going to California, and observed, with a very long face—much longer than a flour barrel—that we had experienced our last of comfort and civilization, as our difficulties and privations were commencing, and that we had better return and be satisfied with the little which Providence had placed in our hands, which would be a great treasure if enjoyed with a contented mind. I admired him for his philanthropic feeling, but considered his philosophy unsound, for I believed that that same Providence was influencing us to seek the gold regions."

McNeil had a very liberal religious view.

"The Lord says that the gold and silver are His, and he does not wish them to remain hidden and unemployed in the earth. While philosophers and religionists are constantly crying for gold to extend their respective schemes, it is certainly no sin to dig it out of the earth to spread it. The more gold there is circulating in the world, the more will it fall into the hands of philosophers and christians for the spread of christianity and philosophy. Although much of it will be expended in scenes of dissipation, we have the faith to believe that it will ultimately fall into the right hands."

Throughout the country, Americans of all denominations were asking this question in their churches: What was God's hand in the Gold Rush? Philosophy, of course, is fine, and meditation is wonderful, but in the end, greed and the determination to find a better life in this life won out. McNeil's practical view of the gold discovery was no different from that of most of his pious countrymen.

"Some preachers have asserted from the pulpit—one in Lancaster particularly, whose name I do not wish to mention—that the straightest way to California is the nearest road to hell; but, as fanaticism never can be right, I must believe that the discovery of California gold will be a general blessing to the earth, aiding in extending religion, philosophy, and commerce—not only benefiting the public generally, but shining gladness into many a private circle.

"I shall blame Uncle Sam a great deal more than I blame the preachers, if he is too hasty in selling the California gold lands in lots to speculators—to rich speculators, who are too wealthy already, that they may place it beyond the reach of our poorer classes, who, as true republicans, should have the full advantage of a republican government. I move that Uncle Sam keep those lands out of the market for several years, that the bone and sinew of our country may have opportunities to increase their little store."

McNeil did not know that his childhood neighbor William Tecumseh Sherman had already done exactly that.

"They [the gold argonauts] have not the talent and genius to fill high offices, and thereby fill their pockets, but, as their genius lies in their hands, let them employ it in digging for gold. Our government should bless all its constituents, both rich and poor. The rich for many years have had chances for filling their pockets—let the poor now have a chance!"

There it was! The class differences in the United States were finally not only being acknowledged, but also discussed. McNeil was simply stating what many were thinking: that the United States should not be a country of rich and poor, that there had to be something *better*. There had to be opportunity for the poor to aspire to a better life for themselves and their children. In the gold fields, under dint of their own labor, all men were equal.

McNeil in his travels cast his eye on everything around him.

"I must relate an occurrence, proving that the Western loafers are as expert in strategy as the loafers of the East— yea, even as the celebrated Beau Hickman who flourished at Washington City, whose exploits in the loafing line would fill a volume."

Well, maybe not a volume, but certainly a paragraph. Robert S. "Beau" Hickman boasted to one and all that he never worked a day in his life. Born to a respected Virginia family in 1813, Hickman was a *gentleman loafer*. Never known to work for his living, he made money through racetrack bets and various filmflammery. Yet McNeil saw somebody in the West to rival Hickman's loafing proficiency.

"A little below Red River, at what is called the *Cut-off*, about nine o'clock at night, a pistol was fired on an island, and the person who fired it swung a burning brand around his head as a signal that he wished a passage. On rounding to, it proved to be a solitary island, without a living soul except the person wishing a passage, who brought on board what appeared to be a trunk.

"He was a Frenchman, who could not, or pretended

he could not speak English. When pay time arrived he coolly observed that he had not a cent in the world, adding that the captain of a boat, for no cause, had landed him on the solitary island. On examining what appeared to be his trunk, it was discovered to be a bundle of old blankets and clothes formed into that shape, proving that he could square his trunk if he could not square his account."

The Frenchman was trying to con a free ride down-river from Captain Logan.

"The circumstance created much laughter and some pity among the cabin passengers. It is well that this *loafer* fell into the hands of Captain Logan, who, instead of cruelly thrusting him upon another desert island, concluded to give him a free passage to New Orleans, considering it more in the light of a good joke than anything else.

"So while one captain voluntarily took French leave of the Frenchman, the other would not benevolently permit the Frenchman to take French leave of him. Although at the lowest notch of poverty, the Frenchman was as gay as a lark. Certainly the French and the Irish are the gayest people in the world in misfortune."

With the latter statement, the shoemaker from Lancaster shows how nativist influence in the country that looked on Irish immigrants as third-class citizens could affect even the most humble of men. Lumping the French in with the Irish was another attempt to dehumanize a nation that the United States had always looked on as an untrustworthy ally.

"About one hundred and sixty miles north of New

Orleans the *South America* ran into trouble. At about 10 o'clock at night, a tremendous storm from the south forced the Mississippi's high waves over the hurricane deck. That exposed us to two fatal dangers, explosion of the boilers and wreck of the vessel in a spot where escape was impossible.

"When the Captain became alarmed, *we* thought it time for us to be somewhat uneasy as well. If the storm was fatal, the loss would be great in life and property, as the passengers in the cabin and on deck, and the crew, amounted to about one hundred and seventy-five, and we had a very valuable freight on board. But few had the courage to swear, and many had the wisdom to pray, who afterwards were the foremost in drinking and gambling, like the person in a storm at sea who prayed to the *good Devil* as well as to the *good Lord* that he might be sure of safety.

"In fact, those storms coming from the Gulf of Mexico are not to be laughed at by the most courageous, as they sometimes extend their ravages almost to the sources of the Mississippi and the Missouri rivers, and then branch off to play a few tricks in Illinois, Indiana, and Ohio."

McNeil is referring to the hurricanes and tropical storms that during the fall months in particular come in off the Gulf of Mexico and drift north, sometimes losing power, sometimes picking it up, always leaving devastation in their midst. People in the United States of the middle Nineteenth Century were fully aware of the ferocious power of those storms, but they could not predict when they would arrive, which constantly put life and property in jeopardy.

Sailors knew the power of the storms intimately, and Captain Logan was no exception.

"To preserve our vessel from being broken asunder by the mountain billows or whelmed beneath the raging waves, the captain caused the steamer to be anchored near a high shore, so that we might be some what shielded from the raging storm, where we remained until morning."

The following morning saw the storm abate. The sun came out in true gulf style; the air became moist and hot. Captain Logan took the opportunity of good weather to his advantage. The *South America* needed to be serviced after its trip through the hurricane, so it anchored in Baton Rouge for five hours while repairs were made. While awaiting the repairs, McNeil and party played tourist. They found it at the nearby residence of General Zachary Taylor, or rather President Taylor.

"Of course, he was absent, but he had left his glorious mark on the place, everything being good and in its place according to regimental rule."

Riding back to the steamer in a hansom cab, the party from Lancaster got their sea legs again. It gave McNeil a chance to compose his thoughts about their trip thus far.

"During our passage, the Mississippi river was unusually high, in some places running over the levees, and occasionally over the highest of them. These levees, or artificial embankments, formed to shield the farms from the water, commence somewhere about eight hundred miles above New Orleans, and are erected and repaired during the winter by gangs of slaves.

"It is supposed by some authors that the channel of

that river is gradually filling from the floating mud and drifting trees conjoining and forming a solid bottom, so that as the descending water is the same in quantity, it must eventually rush over the highest levees that can be formed, and flood all that portion of Louisiana along the river, especially New Orleans."

It was a matter the Army Corps of Engineers eventually looked into. Repairing, building. and maintaining Louisiana levees became one of its essential jobs. As for McNeil, it was time to sail once again.

"On the 20th of February, we arrived at New Orleans, and sojourned at the Planter's Hotel, conducted by Chandler, who is the most accommodating and most reasonable host I have met in all my travels. To be a little jovial, we soon found that the inhabitants of New Orleans are the most patriotic people in the United States—that is, they have Fourth of July every Sunday, closing the stores on the occasion that the people may have a better opportunity for frolicking, frequenting the horse-race ground, the cockpit, the gambling establishments, soldier parades and engine company celebrations, circuses and theatres; carrying on balls, and sending up blazing sky rockets and balloons at night."

This was the New Orleans barely thirty-five years after the corsair Jean Lafitte, the hero of the Battle of New Orleans, held sway. The city was still as gay and as corrupt as ever. The miners could dawdle if they wanted, and lose everything they had in the city's whorehouses and opium dens, or they could continue on and hope to strike it rich.

"Understanding that the steamship *Maria Burt* was about starting for Chagres (Panama), we employed our comrade Stambaugh to engage passage for us." But Stambaugh had an angle. "He desired to place some of us in the steerage, while himself and a few select friends wished to occupy the cabin." McNeil, Ewing, and most of the others turned the tables on Stambaugh, "by bringing all together into the cabin, wishing to bring all on a level both as to comforts and privations. Perhaps he thought some of us could not bear the cabin expenses—if so, he is excusable; but if any other motive impelled his movements, he is willing to have a burden on his heart which we would not have on ours for a considerable sum.

"Feb. 28th, we started from New Orleans in the *Maria Burt* bound for Chagres. Shortly after passing Balize in the Gulf, the vessel sprang a leak, and leaked so much that we returned with difficulty to New Orleans."

McNeil and the Lancaster men were hoping to take the isthmus route, but now they were forced to improvise if they didn't want to waste time waiting for another steamer to the isthmus. Instead, "We took passage in the steamship *Globe* going [through the gulf] to [port] Brazos in Texas." The idea, now, would be to strike across northern Mexico by land; then up the Pacific Coast by boat. It was a way to save time by not having to go farther south, but it also meant a difficult trek across the desert of northern Mexico.

"On that vessel, we found Col. Webb's company, consisting of one hundred men, bound for California. They were fine looking intelligent gentlemen, well calculated

to be successful in such an expedition. Also, Simons'
New Orleans company, comprising forty stalwart adventurers, bound for the same promising land, our own
company at that time consisting of twenty persons, all
inspired by hope and joviality. But, in the course of
ocean events, this hilarity was doomed to come to an
end, when the mountainous billows of the Gulf commenced operating on the susceptible frames of the
landsmen, all suffering from sea-sickness except myself
and another person, which afflicted them until our
vessel arrived at the Brazos on March 4th."

Brazos was a small town consisting of about fifty
houses at the mouth of the Rio Grande, from Fort
Brown twenty-five miles by land, and sixty by water.
There, forty men from Colonel Webb's company caught
cholera and died. The rest returned to New Orleans,
"the very pictures of despair, without money and without
health." McNeil and his companions stayed on. Brazos
was a place where argonauts could get fitted out with
transportation for the journey west.

"I had before frequently advised my companions not
to take so much provision and baggage with us, but was
constantly opposed; but they found at last that the Shoemaker prophet was inspired for the occasion. At the
Brazos, we purchased a wagon and six mules for the conveyance of our goods, and a horse for each, the horses
costing from ten to fifty dollars."

McNeil and company followed the coastline south
until they got to Fort Brown, on the Rio Grande, in
southwestern Texas, where "we were obliged to purchase

an additional wagon and four mules. I tried there to pursuade [sic] them to sell the wagons and mules, and proceed on horses, but without effect. The others concluded to elect a captain, which I opposed, stating that if we could not rule ourselves for the good of the whole, and each take care of his own money, we were not fit for the journey to California, but I was not successful in my argument.

"We then elected for our captain, a Mr. Perkins of Cincinnati, an overbearing ignorant Englishman, who did not suit my strict republican principles."

Mr. Perkins of Cincinnati was definitely the kind of stuffy, ignorant Englishman who could only be characterized as plain stupid. "Six of the mules Mr. Perkins of Cincinnati was permitted to purchase soon dropped dead. The company was then displeased with me, because I would not permit him to purchase one for myself."

The shoemaker knew mule flesh.

"I selected and bought one which I rode safely and happily one thousand miles. On 8th of March, we started from Fort Brown for Reynosa [Mexico] 60 miles [west]," paralleling "the Rio Grande, experiencing much difficulty in keeping the road, and finding water for ourselves and mules. At Charcoal Lake, about half way, we hired a guide and interpreter, for $300, to take us through to Mazatlán, on the Pacific Ocean, one thousand miles from the Brazos.

"We remained at this lake three days. Although the water was so stagnant that the fish were lying dead upon its shores, we were obliged to cook and drink with it. We then proceeded to Reynosa, at which place we arrived on the 20th. Finding there that our complement of wagons would not conveniently carry our goods, obliging us to drag along at the rate of ten miles per day, we purchased another wagon and four mules, which I also opposed, but with the same want of success. I was actually enraged at the increase of our expenses.

"We had then about $1000 worth of wagons and mules, and were now obliged to pay a duty of $60 on each wagon on passing from Texas into Mexico, our personal baggage having already cost more than its value. Firmly believing that Perkins would wastefully spend all our money, if permitted to have his own way, we ejected him from his office, electing in his stead, to act as governors, a committee of three persons, viz: Stambaugh, Hart, and Perkins."

And then, just as the argonauts from Lancaster, Ohio, were about get matters settled, cholera struck again.

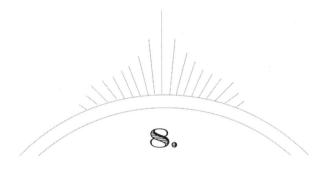

8.

ACROSS THE MOUNTAINS
AND THE OCEAN

O ver the border was Mexico. The path from there to California was across the Sonora Desert. Even before they got a chance to face those deprivations, disease struck McNeil's party.

"The cholera appeared in our band, attacking Brown, of Alabama, who joined our company at Brazos, and Stambaugh, from Lancaster, but fortunately both recovered. So frightened was Brown, that he left our company and returned home."

Brown was one of the lucky ones. Most victims of cholera died from severe diarrhea: the proper medical diagnosis would be dehydration.

"We remained ten days encamped on the bank of the river opposite Reynosa. From our encampment every morning and every evening, we heard about three hundred bells ringing in Reynosa, so terrifically that we thought at first the town was on fire, or about to be attacked by some enemy, and felt inclined to cross the river to render our assistance; but found afterwards they were ringing for religious purposes. The Mexicans called them *Joy Bells*, but it was an obstreperous joy to which we were not accustomed.

"On the second day of our stay there, we were surprised on seeing a Hungarian gentleman ride into our camp, stating that he belonged to a company of traders from Mexico, returning to the United States, with three wagons laden with silver in the bar and coin, which they had received for goods during their expedition, adding that they had smuggled it across the river three miles above Reynosa, and wished to encamp that night with us for protection, which we readily granted. We were glad we did so, for the Hungarian adventurer gave us much valuable information respecting our route.

"As we are encamped on the bank of the Rio Grande, the shoemaker must have a little liberty to *shoe* some of its traits. Rio Grande, in English, means the *Great* River, and I can assure our readers that it is the *greatest* river for winding I ever saw. Descending this river the first prominent town is Santa Fe, an old Spanish town. It is a great trading place, where most of the goods sold and stored there were brought overland from St. Louis, 1500 miles distant in the United States."

Traders from the East would return with rich furs, peltry, Mexican silver, and gold. Matamoros, opposite Fort Brown, is another of the principal towns on the Rio

Grande's banks, "60 miles above its mouth, containing a population of 8,000. One of its principal curiosities is a *barberess*, a French girl, pretty and smart, who cuts the heart and the beard at the same time."

The idea of being entertained by an exotic French *barberess* must have filled the parochial shoemaker from Lancaster, whose eyes were rapidly being opened, with much glee. But once the barberess finished her ministrations to McNeil's person, and the others in the Lancaster party who wished to partake of her wicked, scissor-filled fingers, it was time to move on.

In traveling west, Lewis and Clark sometimes had to collapse their entire party into boats that would transport them over liquid terrain that could not be traversed in any other way. McNeil's band was forced to adapt similarly.

"On the 30th we crossed to Reynosa, in canoes, taking our wagons to pieces and crossing them in the same way, swimming over our mules, which occupied us three days. Of course, we were soon saluted by the custom house officers, for their dues. While our committee waited on them to settle that matter, the rest of our company rushed into the Rio Grande to bathe, which proved a delicious treat.

"Some senoritas, married and unmarried, I presume, had been watching us, and came down to bathe and show off their celestial charms, stripping to the skin while talking like so many parrots, and then mingled with us in the nautical amusement. As we had too much modesty to do in Mexico what they do there, we left the watery angels to their sweet selves, and going ashore, dressed, and watched them a considerable time while they scrutinized us critically."

McNeil goes quickly from the philosophical to the sublime, anticipating this question: With so many beautiful senoritas and so many horny men, not one of them *attempts* a seduction?

"One cause why we did not stay in the water with them was this—We were aware of the excessive jealousy existing in the Spanish Mexican character, knowing, that although it would have passed unnoticed had we been Mexicans, that, being Americans, it might have ended fatally had we remained with them in the water, and we should have experienced from their male friends the stiletto or pistol instead of words of friendship.

"I love to follow the advice of a celebrated traveller [sic], who says, that in order to get along safely with the males in foreign countries, he avoided the females as much as possible, knowing that jealousy is accompanied by the same fatality in every land."

Considering that murders are frequently committed because of jealousy, McNeil showed good judgment.

"Reynosa contains about 3000 inhabitants, who were terribly frightened and scathed by cholera, during our stay of three days in the place. The day we left, sixty persons died in the place from its effects. In fact, every house we passed in our progress from Fort Brown to Saltillo had one or more persons in it dead from cholera. Eight of our company, who were Romanites [Catholics], before leaving, fearing that disease, purchased from a Spanish priest a sufficiency of prayers that would last them till we got to Monterey or to some other place in the other world if they died on the way."

But one member of the company was not as circumspect as McNeil.

"While those Catholics were absent purchasing prayers, a Lancaster lawyer, of our company, asked a splendidly dressed and lovely senorita, if she would go into another room with him, stating that he wished to have some private conversation with her. She understood enough of his speech to reply, '*Sí*, Senor.'

"He thinking that she said that some one would *see* them during their innocent interview, I told him that '*Sí*' did not mean *see* but 'Yes,' and that she was perfectly willing that he should have a harmless kiss. On returning from the interview, the lawyer, thinking that her sweet lips might have imparted the cholera or some other awful disease, requested me to give him some linament immediately, with which he rubbed himself all over, but, it smarted his tender flesh so excessively that he howled around the room like an old wolf, caught at last in a baited trap.

"Oh! these attractive women! whom we find at the *bottom* of every evil prevailing in every land. The lawyer paid dear for his whistle, and he surely whistled with excessive pain for about one long hour, and then had to receive jokes about it forever afterwards!"

Then it was on the road again.

"Proceeding we reached, after two days travel, a town called Chenee, on a river pronounced San Whan, (San Juan) one of the tributaries of the Rio Grande, 50 miles from Reynosa."

The shoemaker and company had arrived someplace near present-day Los Aldamas, about 100 miles north-east of Monterrey, the provincial capital.

"We arrived at 11 o'clock at night. Progressing, we lost our way, in attempting to find the ford across the San Whan, so that we were obliged to encamp on this side of it. A singular occurrence happened that night."

The shoemaker was on guard duty when, he was "suddenly startled by the screaming of Strode, who, in his fright, declared that he saw a Comanche [sic] Indian or Mexican crawling towards the encampment. Leverett, who had slept in the same tent," descended into a wild, racial hysteria, "wrapping a blanket around him, rushed into the chapparel [sic], shrieking that the Indians were about massacreing [sic] the whole band. Of course, we awakened the others, and all who remained, prepared in military order for the expected combat."

Looking into the gloom, McNeil could have sworn that he heard and saw something threatening moving toward them. If he had known Indian ways, he would have known that if Comanches had intended them harm, they would already be dead. But something was coming toward them from the darkness of night, and assuming hostiles, they marched out to meet it, determined to fight and die, "in the defence [sic] of our rights," even as Strode and Leverett continued rooted to the spot, screaming in fear.

Handguns had cleared leather, rifles were up with keen eyes gazing down the barrels. Good with a blade, McNeil made sure his bowie knife was at the ready. "We boldly advanced—advanced—advanced—and found the enemy to be—not a Comanche Indian, not a renegade Mexican, or a wild beast—but an expanded umbrella rolling on the ground towards us, moved by a gentle breeze."

Strode and Leverett slept well that night. The next morning they forded the San Juan River.

"Leverett was on a very small weak mule. The force of the current swept both away into deep water. As he could not swim, his situation was a critical one. Stripping as fast as possible, I leaped in to his rescue, and succeeded, after much difficulty, in bringing him to shore. The mule, after losing the saddle, swam out."

On April 10, 1849, the McNeil party finally arrived at Monterrey.

"As the Cholera was raging badly in the town, we disputed whether we should remain or proceed to a mill five miles farther, where there were many conveniences both for health and comfort. The committee determined that we should remain there, which highly displeased the rest of the company.

"That night, about 6 o'clock, a colleague and myself were attacked by cholera. At 6 o'clock the next morning my colleague died, but fortunately I recovered to tell the readers my adventures. We buried him at the Walnut Springs, about eight miles from the city, as we could not be permitted to bury him in a Catholic burial ground in Monterrey, the deceased having been an Episcopalian [sic].

"O cursed hell-born bigotry that separates the living, and then separates the holy dead! A Mr. [Henry] Hyde, from the same place in Virginia, and belonging to the same Episcopal Church, after helping to drink or finish three kegs of the best 4th proof French brandy, preached an appropriate funeral discourse over our deceased comrade before starting to the grave."

By now the McNeil party from Lancaster had traveled more than two thousand miles of a none too hospitable continent. One of its members was dead, one had turned back, and many others stricken with terrible disease, in addition to the daily deprivations all of them went through. Worse, they were not yet to the gold fields. There was more wild and unfriendly country in front of them.

"Passing from Monterrey to Saltillo [across northern Mexico], we proceeded to Paras, finding the road skirted luxuriantly with the palmetto, prickly pear, and a plant called the King's Crown. We stayed three days at Paras, where we got our wagons repaired and the mules shod, and disposed of some of our loading in order to facilitate us on our journey. At this point the Comanche [sic] Indians became numerous."

McNeil and company now had the misfortune of encountering the most skilled and fearsome cavalrymen of the Great Plains tribes, the Comanche. In pre-Colonial times the Comanche had been on offshoot of the Wyoming Shoshone. The Comanche moved south in stages, attacking and defeating other Plains tribes, until by 1800 they had a total population of seven thousand to ten thousand, many of whom were warriors.

The Comanche were different from the other Plains Indians. Rather than functioning as a true tribe with a central group of traditions and elders, the Comanche were organized into twelve totally autonomous bands. Fitting in well with their nomadism, they had acquired horses from the Spanish in the seventeenth century and were one of the few Plains tribes to breed them.

Comanche bands raided frontier towns and settlements, killing whites and looking for booty and captives to ransom. Their raids took them as far south as northern Mexico, where the men from Lancaster ran into one of those twelve Comanche bands.

"Eight miles from that town before reaching it, nine of those [Comanche] Indians attacked a Mexican train, consisting of mules packed with silver, which thirty Mexicans were taking to Durango. We saw the transaction. The Indians left the silver on the ground and drove off the mules, as the Mexicans ran to us for protection. We tried to save a wounded Mexican, but seeing us hastily approaching; the Indians killed him [with lance and arrows] and rapidly fled," leaving a mutilated, bleeding corpse in their wake.

"The inhabitants hailed us as if we were delivering angels. The Alcalde offered us $50 each, if we would lead the citizens against those Comanches. But, we concluded not to interfere as it might afterwards hinder our journey and endanger our lives, should those Indians hear of our interference."

McNeil's prescience was proven that afternoon when the Mexicans had a battle with Comanches in which five Mexicans were killed and twelve wounded, while only one Comanche bit the dust, literally.

"He [the Comanche] was dragged into town at the end of a lasso, the other end being affixed to the horn of a saddle occupied by a vaunting Mexican."

McNeil notes nothing special about this treatment of the hostile, but that is not surprising. While Lewis and Clark had tremendous respect for the Indians and showed it, subsequent generations had begun to systematically take the Indian land by force, resign them to poor reservations, and try to eliminate by gunfire the rest who wouldn't come to the treaty table.

Like all "foreign" enemies, the red Indians had become dehumanized by the now white majority spreading across the continent. The Gold Rush hastened this demise by decades because the Plains had to be made "safe" for white men to cross in search of California gold.

"Thence to Durango, where we arrived April 19th. It is one of the largest and oldest cities in Mexico, containing, as I thought, about 125,000 inhabitants. The houses look like prisons, the doors and windows being plentifully supplied with iron bars, as if to prevent the beaux from carrying off the ladies or the Indians from capturing the whole family. The churches are among the most splendid in the Roman Catholic world. On entering one of them I thought that I had prematurely got into California, so valuable and splendid were the ornaments glittering with gold and silver."

On that Sunday afternoon, the shoemaker from Ohio attended his first bullfight. Anti-Catholic feeling was then high in America, and McNeil represents those dominant feelings in some of his subsequent observations about the bullfight and its aftermath:

"I there saw, among the gayest of the gay, the [Catholic] bishop and his entire congregation. He had licensed the fight and was determined to see it out, believing that it is as good to act proudly in sin as it is to act humbly in religion, a very accommodating faith to those who worship *God* and *Devil* at the same time.

"About fifty wooden spears, saturated with brimstone, were pierced into different parts of his [the bull's] body. Those were ignited, when the bull in a perfect blaze, rushed furiously around the enclosure, still further persecuted by three Mexicans on horseback, who occasionally speared his flesh as they rode around and jumped over him, escaping sometimes almost miraculously from the horns of the animal, finally killing him by slow torture.

"In this way six bulls were killed, but not until three horses had met the same fate and one Mexican wounded. The bishop, who delighted in such barbarity, and led his congregation to admire the same brutality, professed to be a follower of that Jesus Christ who on earth would not willfully harm a fly or tread upon a feeble worm. The next morning, while passing along the street, we witnessed the following scene.

"Twelve soldiers on horseback, armed with muskets, pistols and cutlasses, a priest walking in the midst of them, while a musical band, in full operation, brought up the rear. The citizens, wherever the procession went, fell down upon their knees before his Heavenly Majesty. The soldiers motioned to us intimating that we had better pull off our hats in honor of that cunning priest, who was thus showing publicly that the military power could at any time be brought out to sustain their interests."

All of the McNeil party complied except the redoubtable Leverett, who, holding his hat on his head firmly with both hands, swore audibly that he would not take it off for any such purpose. The soldiers threatened to knock it off with their cutlasses, but thought twice about it when Leverett told the captain that he had obtained from the Mexican consul at New Orleans permission to travel through Mexico with his hat on and with a sound head!

It was at Durango that McNeil, thinking ahead, finally convinced the party to become more mobile, by selling their wagons and using pack mules to the Pacific Ocean and the journey north. That done, they headed the 160 miles west to the Mexican port of Mazatlán. Travelling [sic] on nothing more than a mule path, "I must here relate a laughable circumstance to relieve the tediousness of the journey.

"Fennifrock got sick at Durango with diarrhea. Previously, he had purchased some boiled beans, fully peppered and compressed into a small space. As he was sick, he could not eat the luscious mess, and gave me permission to eat some of them. I ate a small quantity, but Strode swallowed the rest at a meal.

"On Fennifrock enquiring who had eaten his stock so voraciously, Strode told him that I had eaten all of them *up* or rather *down*. Fennifrock attacked me for the deed, when I observed that I could soon prove my innocence.

As I expected, the huge meal of beans made Strode dreadfully sick. Murder will out, and beans will keep in, and extended Strode's stomach to the size of a small barrel."

McNeil was not a man to take lying lightly, especially when someone questioned his word, even if the matter was about something as innocent as beans. Yet those beans represented more than a gaseous quantity of stomach-churning delight—they were a meal in a country where food was not plentiful. Any man accused of stealing food could not be trusted.

"Strode applied to me for medicine, but I told him I would give him none, and that he might die of the bean disorder for slandering me. However, on some one's applying a hot stone to his stomach [a queer folk remedy for upset stomach] he vomited out the whole of the beans before the eyes of Fennifrock, who was then convinced that I had spoken the solemn truth. Some have a hell upon earth for their misdeeds, but Strode had a young hell in his belly for his crime!"

Three nights out from Durango, Strode and Denman lost their mules. Obliged to foot it, "Denman and myself being on very good terms, I permitted him to ride my mule occasionally while I walked. On the third day I walked considerably ahead, and stopped to rest until the train reached me, when I found Strode riding my mule and Denman walking." Denman had acceded to Strode's sore feet and let him ride awhile rather than walk.

McNeil was furious.

"I observed that I wished only to oblige Denman, and that Strode might walk to the devil if he pleased, even if he wore away his legs to the knees in so doing. This so much displeased me that I would neither let Denman nor Strode ride after that. I remembered the bean affair in which Strode slandered me, and, as the Universalists say, every man must suffer in his body and feet for the evil deeds he does on earth."

The mule path snaked around a mountain. If one of the mules stumbled, or the rider made a mistake, there was nothing to stop his descent over the edge and down thousands of feet, to be smashed on the rocks below. While McNeil had no fear in riding up and down the precipices, Stambaugh did, to such an extent that he told McNeil to quit "showing off." McNeil, who was riding a rented mule replied:

"Stambaugh, I will ride any way that I want to. I have given $1 per day for the privilege of driving a mule up hill and down, for the privilege of riding whenever it suited my convenience, and that is all the time."

They were traveling over high mountains. At one spot they passed over many acres of lava, which had been thrown out by a neighboring volcano, "which proved very troublesome to the feet of our mules. We visited a warm spring, apparently hot enough to scald a chicken or boil an egg, showing that the internal fires were burning beneath. But volcanoes are great blessings instead of curses, and should excite our gratitude instead of our fears. If a man has a colic, and applies no physic to remove the cause, he dies. So has the earth the colic at times, but those volcanoes remove the origin of it, or otherwise the globe would burst."

On the fifth day out from Durango, they reached the summit of the highest mountain, "where I thought I was nearer to the good world than I would ever be again. We enjoyed a glorious prospect of mountains and plains, and, towards the west, a glimpse of the Pacific Ocean, which seemed to be pacifically inviting us to its borders.

"As we progressed, we had ice and snow on the mountains, where we encamped at night. By day in threading the valleys we enjoyed a delicious climate: watermelons, peaches, grapes, cocoa nuts, oranges, lemons, bananas and plantains. This truly romantic and solemn scenery affected us considerably.

Previously, we had almost constantly passed through scrubby chapparel [sic], and frequently could not find enough of wood to cook our meals. But here, almost for the first time since leaving the Brazos, we were traversing primeval forests. Some of the trees had witnessed, trees have eyes, the exploits of the soldiers of Cortez and Pizzaro, centuries earlier."

On May 10, they arrived at Mazatlán, on the Pacific Ocean. There was a dispute among the party about taking passage to San Francisco, with the crooked lawyer in their party arranging the passage, and in return, traveling for nothing. McNeil had had enough of such shenanigans and decided to quit his party and travel north to the gold fields alone. It was a fateful decision.

"Before leaving, Stambaugh told me that I could do nothing without the company, and that I would certainly be murdered in California without its protection. I observed that I would rather die than travel any further with such a swindling company. This greatly enraged him, and the Lancaster lawyer picked up a gun to shoot me."

The lawyer took a closer look at McNeil the shoe-maker. In the months since they'd left Ohio, the shoe-maker had grown a waist-length beard. He wore buckskins and a stained, creased Stetson hat. Across his silver saddle, picked up in Mexico, was a Sharps buffalo rifle that spit out a large caliber bullet and could stop a buffalo at a distance of one mile. Casually, he moved the weapon in the shyster's direction in a decidedly unshoe-manlike posture.

"I do not wish wilfully to kill any body or to be killed in an ordinary brawl," said McNeil coolly, "but I am stout and stout-hearted, and either with rifle, pistol, or bowie knife, I am honorably willing to fight you on the spot."

The lawyer quickly retracted his statement and McNeil, alone for the first time since leaving Ohio, boarded a ship for San Francisco.

"I took passage on a Danish schooner, named *Joanna Analuffa*, commanded by a gentlemanly German, paying $75, the distance from Mazatlán to San Francisco being 1500 miles. There were 200 passengers on board. I left $100 worth of articles with the company which went in a French vessel [instead] for which I never received a cent.

"After getting far out into the ocean, we ran a north-east course towards the destined port. When a week from land, we were supplied with wormy bread, putrid jerked beef, musty rice, and miserable tea. There not being enough tea to color the water, we were too wide awake for the captain, and, being 200 in number, we determined to have the worth of our money, as the Yankee boys are number one on sea as well as on land."

The Yankees threw the putrid beef and other "vittles" overboard and told the German captain they must have better. Infuriated, the German swore that if they did not become satisfied with the food he gave them, he would take them back to Mazatlán, and have them tried and imprisoned for mutiny.

"Hunger knows no law," McNeil told him. "We will shoot you, and moreover, you must not only keep on the proper course to San Francisco, you must give us proper food, or we will take all the ship matters into our own hands."

McNeil had once again found force in numbers, this time the two hundred passengers who agreed wholeheartedly with his pronouncements. The German, for his part, "became as cool as a cowed rooster, kept on his course, and afterwards gave us the best he had. We caught and ate a few sharks on the passage and I saw for the first time in my life, whales every day, and porpoises darting about in every direction, like artful politicians, turning summersaults [sic] occasionally to suit their respective views, and show the other fish their superiority.

"On the 30th I arrived at San Francisco, not knowing a single person there."

That first night in San Francisco, McNeil experienced his first rain since leaving Ohio. He turned his face up to the cool water flowing from the sky, the first rain he'd seen and felt since leaving home. Looking out at the harbor filled with ships flying flags from all over the world, McNeil knew he was anyplace but home.

9.

THE DIGGINGS

San Francisco in 1849 was still a tent city amid scattered wooden buildings high on the bluffs overlooking San Francisco Harbor. But its harbor had begun to look like a big city's.

"I saw anchored in the harbor about five hundred vessels belonging to different nations," Samuel McNeil wrote. "The sailors had all ran off to the mines, averaging at that time but one man to a vessel to take care of them. Some of the vessels were rotting, and I suppose the majority of them would be destroyed by the N.W. hurricanes."

The men on those ships, the ones that streamed into the tent city, whose money would help eventually build it into one of the foremost in the world, those men wanted one thing and one thing alone: California gold. Gold had caused rooms to become scarce and food expensive.

Even the earthen floor of a tent became prime real estate.

"On arriving, I went into a tent asking the proprietor what would be his charge for permitting me to sleep on the bare ground that night," McNeil continues. "He replied 'fifty cents,' to which I instantly agreed."

In walking around town, McNeil saw evidence of little or no crime. "There is no law there and no need of it at present." He was right.

During 1849, robbery in San Francisco and the Gold Rush boomtowns was rare. Boxes and bales of goods were left open and exposed, with impunity, in the crowded streets. There was no law to coerce anyone into honesty, yet stealing from miners was rarely heard of. Gold did not seem to tempt the darker side of men. As for rustling, cattle, horses, and mules remained safe on ranchos. People writing home from the gold fields usually remarked that property was safer in California than in the older states at home.

The popular explanation was that the recent migrants came from "good stock," and had not so soon forgotten the principles under which they had been educated. Those principles included respect for others' rights, including property rights. Sutter's attempt to get the U.S. government to legitimize his claim to the sawmill and other interests, all of which he had improved on what was there before, supports this belief.

True, if you were found guilty of something less than murder, such as stealing a horse, you could face a miner's court and a hangman's rope. But that was for the worst of crimes. The real reason why crime was so low was just pure numbers. It wasn't until 1850 that people started streaming en masse to California.

In walking through town, McNeil saw people from all quarters of the globe; San Francisco had already become the landing of the world. There were "Americans, Englishmen, Hibernians, Scotch folks, Chinese, Sandwich Islanders, South Americans, New Granadians, Mexicans, Polanders, and Sonorians."

In the morning, he quickly vacated his earthen bed and went to another tent to get breakfast, for which he paid $2.50. The owner of that tent offered him $8 per day if he would aid in erecting a muslin house. As he had never earned more than $1 per day, McNeil thought that high wages, "But, rejecting his offer, I started for the mines that day." Paying $20 for passage on a schooner up the Sacramento River to Sacramento City, 160 miles from San Francisco, McNeil soon encountered another problem.

McNeil and sea captains just didn't mix. This time, about 50 miles upriver, the captain got drunk and ran his schooner aground. It took a few hours before the rising tide rescued the vessel and carried it back out into the river channel.

"The captain being still intoxicated, and, being fearful that he might delay us to our loss, five or six of the stoutest passengers (I being one of the number) attacked the little Irish captain, knocked him down, and tied him with ropes. By our orders, the vessel was safely and rapidly steered to our port of destination."

McNeil once again seems to be showing the popular taste in attacking the captain not just for his drinking and poor judgment but also for his Irish lineage. Regardless, it was clear that whatever he may become, McNeil would not soon fit in as a sailor.

When he got to Sacramento, "I entered a tent, kept by Mrs. Moore, the first American woman I had seen since leaving the States. She swore her brandy was better than any *other man's* in that renowned city. Her price was fifty cents a drink. I soon found she had a great deal of the masculine gender about her, and that she permitted other things (more expensive) in her tent than drinking brandy, considering one of her sweetest smiles worth an ounce of gold or $16."

After refreshing himself at the well of Mrs. Moore's brandy and "smiles," McNeil began the final part of his transcontinental trek.

"I proceeded immediately to the gold mines or diggings on the North Fork of the American river, which empties into the Sacramento river, being 45 miles from Sacramento city. That distance I walked, paying $20 for the conveyance of my baggage on pack mules. The next day, about 10 o'clock after leaving Sacramento city, I reached the mines."

McNeil doesn't mean mines literally. Mines refer to the actual sites on the river where the prospectors panned for gold, or dug directly into and sifted the "pay dirt." Actual mines sunk into the ground would come later, as the true worth of the find became known.

"I passed the first day in observing how five hundred

persons dug and washed the gold. This place is called Smith's Bar, because a man named Smith has a store there, where he sells provisions and mining implements. There I paid 10 dollars for a small pan for washing gold, 7 dollars for a pick, and 8 dollars for a small crow bar, renting a cradle for 6 dollars per day. I had then but seventy-five cents left."

In the brief year and a half since Marshall's find, a modern phenomenon had begun in and around Coloma. Mining camps sprang up overnight as men converged on the river, seeking El Dorado. Prentice Mulford, an early miner, later wrote, "The California mining camp was ephemeral. Often it was founded, built up, flourished, decayed, and had weeds and herbage growing over its site and hiding all of man's work inside of ten years from its inception."

From 1848 to the mid-1850s, hundreds of these camps sprung up and, as Mulford says, disappeared over a short time span. They would have the most colorful names: Rough and Ready, Crimea House, Chinese Camp, Jackass Hill, and Rich Bar, to name just a few. Rich Bar had been founded by a man from Georgia who struck it rich at the diggings on the Middle Fork of the Feather River, about twenty-five miles from Sacramento.

When Louise Amelia Knapp Smith Clapp, a doctor's wife and aspiring writer, arrived at Rich Bar with her husband, who was seeking mountain air for his health, she observed, "Part of the adventurers camped there, but many went a few miles farther down the river. The next morning, two men turned over a large stone, beneath which they found quite a sizable piece of gold. They washed a small panful of the dirt, and obtained from it two hundred and fifty-six dollars."

Writing under the nom de plume, "Dame Shirley," she continues:

"Encouraged by this success, they commenced staking off the legal amount of ground allowed to each person for mining purposes, and, the remainder of the party having descended the hill, before night the entire bar was 'claimed.' In a fortnight from that time, the two men who found the first bit of gold had each taken out six thousand dollars. Two others took out thirty-three pounds of gold in eight hours, which is the best day's work that has been done on this branch of the river.

"The largest amount ever taken from one panful of dirt was fifteen hundred dollars. In a little more than a week after its discovery, five hundred men had settled upon the Bar for the summer. Such is the wonderful alacrity with which a mining town is built.

"Soon after was discovered, on the same side of the river, about half a mile apart, and at nearly the same distance from this place, the two bars, Smith and Indian, both very rich."

Smith's Bar, where McNeil finally found himself, was at the base of the Sierra foothills.

"I slept at night on a rock, between two high mountains, with a blanket over and one under me, reflecting in wakeful time that I was 3,500 miles from home, my mind running back to my boyhood and my playmates, remembering the delicious seasons I had enjoyed with my father and mother, and particularly with my bosom friend and wife, Ellen, and my children in Lancaster, Ohio."

McNeil was a man on the brink of something fateful.

"The next morning, I commenced working in earnest, and laboring incessantly for four weeks, finding, after deducting expenses, that I had cleared ten dollars per day, that is $280. I then sold my mining implements and returned to San Francisco, expecting to get a letter there from my family. I received one, being the first I had got. After blessing the steamer that brought it, I addressed a letter to my wife, inclosing $200 and a sample of the gold dust. I then went to the gold mines at another point, on a river called the Stanish Lou, 200 miles south of the mines I had previously visited.

"I found the miners generally making, on an average, $16 per day. I saw three men dig out $9000 in seven days, and two men dig $2500 in two days. But these are rare circumstances. I saw a Spaniard having a lump of gold he had found weighing one pound and a half. Finding gold digging too hard labor for me, I returned to Sacramento city."

When James Marshall made his find, it had been pure accident; he didn't have to work for it. All the publicity it had received worldwide made it appear that all you had to do to get rich was reach down and pick up a chunk of gold from the water or the land. It was actually much harder than that.

Gold wasn't found just anyplace. Little gold was found on the sides and tops of mountains nor on the plains.

"But dig wherever you may think proper in that country, you will find some," McNeil asserts. "You will hit pay dirt.

"The explorer, if passing along a river when the water is high, may correctly judge that gold may be found at the foot of a fall or eddy, where he will or may be very successful when the water is low, the swiftness of the eddy having accumulated the gold scales in piles, in places called 'pockets.' In such places, the diggers should not be discouraged if at first they find none, but dig on until they get to the rock where they will find it the most, as gold, being the heaviest, passes through the sand and gravel, and settles on the rock.

"In those pockets, formed by the current of the river, some not aware of what I said, will dig down one, two, or three feet, and finding none will leave the spot, while an old miner, coming afterwards, will dig deeper in the same hole, and find thousands of dollars safely deposited on the rock. In the slate rock it is only found in the crevices, as if it had been melted and poured into them by the hands of the Almighty."

While McNeil was at the mines, companies of miners from New York and Massachusetts arrived, bringing with them patented gold washers. This was a newfangled invention that promised to mine gold even faster than anything that came before it. But they had been manufactured so quickly, they were no more than a prototype; they worked infrequently. The Easterners were compelled to throw them away and use the simple, common cradle.

The cradle was the popular implement for extracting placer gold. Resembling a common baby cradle, it was about four and a half feet long, made of white pine, having bottomed sides and headboard, but none at the foot. On the bottom, three cleats, an inch wide and eighteen inches apart, were nailed. A kind of hopper, the bottom of which is sheet iron perforated with half-inch holes having a low raised board around the edge, is fastened across the top of the cradle.

To mine for gold, the sand and gravel in which the gold is hidden, are poured into this hopper. Then, while water is poured on these with one hand, the cradle is rocked with the other, by which motion the gold, sand, and gravel are forced into the body of the cradle. There, the gold, being the heaviest, lodges against the wooden cleats. The sand and gravel pass onward and out by the foot of it. Then the gold along those cleats, and the little sand and gravel still mingled with it, are taken out, put into a pan, and washed at the edge of the river as clean as the miner can get it without wasting any of the gold.

"After that, the sand left is placed on a handkerchief spread in the sun. When it is dry, the remaining sand is blown from it as one blows the dust from beans. This sand is as black as powder. The fact is that gold is only found in black sand. The pure gold is then put into a double-sewed buckskin bag or purse and is then ready for preservation or exportation."

While McNeil was lucky to borrow enough to buy a cradle, many of the 49ers were not so lucky. Instead, they used the most common method of extracting placer gold from sand: a simple pan with a round depression in the middle. This method of extracting the gold depends more heavily on the element's specific gravity—the ratio of the weight or mass of a given volume of a substance to that of another substance. For solids, water is usually the other substance used for comparison. For example, gold has a specific gravity of 19.3, making it nineteen times heavier than water.

To get the gold, miners would generally wade out in the water of the American or Feather River, on a narrow strip of land (the "bar") that was their claim. On either side would be other miners doing exactly the same thing, only they would be confined to their claim, which had a specific boundary line. While the government owned the land, the miner owned the mineral rights by simply filing that claim with the government.

To pan for gold, the miner would simply bend down and scoop out with his hand or shovel some of the black dirt that had settled on the river bottom, and deposit a big dollop of it in the pan. Then the pan would be placed in the water to fill it up, making sure the dirt stayed put.

The next step is to take the pan out of the water and shake it to settle the gold to the bottom of the pan. Gold is the heaviest thing in the pan, and if it's there, it'll settle to the bottom. It takes thirty seconds for this process. Then it's on to shaking and swirling the pan to a working angle at about forty-five degrees to the ground or water. Stop those actions and while maintaining the working angle, submerge the pan back in the water. It is then immediately lifted out of the water, taking care not to lift the front lip. The idea is for the water to rush out of the pan and wash off the top layer of dirt.

Now comes the dipping sequence. Every few drops, swirl the sand while maintaining the working angle. That'll keep any gold present trapped in the crease of the pan. The miner keeps dipping and swirling until only about a tablespoon of black sand is left. Moving to the last part of the process, the miner places about half an inch of water in the pan, then slowly swirls the water over the sand. As the sand is moved away by the water, if gold is present, the miner will immediately see its glittering presence.

In their excitement, some miners actually washed the gold out of their pans! Those who didn't then placed it on a handkerchief to dry in the sun. Once dry, it could be transferred to a rawhide pouch.

Whether using the cradle or the pan, gold mining was backbreaking work. McNeil quickly learned that making it rich at mining required a combination of luck to both find the stuff and to survive the cholera and other epidemics that swept the mining camps.

"None but the stalwart and gigantic laboring man, who can work from sunrise to sunset and withstand the hot sun, is fit for such an occupation," McNeil later wrote.

McNeil was one of the smart ones. Realizing that gold mining required luck and a back as strong as the Kentucky Giant, McNeil decided that instead of getting rich panning, he would be better off making his money doing something else. So he set off to Sacramento City with an idea: he would sell one of the two things men always craved.

Halfway between the ship landing in Sacramento and the main street was a singular sycamore tree, which, with age and honor, had bent down to the shape of a half circle, while from its curved trunk rose branches, casting "a delightful shade around. This curve I made the entrance or front door of my tent, building back of it with muslin until it was sufficiently large for every purpose. Between the two sides of the trunk ran my counter, leaving a small passage on one side for entering and going out."

Surrounded by other "liquor houses," McNeil's Sycamore Tree Establishment became famous far and near as one of Sacramento's better run saloons.

"I sold some brandy at my tent at twenty-five cents per drink. When a person came to me for brandy, I invariably observed that if he must and would have it, and was determined to die, that I had the stuff that would kill a man as quick as any other liquor in California. This I done fully one hundred times a day."

McNeil supplied not only liquor but also a unique atmosphere to the miners and traders who populated the city. If there is any business through which a person can see into the heart of the human character, it is saloon keeping. McNeil soon found this out and kept careful notes on his customers.

"An Irishman, who lived on the opposite side of the river, came over to the City to have a spree, for the Irishman is the same jovial personage every where.

Excited by ardent spirits, he had been swearing that he would kill somebody that day. From my tent, I saw him, with uplifted Bowie knife, pursuing an individual. When he had almost reached his expected prey, the latter turned on him and wounded him severely with a pistol. His wife was sent for, who came over in a canoe.

"With assistance, she had her husband placed in the bottom of it, and started for home. As the wound made him restive, she swore that if he did not be still she would throw him overboard. He died about four hours after reaching his dwelling. Elder, the man who shot the Irishman, was immediately arrested, and tried before a miner's court, and acquitted."

Miner courts were the only law and order in the boomtowns.

"A few days afterwards a man was arrested for stealing $50 worth of gold dust. A jury was called and a judge appointed, and he was found guilty, his sentence running thus: that he should have his ears cut off, receive fifty lashes on the bare back, and leave the country."

Such penalties were barbarous leftovers from seventeenth-century Colonial times, when crime against property warranted a pious society's fiercest punishment. Things changed with the introduction of criminal codes in the eighteenth and nineteenth centuries in the states. But in California gold country, with the law hundreds of miles away, mob rule took over and penalties for crimes were, to say the least, a throwback to what was.

"Lots were drawn to discover who should cut off his ears," McNeil continues, "and it fell upon a person named Clark. The prisoner prevailed upon a doctor sojourning there to do the job instead of Clark, knowing that he could do it more skillfully and with less injury; but the difference was that between a little hell and a big hell. The doctor complied with great good nature and willingness, and with a well-sharpened glittering razor, cut the scoundrel's ears off close to his head."

Apparently the Hippocratic oath, too, could be put aside in favor of mob justice.

"With bleeding head and back, and, no doubt, with an agonized heart, if such a villain could feel, he stole a mule the same night, and was never heard of afterwards."

On another occasion, "A [different] doctor stepped into my tent for refreshment. He was just from the mines with a gloomy countenance and apparently with almost broken heart. He stated that he had left a profitable practice in New Orleans for the life of a gold-seeking wanderer—a splendid carriage, to walk on foot over barren hills and valleys—an ample table, to cook his scanty worm meat and eat his musty bread—a feather bed and lovely wife, to sleep on the hard ground serenaded each night by howling starving wolves."

Such tales of woe were common.

"A young man named Samuel Anderson, the son of a wealthy gentleman in New York, came to my tent sick and without a cent. I gave him something to eat, medicine and money to pay his way to San Francisco. He was direct from the mines. I never saw him since and never learned whether he lived or died."

On another occasion, still another doctor rode up to

McNeil's bar and asked if he would like to purchase his horse.

"I am from Illinois," the doctor said.

"Have you been to the mines?" O'Neil asked.

"I have been to the Mormon Island. I am going home, as I had only visited the region for my health. That's why I am going home."

McNeil looked him over; the stranger looked healthy. The mountain air must have worked.

"Any person who can endure the fatigues consequent on traveling across the Plains must have been very healthy at home," McNeil observed shrewdly.

"I would like to give [John] Frémont, and all the letter-writers who had extolled California, a [dose of] arsenic, as the intelligence about the gold was designed to humbug the people of the United States," the doctor replied bitterly.

"He rode off and I saw no more of him. On another day, two New Yorkers were eating dinner at my tent. In stepped a Massachusetts man, who said that he had just returned from the mines. The New Yorkers, to have a little fun with him, commenced asking him questions, and found that he, like the celebrated doctor, was bound for home. They pretended they had a diving bell, and offered him $16 per day and board, for working only two hours a day with it. This offer he refused.

"They then offered him wages for that purpose from $25 up to $50. He swore that he would have nothing to do with the under-taking, as he believed they wished to drown him. He said that he could live better in a

Massachusetts poor house than he could in California; home he would go, and took his hasty departure, followed by the laughter of those who had tried to hook the land gudgeon.

"A gentleman, named Francis Shaeffer, whom I had known from a boy, stepped into my tent. He was born and raised in Lancaster, Fairfield County, Ohio. His father keeps the finest hotel in Lancaster, and, I think, is worth $100,000. I was considerably glad to see Frank, as he was the first of my acquaintance I had seen in the gold regions. He came the overland route from Fort Independence, one among the first who got through. I asked him, why he had come to that desolate place, as his father had enough at home to sustain him during life without laboring.

"He answered, 'I knew that. I wish to make with my own hands as much as my father possessed.'

"I could not help sincerely pitying him when I saw his fine form and expressive countenance, with an intelligence that might have realized him a fortune in any other place, knowing and feeling that the hardships and privations of that region would be severe on one who had been so delicately raised and liberally educated. Yet, feeling confident that by his extraordinary energy and ability, he would acquire an independent fortune at the mines, and would go to his home with one of the largest treasures on earth.

"A New York lawyer stepped into my tent one day, without the usual haughty swagger he had previously exhibited on Broadway, and without the usual gloves on his hands and umbrella under his arm, which he had displayed there in going to perform some peti-fogging business. I never heard his name, and perhaps he was so ashamed of the mines he wished to conceal it.

"He said there was no law in that country, and that gold digging was too severe for his delicate hands and body. I observed that the more law there is in any country, the more trouble there is among men.

"He said, 'I am without money and without hope,' showing me a splendid gold watch, saying that he wished me to purchase it from him, asking $50 for it, observing that it had cost him $110 in New York.

"I told him that I would give him $20 for it. This he took and spent $5 of it with me, in eating and drinking, before he left."

It was an everyday occurrence for McNeil to wait on men coming to and returning from the mines. Most did not stay long enough to learn how to find the gold and wash it properly. Frequently they stayed only a few hours in the gold fields. Without the prerequisite patience for the boring, repetitive, backbreaking labor of pan and cradle, they instead retired in disgust.

"A sailor was at my tent. The captain of a vessel wished to hire him to accompany the former to Oregon. The captain offered him $250 per month. The sailor asked $300. The captain observed that that was too much, and he could not give it. The sailor then retorted that if this captain would accompany and help him at the mines, he would give him $300 per month and board. This is the only country in which I have seen true democracy prevailing. The poor man can give as high wages as the rich man, and the former can hire the latter as readily and as liberally as the latter can hire the former."

The Sycamore Tree Establishment, with its philosophizing bartender/owner, the shoemaker from Lancaster, became so popular that one day the great man himself, John Sutter, showed up for a drink. After he'd had a few, Sutter began complaining to McNeil.

"On his first expedition to California, Colonel Frémont come to my fort, and took by force, horses, cattle, and provisions, for which he I have never been paid by the government," Sutter said bitterly.

"What about the great crops of wheat you were raising when the gold excitement commenced?" McNeil asked.

"I only raised it for the use of my own stock, as there was not at that time a mill in that region for grinding wheat. I have not a fence on my farm, the Fort is in ruins, its walls having been formed [as those of his house in which there is now a tavern] of adobe brick, or clay bricks not burnt. I live now at Suterville [sic], a town of about one hundred buildings, one mile and a half below Sacramento City.' "

Sutter was lying. This was the beginning of a myth that began that day in 1849 when Sutter visited McNeil's establishment and extended throughout the rest of his lifetime, beyond his death, and into the twenty-first century.

Sutter would tell any and all that the Gold Rush ruined him, which wasn't true. He just didn't have unfettered control of northern California like he used to have. While it's good to be king, when you're kicked off your throne, it's a hard fall. Now his fort wasn't the only game in town for the kinds of civilized services men needed before going into the gold fields. He had competition, and he didn't like that very much. McNeil barely had time to think about Sutter's expressed condition when he came in for a surprise.

"The Lancaster boys are arriving. The vessel I sailed in from Mazatlán arrived at San Francisco two months before the French brig in which they voyaged. The Catholics have their hell in purgatory, the Universalists theirs on earth, but the Lancaster boys were to have theirs on the Pacific Ocean for their conduct towards me.

"They arrived at Sacramento City without money, and wished to borrow $50 from me. I readily agreed to let them have it. They wrote a joint note, not with a pen, but with a pencil, that through rubbing in the pocket book, it would soon rub out. I observed to them at the time that they need not think I am a fool because some may consider me an ignorant shoemaker, for I had discovered why they wished to have the note written with a flimsy pencil, and would not, in consequence, let them have $50 on any terms.

"After wishing to shoot me at Mazatlán, they tried to borrow money from me at Sacramento City! But the reader will see that the same principle, or rather want of principle, was exhibited both in the shooting business and the borrowing affair. They then took a pleasure trip to Smith's Bar."

It was then August 20; McNeil had landed in San

Francisco on June 1. In almost three months, he had accumulated $1,500, "that is, cleared that sum, after paying all expenses. I firmly believe that, if I had not been bothered and delayed through Texas and Mexico by the Lancaster boys—that is, if the wagons had been sold, and we had muled it in 30 days instead of the two months the trip occupied, I might have doubled the $1,500 between the dates I mentioned."

To show how social class was in a constant state of flux during this period, McNeil cites this example:

"An English vessel was lying at that port of the muslin houses. Although the sailors had been receiving good wages, all of them run away from the ships to the mines. The captain, who was receiving $50 per month from his employers in England, being an honest man and true to their interests, remained on board. He hired at that port a cook, for his own eating, to whom he gave $250 per month. This is the first time I ever saw a cook get more wages than the captain of a vessel. No other country can exhibit such a singularity as that. In fact, California has turned the world upside down in every department of life."

California had not been the boom place it was for some, nor did he lose his shirt like most. McNeil saw the reality. It invaded his feelings with an intense and profound sense of loneliness. He missed home, he missed family, he missed his children, and he missed his friends.

"A New York gentleman walked pompously into my tent, and asked me what I would take for the now universally celebrated and appreciated Sycamore Tree Establishment and all its appurtenances, the latter consisting of as much as an ordinary man could carry on his back, and would be worth in the States about $50.

"I told him $500, considering that the credit of the establishment was worth a small fortune. He offered me $400 in cash. I observed that it was useless to multiply words between gentlemen, and he might count out the $400 in sterling gold, and he could take the whole concern and possession at the same time.

"Now I am ready to start for home."

As it turned out, McNeil would once again have a traveling companion. A countryman named Walker from Cincinnati, who had traveled with him previously from Mazatlán to Sacramento, showed up at the Sycamore Tree Establishment just as McNeil was selling the place. The last time they had seen each other, Walker "got drunk soon after arriving in Sacramento and went off intoxicated to the mines. When I saw him last he was making a perfect worm fence along his route.

"I did not hear of him afterwards until the moment I was ready to start towards home. I asked how he had progressed after leaving me. He informed me that he had found a rich spot, and had dug out $8,500. He showed me the dust. Both of us then proceeded to San Francisco, where, getting as beastly drunk, as ever, he gambled and soon lost $1,000. Then he had $7,500 left, which I took care of for him. As to fortune, there was a great disparity between us, as I had only $2,000.

"It is now August 20, and Walker and myself are at San Francisco, waiting for a passage to the States. The U.S. Mail steamer *Panama*, is anchored in the bay, three miles from the town, appointed to sail Sept. 2d. She is commanded by Capt. Baily. Our tickets for the steerage, in that ship, cost us each $150. I could have sold my ticket for $250, as there were about one thousand more than the steamer could take, wishing passage to the States.

"Before catching the steamer, several of the Lancaster boys showed up. I call them *boys*, for *men* would not have acted towards me as they did. They had not, as yet, made one dollar. They tried to persuade me to stay longer in that country, but they could not succeed.

"I told them that I had seen the elephant, which had a longer tail and a bigger snout than the usual elephants. That I was satisfied with the small bucket full of gold I had accumulated, and would not stay to see it running over the sides like milk from a pail, as I was no advocate for wastefulness.

"Perhaps they had not sense enough in their contracted skulls to understand the homely illustration of the Lancaster shoemaker. If so, they may die with their wisdom, as its loss will be not the least loss to the world."

10.

CRIME WAVE

As he boarded his steamer in San Francisco Harbor for the trip south, Samuel McNeil noticed all the foreigners emptying off the five-hundred-some ships in the harbor. Being a parochial people, Americans like McNeil were afraid and distrustful of foreigners. Among the latter who came to America's shores in the wake of the discovery were the dissolute and dishonest from all countries of the civilized world.

"Situated within reach of the penal colonies of Great Britain, as well as being in proximity with the semi-barbarous hordes of Spanish America, whose whole history is that of revolution and disorder, it was soon flooded by great numbers from those countries, who were accomplished in crime, and who, without feeling any sympathy for our institutions, and contributing nothing for the support of our government, their only aim seemed to be to obtain gold, by any means, no matter how fraudulent; and owing to the weakness of the constituted authorities, joined to the vicious among our own people, they succeeded in their frauds and crimes to an amazing extent, and rendered the security of life and property a paradox on legislation, hitherto unprecedented in the annals of modern history," wrote Alonzo Delano in his popular 1857 book *Life on the Plains and among the diggings.*

The book is based largely on letters from Delano published in Ottawa, Illinois, and New Orleans newspapers. The Aurora, New York, native had moved to the Midwest as a teenager. By July 1848 he was a consumptive storekeeper in Ottawa looking to extend his life by going someplace where the air was drier. Delano joined a local California company and migrated west, where he won fame after the Gold Rush as an early California humorist.

Delano's view that Gold Rush crime was perpetrated by "the semi-barbarous hordes" was a popular belief. And yet, like most prejudicial racist tracts, "In the early part of the winter of 1850, however, some of those who left the mines early for fear of starvation, or because they preferred the comforts and pleasures of the town to a winter seclusion in the mines, being unable, perhaps unwilling to obtain employment, gave loose to their vicious propensities; and about that time, too, Sydney convicts began to arrive, when affairs began speedily to assume another aspect and it became necessary to guard property with as much acre as in towns of the older states."

Gold Rush crime came about because of a variety of factors: sheer force of numbers; the immigration to San Francisco of convicted criminals from Australia and Britain, who came there after their release; and the sheer hunger and deprivations of miners who failed to hit pay dirt. Making things worse was the lack of an effective government and law enforcement program to deal with the burgeoning crime wave.

During the winter of 1849–50, cattle rustling began. The Californios, whose herds the rustlers were stealing, complained, but to no avail, because there really was no one to complain to. Rustling of mules and horses followed with impunity. Naturally, at first the Indians were charged with the thefts. When many of the rustled animals were subsequently recovered and their path from rightful to unlawful owners was traced, it became clear "that the white savages were worse than the red," Delano wrote.

Then pure greed showed itself at the diggings.

"Even as late as June, 1850, I was one of a jury in the mines, to decide on a case of litigation, where one party sued another before a self-constituted miners' court, in the absence of higher law, for flooding the water on a river claim, and thus preventing its being worked.

"The court was duly opened, the proofs and allegations adduced, and the costs of the trial advanced. Judgment was rendered against the plaintiff, in favor of the oldest occupant of the adverse claims, when the plaintiff submitted without hesitation, and paid $102, costs, with as much cheerfulness as if it had been done by a legally constituted court of the United States."

Zachary Taylor had taken office as the twelfth president of the United States on March 5, 1849. For the next sixteen months, Taylor and his vice president, Millard Fillmore, enjoyed unprecedented popularity because of Old Rough and Ready's forty-four years of loyal and popular military service.

During those sixteen months, the South threatened to secede from the Union over the issue of slavery in the new territory it acquired. Taylor encouraged both New Mexico and California to apply for admission as free states. A Kentucky native, Taylor angered his Southern followers even more by ignoring the claims of Texas, a slave state, to territory that had become New Mexico instead of Texas as a result of the Treaty of Guadalupe-Hidalgo.

In February 1850 President Taylor held a contentious meeting with Southern leaders threatening secession. "[People] taken in rebellion against the Union, I will hang," he said, "with less reluctance than I used in hanging deserters and spies in Mexico."

Eleven years before President Lincoln went to war to preserve the Union, President Taylor threatened to do exactly that. Taylor told the South in no uncertain terms that to enforce the Constitution, he would personally would lead the army against the South.

Taylor then lobbied for the Missouri Compromise of 1850, which prevented the South from seceding, at least for the time being. Then a very strange thing happened. Ground was broken on the Washington Monument on July 4, 1850, at which the president presided. It was a stifling, hot day. For relief, the president consumed a bowl of frozen cherries and milk. He became ill almost immediately and died three days later of what appeared to be an acute inflammation of his intestinal tract caused by ingestion of the confection in combination with the heat.

With Taylor dead, Millard Fillmore took over. Fillmore did not have Taylor's enormous experience in the world; he never cast a glance toward California. As a result, crime continued unabated in the Union's newest state.

By the spring of 1851, crime was rampant, particularly on the streets of San Francisco. Robberies and murders were daily occurrences. Organized robber bands terrorized the towns and the mountains.

"I was privately informed by a young man of my acquaintance, that he had been offered seven hundred dollars a month to steal horses and mules. Although he was a wild, daring fellow, he had too much principle to engage in nefarious practices," wrote Delano.

Every morning, San Franciscans awakened to reports of more robberies and more murders as daily newspapers chronicled the crime wave. By June 1850, there were sixty people awaiting trial for a variety of alleged crimes. Ten of them were on indictments for assault with intent to kill. Things were just as bad in the mining camps.

In Marysville in March 1850, a cloth house was cut open with a knife, and a trunk stolen, containing $1,000. Arrested as they were preparing to go down the river, the thieves were taken before the Alcalde, who sentenced them to a public whipping. It was carried out immediately in the town plaza. Despite that, only a portion of the stolen money was ever recovered.

Down in Placer County, two men went into a tent, and finding a woman alone, her husband off at work, proceeded to bind and gag her, and then robbed the tent of $1,500 dollars. These thieves, too, were arrested. As there were no prisons in the country, they were whipped, and again turned loose. This kind of thing happened regularly.

In December 1850 the crime wave spread south, to Monterrey. While the tax collector was absent from his office for only twenty-five minutes, thieves stole in and robbed it of $14,000 in public monies. Five ex-convicts from Sydney were arrested, and a portion of the money found. Captured in San Juan, two others were charged as accessories.

Of these two, one was also charged with horse stealing; he had stolen a horse that belonged to Judge Ord, who was counsel for them on the first charge. It was dangerous to buy a mule off a stranger, for fear the property had been stolen, and might be claimed by another party.

January 1851 saw no letup. Buoyed by their unheralded success, the thieves got even more brazen.

"The sleeping room of Captain Howard, of the police in San Francisco, was entered and a trunk, containing $2,100 in scrip, and $3,000 in gold was abstracted. So adroit had the thieves become, they actually went into a store about ten o'clock at night, and while men were at work overhead, they blew open a safe, took $700 which it contained, and escaped," Delano wrote.

"Cases even more bold and daring than any of these might fill these pages. Such became the insecurity of property, from the hordes of villains prowling about, that men scarcely felt safe under any circumstances, and no man slept in a building without having firearms within reach, well loaded, to protect himself against these ruthless midnight villains.

"In addition to other crimes, was that of arson. San Francisco was four times burned, and every principal city in California suffered severely from fires, when subsequent disclosures proved that some, at least, if not all, were caused by the fiendish incendiary, to gratify a desire for plunder, or from a horrible spirit of revenge.

"Every ship from the penal colonies of Great Britain only swelled the number of English convicts already here; while the vicious from all nations seemed to find a rendezvous in California, and hordes of the most accomplished villains in the world, who had passed through every grade of crime, found a home and congenial spirits in this devoted land."

These individuals were morally bankrupt. They not only wouldn't work to acquire wealth, they were willing to kill for it. They got away with it, the kind of situation that cannot long endure in any civilized society without there being violent repercussions.

With any crime wave, there is always a point where the criminal goes too far. Even ordinary people with no taste for blood get that strange, salty taste in their mouth. Then, in February 1851, San Francisco was thrown into turmoil by one of the most audacious robberies that had ever been committed in the town.

Two Englishmen, Frank Dravat and Smythe Carnahan, ex-convicts from Sydney, had entered the San Francisco store of Tom Brewster. Located near the corner of Washington and Montgomery streets, Dravat and Carnahan came in the store at eight o'clock in the evening. Inquiring for some blankets, Brewster was in the act of showing them, when one of the scoundrels struck him a blow on the head with a slug shot, which some also called a blackjack. Brewster fell unconscious to the floor; the thieves jumped on top of him and struck him again.

Satisfied they would not be bothered, the Brits broke the lock off his desk, robbed it of nearly $2,000, and escaped. A short while later, Brewster recovered sufficiently to crawl next door and give the alarm, but the villains were gone. What made the crime different was that it happened on one of the city's most crowded streets in broad daylight. That not only showed the thieves' courage but also their desperation to make a score.

A few days later, a Sacramento cop, Chris Dalton, recognized Dravat. He was wanted for crimes committed in the mines. Dalton arrested him, along with his companion, Smythe Carnahan. There were inescapable similarities between their thieveries in the mines—where one of the men knocked out the unsuspecting victim and the other rifled his pockets. Carnahan and Dravat retained counsel, Willie Gingrich, who tried to show they had an alibi.

No one believed them, least of all the district attorney and the public who witnessed the testimony in a makeshift courtroom. A row ensued in which the mob attempted to seize the prisoners to hang them. They were rescued by the police and a company of the Washington Guards, and conveyed to a recently constructed prison.

That was it. The mob hissed the Washington Guards and rushed the prison. Stones were thrown through the barred windows, shattering the glass. Some in the mob brandished rifles and revolvers; others, knives and pick-axes. Suddenly, the door to the prison was thrown open and a man in uniform appeared, Captain Bartol of the Washington Guards.

Bartol wore the standard issue scabbered sword on one side, with a holstered Colt Navy revolver in a waist-high leather holster, secured to his thigh by a drawstring of tough rawhide. Bartol addressed the crowd.

"I have acted only in obedience of the law. If the prisoners are guilty, and if required by the authorities, we will march out and assist you in hanging them."

The crowd liked what they heard and backed off, deciding to act with brains instead of brawn. They organized a meeting, and appointed a committee of twelve to consult with the city authorities and to guard the prisoners. A meeting was called for the next day. As the time for said meeting approached, crowds began to gather around City Hall.

The streets and the roofs, windows, and balconies of adjoining homes all filled up with people. About ten thousand in all anticipated the meeting, which finally began with the mayor, as well as several other gentlemen, coming forward to address the mob. The committee of twelve advised the mob to leave the matter with the proper authorities, while pledging themselves that justice should be administered.

During their speeches, the committee members were frequently interrupted by cries of "no more quibbles of law—no straw bail—the criminals all escape—give us justice." But justice won out for the moment, and the mob once again backed off. A few days later, there was a major jail break. Among the escapees were Dravat and Carnahan.

The newspapers were not ignoring the crime wave, covering it in all its sensationalism. It provided a circulation boost and an opportunity for editors to pontificate on the conditions and, occasionally, solutions. From the *San Francisco Daily Courier* of June 10, 1851:

"It is clear to every man, that San Francisco is partially in the hands of criminals, and that crime has reached a crisis when life and property are in imminent danger. There is no alternative now left us, but to lay aside our business, and direct our whole energies, as a people, to seek out the abodes of these villains, and execute summary vengeance upon them."

On September 23, the *Alta California*, one of the state's best papers, published this editorial:

"We do not wonder that the whole city is excited, that every honest man feels indignant against the vile miscreants who have fired our houses, robbed our citizens, and murdered them. This feeling is natural. And the present apparent and expressed determination to take the administration of the law into their own hands is the inevitable result of a shameful laxity in the administration of our lower courts. To them alone is chargeable the present state of public feeling.

"Examinations and trials of criminals have been a miserable tissue of trifling, quibbling, and nonsensical distinctions, and deductions unworthy to be used by a respectable bar, unworthy of any consideration by judges. Any persons have been allowed to testify. Every one of the thieves and robbers who infest our city has witnesses enough to swear an alibi and such evidence has been allowed! Every means, too, has been taken by unscrupulous advocates [usually lawyers] to postpone, and stave off trials, knowing that delay would absolutely destroy all incriminating evidence."

It was an argument that would be used in the subsequent century when a crime wave hit the midwestern United States in the 1930s, and again the 1980s through the 1990s, when cases against members of organized crime fell apart with bought alibi witnesses. California has the dubious distinction to say that it happened there first on a regular basis.

On June 11, a notice appeared in both the *Daily Courier* and *Alta California*, requesting that San Francisco's citizens assemble in Portsmouth Square at three o'clock in the afternoon. At the appointed hour, the citizens assembled there to the astonishing spectacle of a man hanging by the neck from the porch of an adobe home.

Someplace under cover of darkness and civilized law, a shadowy, vigilante organization had formed. Composed of some of the city's wealthiest citizens, who had much to lose if crime continued to run rampant, the newly organized Vigilance Committee was determined to execute justice, and criminals, with their own hands. This hanging was the first by their organization. The *Daily Courier* of June 10 covered the lynching this way:

"It is clear to every man, that San Francisco is partially in the hands of criminals, and that crime has reached a crisis when life and property are in imminent danger. There is no alternative now left us, but to lay aside our business, and direct our whole energies, as a people, to seek out the abodes of these villains, and execute summary vengeance upon them."

A week later, Sam Jenkins, a Sydney convict, was arrested while robbing a safe. A jury was selected, "indubitable proof of his guilt was adduced, and he was hung immediately, about two o'clock in the morning. Shortly afterwards, the people of San Francisco were summoned by the most respected men of the city, to a meeting in the Plaza.

"The meeting was duly organized, and several among the most highly esteemed citizens addressed the people, briefly stating the condition of affairs and advocating the necessity of taking steps to arrest the career of crime. The existence of a Vigilance Committee was [publicly] announced."

A resolution was then offered, approving their acts in hanging Jenkins. By loud acclamation the crowd accepted it, with one lone dissenting voice, from a lawyer, "whose interest it undoubtedly was to perpetuate this unwarrantable condition of things in our community. The meeting adjourned over to the next day, at the same hour and place, when, it was understood, a series of resolutions would be presented.

"At the appointed time, the Plaza was again filled with anxious but not excited citizens, and there was a determined calmness in their demeanor, which plainly told that it proceeded from long suffering, and that they would coolly, deliberately, and surely protect themselves from further insult and outrage."

The following eight resolutions were offered for public approval:

1. On account of circumstances over which we have no control, we are constrained to believe that the crimes of grand larceny, burglary, and arson should be punished with death, disclaiming the right to inflict this penalty after a proper time has elapsed to obtain the voice of all the people, through the ballot box.

2. That a committee of seven be appointed to call an election of the citizens in each ward, to decide whether or not these crimes shall be punished with death, appoint the officers of the election, and define the form of the ticket.

3. That at the same time and place, a judge and sheriff shall be elected (unless one of our judges and sheriff will serve), who shall enforce the will of the people in punishing the guilty, who shall have jurisdiction only on those criminal cases above-mentioned.

4. That we pledge our lives, our fortunes, and our

sacred honors, to protect and defend the people's court and officers, against any and all other jurisprudence.

5. That any person charged with crime shall have a fair and impartial trial by jury, nor shall he be deprived of the privilege of giving any evidence he can bring to prove his innocence.

6. That in case of any doubt as to the guilt of any person, he shall have the benefit of such doubt, in accordance with established usage.

7. That the people's court shall have no jurisdiction after the next legislature has been convened five days.

8. That all expenses of such court shall be paid by the contribution of citizens.

Once again by loud acclamation the resolutions passed.

The Vigilance Committee controlled San Francisco. It was 1850, California was a state, but the seat of government was still Monterey, far south. It was therefore no surprise that San Franciscans saw the handwriting on the wall.

Soon, the vigilance organization's ranks were swelled by the voluntary enrollment of great numbers of the best and most effective citizens. Opposition was offered at various times to the Vigilance Committee's holding sway, usually by lawyers "who were losing a fruitful source of revenue in the defence of scoundrels." But the vigilantes maintained their ground.

Within ten days, criminals seemed to have gotten the message. They could be hung quickly for a variety of crimes. Suddenly the crime wave stopped. Assaults, robberies, and murders were dramatically lowered. An effective and active police force was formed. The rogues were caught, killed, or kicked out of the city. Change was not felt in San Francisco alone. Taking a page out of justice in the big city, in the mining towns, vigilante committees were organized and also held sway. Those found guilty by a miners' court were summarily punished, including by hanging.

The most famous of these hangin' miners' towns was Placerville. Its nickname was, and is, Hangtown.

It hadn't taken long. Coloma was so crowded with gold seekers by the summer of 1848 that prospectors had no choice but to search elsewhere for gold. Three ranchers from the Sacramento Valley—Perry Macoon, William Daylor, and Jared Sheldon—traveled east of Coloma, ten miles down the American River, onto a branch of Walnut Creek. There they discovered pay dirt. In one week in June 1848 they took out $17,000 from a small ravine "not more than a hundred yards long by four feet wide and two or three feet deep."

The creek tended toward dryness in the summer. The dirt had to be physically transported to water for the washing. The miners thus named their new camp "Dry Diggings." With rumors spreading throughout the area that Dry Diggings paid a man six ounces of the gold dust every day, miners came by the droves, some even abandoning already good claims to join the second phase of the Gold Rush, to Dry Diggings. Maybe there they could get even richer.

By December 1848 fifty log cabins had been built. During the following year, the population multiplied to a total of two thousand hearty souls camped out on every conceivable patch of ground, from ravines to hillsides, in all manner of protection from the elements. There were muslin tents, the aforementioned log cabins, lean-tos with one wall opened to the wind and rain, and then the more commercial establishments—saloons, whorehouses, restaurants, gambling houses, all charging exorbitant prices, anything to get that previous gold off the miners.

Crime flourished in the lawless environment as it did in San Francisco. Here, too, people decided when enough was enough. The change occurred in January 1849, when five men entered a gambling hall without the best of intentions. They stole their way into the office of the owner, John Vivyan. They put a gun to the unlucky man's head and rifled his office and clothing for gold.

In some way, Vivyan managed to tip off his employees, who waited for an opportunity and then crashed into the room, catching the robbers without firing a shot. The following day the five were found guilty of attempted robbery by a miners' court and sentenced to receive thirty-nine lashes.

Public punishment for crimes was still common in many other states as well as in California; people were used to viewing it. A large crowd of miners came out the next day for the spectacle. Each of the robbers in his turn was tied to an old oak tree, and the shirt ripped off his back. The man representing the state flung his cat-o'-nine-tails made out of toughened cowhide and leather. It flashed across bare backs thirty-nine times, baring some of the flesh close to the bone.

No sooner had that sentence been carried out than new charges were made against three of the five, Manuel, a Chileño and Frenchmen Garcia and Bissi. The charges were robbery and attempted murder in Stanislaus County. Too weak to stand for an arraignment, they were taken to a nearby house to "recover" while they were tried in absentia by a lynch mob. The trial took thirty minutes, and the sentences were immediate.

Of course, that left the issue of punishment. Someone in the crowd who looked like he himself had killed a few people shouted, "Hang 'em!" The mob roared its approval. Three ropes materialized, hanging from the limb of a sturdy white oak.

Half an hour later, the condemned men, barely able to stand and their backs still raw from their public flogging, were marched out and put into the back of a wagon, which then progressed a few feet to the hanging tree. A black handkerchief was put around the head of the three condemned men. Their arms were tied behind them. At a prearranged signal, the wagon was drawn out from under them, and they dangled into eternity.

The lynchings of those men, who became known as the Stanislaus Three, are among the first recorded homicides ascribed to vigilante justice in the Gold Rush camps. Shortly after the three met their Maker, a notorious character, "Irish Dick" Crone, was hung at the same tree for gutting a man and killing him over a disagreement at cards. Other bad men also were hung for assorted crimes.

Thus Dry Diggings became infamous throughout the gold diggings as "Hangtown."

Thirty days after the first hanging in San Francisco, "a security of life and property was felt throughout the whole length and breadth of the land, which had not existed since 1849. When, at length, order had been restored, and the courts began tardily to administer that justice for which they were designed, the Vigilance Committee, instead of executing the law themselves, acted as a people's police, to aid the constituted authorities in detecting villains, and left their condemnation and execution to the conservators of the law."

The state legislature passed a criminal code similar in nature to the resolutions of the San Francisco Vigilance Committee. Crime in San Francisco and the mines slowed to a manageable crawl. But that wouldn't last for long. A man was about to emerge from the mass of "foreigners" who had come to the mines, a man who was not going to tolerate discrimination, and a man who would become a champion to his people and to oppressed people everywhere.

THE OVERLAND ROUTE.

Top: Contemporary woodcut showing the "overland route" to California by wagon train, circa 1849. *Bottom:* An illustration of Sutter's Fort drawn from an old print.

General John Sutter of the Swiss Guard.

General M. G. Vallejo of the Mexican Army.

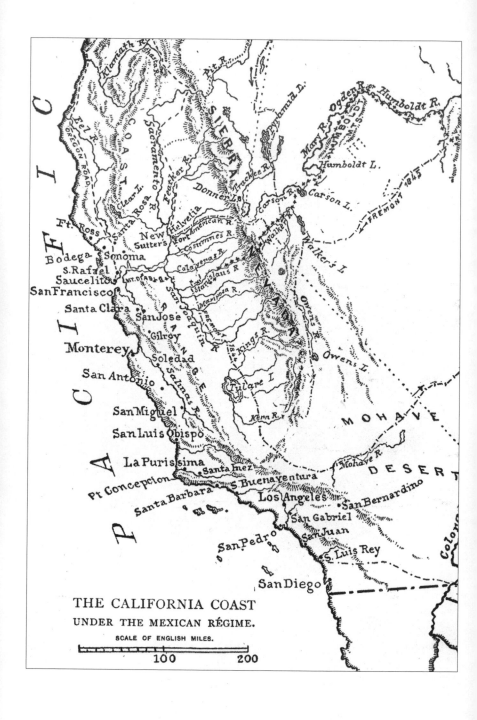

THE CALIFORNIA COAST
UNDER THE MEXICAN RÉGIME.

SCALE OF ENGLISH MILES.

100   200

Top: Sutter's Fort circa 1890 (redrawn from a photograph by H. S. Beals).
Bottom: U.S. soldiers fighting in Mexico during the Mexican-American War.

Top: The tailrace today. In foreground is where Sutter's Mill stood.
Left: The actual site where Sutter's Mill stood.

Top and Bottom: Views from Sutter's Mill and the surrounding area as it appears today.

Top: Looking out into the American River from the spot where Sutter's Mill once stood.
Bottom: The actual site where Sutter's Mill stood.

Top: The reconstruction of Sutter's Mill, not far from the actual site.
Bottom: The statue in Marshall's honor, erected up the mountain road from his cabin.

Top and Bottom: Marshall's cabin, which evidences his fine work as a carpenter.

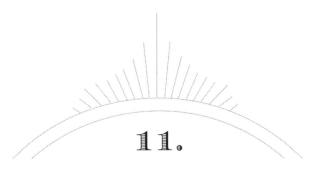

11.

THE FIVE JOAQUINS

Disagree as you would with whatever national policy the president of the United States set. The French were not enamored when Jefferson set Lewis and Clark on their westward trip; they knew the result would be forfeiture of their American territory. The Spanish knew even earlier, when the colonies declared independence from Britain, that eventually that would cost them their possessions in the New World.

Regardless of the president's policies, what no one in the world of the 1850s disagreed with was that the president of the United States told the truth. Period. The president was not a liar. President Polk's statement assured the rest of the world that gold had been discovered in California, and neither Taylor nor his successor Fillmore, said anything to the contrary.

It was there, a holy grail now to be found. To Americans in the slums of New York; on the Kansas prairie; in the Mississippi Delta, where slaves, fully aware of the gold strike, could look up and look to the West to a place where they could be free.

Even in 1849, before California became a state, slavery wasn't tolerated in the freewheeling Gold Rush. That's how Nancy Gooch got her freedom. Nancy was a slave who came to California with her owners, the Monroe family of Missouri. When they got to Coloma, Nancy was given her freedom. It was either that or the Monroes would face a lynch mob. Despite its isolation from the rest of the country, California had already grown in some ways into a politically progressive place that philosophically favored the North over the South.

Nancy Gooch was an industrious person, not surprising considering that she had been a slave to white people one minute, always at their beck and call, and the next, she was free. Whether she threw up her arms and danced a jig is unlikely. Nancy was pretty level-headed and was concerned about her son Andrew Monroe. He, too, was a slave.

Andrew had been sold to a different family and was still back in Missouri. Nancy's foremost identity was as a mother, but now, she realized, she could be a mother with a white person's freedom to earn money and turn it toward breaking a black man's chains. Nancy determined to earn enough money in the Gold Rush to buy Andrew's freedom.

Looking around her, she saw people in a pitiable state. The miners lived and worked in total filth. They could certainly use some clean clothes and good grub. Nancy began hiring herself out as an independent, doing laundry and other domestic chores for the miners. She lived in a shack that didn't cost her very much, and she had no real needs except food and drink.

It took almost a decade until Nancy had accumulated enough money to buy the freedom of her own son. Nancy contacted Andrew's owners, negotiated a price for his freedom—and putting in something additional for Andrew's recently taken wife, Sara Ellen—and then sent them the agreed-upon sum.

Andrew and Sara Ellen traveled over the Oregon Trail to California by covered wagon and joined Nancy Gooch in her Coloma home. It was a joyful reunion; the Monroes moved in with Nancy. Soon the family prospered. As the placer gold ran out in the late 1850s and miners went to the new boomtowns, land could be had at a low price. The Gooch Monroe family began buying land, which could be had at deflated prices. Some of the land was later turned into orchards that were worked by Andrew and his sons Pearly and Jim.

The Monroes were well liked and respected for their integrity and honesty. All through the Gold Rush boomtowns, blacks were treated most equitably. The same did not hold true for the Chinese.

In 1849, thirty-five Cantonese miners arrived at Camp Salvado to prospect. They struck it rich, pulling out thousands from the pay dirt. The thing about rich claims is that they attract prospectors who think that they, too, can strike it rich. Never mind the majority who don't; all it takes is one for people to flock like vultures to flesh. Soon white miners came to Camp Salvado and pushed the defenseless Chinese out.

In 1850 there were three thousand Chinese miners in California. The number doubled by 1852. Americans feared the Chinese because they would do any job to survive. That lowered the wages for all. Many camps chose to banish their Chinese rather than allow them to affect their pocketbooks. The Chinese could not even expect relief from the courts.

California state courts treated the Chinese as nonentities. They were not allowed to testify. But that still didn't stop them. The Chinese organized their own district unions to deal with disputes, to take care of the sick and infirm, and to bury their own.

The mining camps had a uniform ethnicity, but not every white man was a racist. Ironically, the American camp known as either Washingtonville or Camp Washington, located opposite Rocky Hill from Camp Salvado, accepted the outcast Chinese miners without problems. Camp Washington turned out to be a rich site. Other Chinese, who knew they would be accepted, flocked to the camp. Like the Lancaster boys, the Chinese knew that there was strength in numbers.

Unfortunately, the area they had gravitated to lacked water. The dirt had to be hauled out for cradling. Even the strong Americans who mined the placers pailed when it came to pailing dirt. But the Chinese didn't. Whatever it took to get the gold out of the dirt, they'd do it. They even made money on claims abandoned by non-Asian miners.

The mines around Camp Washington were mostly diggings, the rich gold scattered in the dirt. Mine a hilltop or a gulch, it made no difference; it was guaranteed to be pay dirt. Hilltops as well as gulches paid good money. That was only after the dirt had been brought out by muscle and mule to the Sims Ranch or Six Bit Gulch, where a creek was used to wash the dirt.

It seemed a lot easier to apply some basic tenets of irrigation. Trenches and flumes were built to allow a connection with Woods Creek. Water thus came to the camp, and with it, a new batch of miners. As the camp grew, and with it the Chinese population, it eventually became known as Chinese Camp. Its location made Chinese Camp a transportation center. Freight and stage lines used the place as a regular stop. By that time, the mid-1850s, most of the Chinese had been forced off their claims.

That kind of prejudice was tolerated because there was a dream that despite all of that, you could still get rich regardless of your ethnicity. It didn't make sense, given the facts, but then greed never does. As with any great upheaval, forces had been building below the surface and were now threatening to erupt. It came down to greed under the guise of racism.

From 1848 to 1851, fifteen thousand Latin Americans came to the gold fields. Most came from the Mexican state of Sonora, the rest from other parts of Mexico as well as Chile and Peru. The Mexicans and South Americans had centuries of experience as miners and easily surpassed their American competitors, who were jealous of their expertise that increased their profits.

Many of the Mexicans weren't even keeping the majority of the gold they mined. They came as encumbered peons, day laborers paying debts to their creditors by working in the mines. The peons were paid wages. To the "native" Americans, not only were they taking up valuable claim space, they were also doing it for an absentee owner.

Added to this racist brew were the Californios, the Californians of Spanish or Mexican descent whose families went back to the mission period of previous centuries. They became reluctant American citizens by the Treaty of Guadalupe-Hidalgo. They were already recipients of white settlers' enmity; the whites coveted their well-tended lands. It was as if, by some divine right, it belonged to them! These same Californios streamed to the mines, too, and of course, bringing their centuries-old experience, from their Spanish and Mexican cultures, were more successful than the "Americans" in mining.

When anti-Mexican and anti-Californio feelings were at their highest, the state began to act. The governor, Colonel John Mason, decided by executive order that foreigners working at the mines be treated as trespassers. That is, no foreigner could have a first "dibs" claim. They could only mine a claim after an American left it. Of course, Mason's edict was a contradiction in terms, since all the land being mined was public land, owned by the state and federal governments. His memo to Sutter, composed by Sherman, had seen to that. Therefore, all miners were trespassing, whether they were black, white, yellow, red, or any other color. But that made no difference.

Politicians did what politicians usually do: the cowardly thing. The California state legislature passed the Foreign Miners License Tax in 1850. Whereas Mason's edict had been just that, the tax was actually codified, albeit a racist law. Foreigners who were not U.S. citizens had to pay a monthly tax of $20.

Europeans frequently managed to avoid paying because they were the right skin color. The Mexican miners, who weren't, immediately protested. As peons they made all of $6 a month when they got lucky. Mexican-American War veterans gathered, fully armed, to help the tax collectors enforce this new law. They had no problem firing on the Mexicans, whom they still considered their enemy.

The state legislature, seeing they might just be fomenting a genocide they weren't prepared to accept, changed the law and made it $4 a month. That still was two thirds of what the Mexicans made, leaving them barely enough for anything in a place where everything cost a lot.

Despite the prevalent racism, many U.S. citizens, particularly traders, supported the foreigners by opposing the Foreign Miners License Tax, understanding that it was based only on racial prejudice. Nonetheless, the lines between the ethnic groups had been harshly drawn. Violent encounters between the races became common. Mexicans, whom the miners referred to as "greasers," who had disagreements with whites, could expect little relief from the courts. While thefts committed by Americans were ignored, those committed by Mexicans faced the harshest punishment.

The idea of the tax, of course, was to drive the foreigners out, particularly the Mexicans. By 1851, not coincidentally when the state legislature came to its senses and repealed this "legislation," ten thousand of the fifteen thousand Latin Americans who had been prospecting for gold gave up and went home. The remaining five thousand faced an intense hatred from the indigenous white "culture," which was still jealous over their mining prowess.

Among the remaining five thousand were five Mexicans who became bandits. When Governor Mason later put a bounty on them, he referred to them as the Five Joaquins, because each had Joaquin as his given name. Only one became a revolutionary legend to his people.

There was no immediate indication that the Gold Rush was about to produce the first, legitimate, home-grown revolutionary since Revolutionary times seventy-four years earlier. Instead, everyday events proceeded at a rapid rate. Miners came in; miners came out. Some got rich; most didn't. But that *hope* was still there. You could see it in the golden glint in the stream, or the rock on a weight scale.

Then, Joaquin Murieta came to the Gold Rush.

In October 1852 the steamer *Sea Bird*, with Captain Haley at the wheel, landed at San Pedro Harbor, south of Los Angeles. Passenger Horace Bell, twenty-three years old, took a hansom up to Los Angeles, where he took a room in a boardinghouse. Bell had every expectation of heading north for the gold fields immediately. Writing later in his *Reminiscences of a ranger; or, Early times in Southern California*, published in 1881, Bell takes up the story of what happened next:

"On the morning following my arrival in the city of the Angels, I walked around to take notes in my mind as to matters of general interest. First I went immediately across the street to a very small adobe house with two rooms, in which sat in solemn conclave, a sub-committee of the great constituted criminal court of the city.

"On inquiry I found that the said sub-committee had been in session for about a week, trying to extract confessions from the miserable culprits [of recent crimes] by a very refined process of questioning and cross-questioning, first by one of the committee, then by another. When the whole committee had exhausted their ingenuity on the victim, then all of their separate results would be solemnly compared, and all of the discrepancies in the prisoner's statements would be brought back to him. The prisoner would then be required to explain and reconcile them to suit the examining committee.

"The poor devil, doubtless frightened so badly that he would hardly know one moment what he had said from the moment previous, was held strictly accountable for any and all contradictions. If not satisfactorily explained, he was invariably taken by the wise heads of the said committee to be conclusive evidence of guilt."

Bell had walked into the Spanish Inquisition, California style. Six men were being tried, all Sonorans, except one, Felipe Read, whose mother was an Indian, and whose father was a Scotchman. All claimed, of course, to be innocent. Finally one Reyes Feliz, made a confession. He was probably under the hypothesis that hanging would be preferable to such inquisitorial torture as was being practiced on him by the seven wise men of the Angels.

"Reyes said in his confession that he and his brother-in-law, Joaquin Murieta, with a few followers, had, about a year previous, ran [sic] off the horses of Jim Thompson from the Brea ranch, and succeeded in getting them as far as the Tejon, then exclusively inhabited by Indians."

After that, Zapatero, the Tejon chief, recognized Jim Thompson's brand and arrested the whole party, some dozen in all, men and women, and stripped them all stark naked. Zapatero tied them up and had them whipped half to death. He finally turned them loose to shift for themselves in the best way they could.

"Fortunately for the poor outcasts, they fell in with an American of kindred sympathies, who did what he could to relieve the distress of the forlorn thieves, who continued their way as best they could toward the Southern Mines on the Stanislaus and Tuolumne [rivers], no mining being done south of those points at that time. In the meantime, brave old Zapatero, who was every inch a chief, sent Thompson's herd back to him—an act for which I hope Jim is to this day duly grateful."

While the confession was being given by Reyes, his brother-in-law Joaquin Murieta was walking around as unconcerned as any other gentleman—as he should have been. If he had received the flogging from the chief, there would have been scars on his back. But there were none; Reyes had lied.

Murieta was of proud Mexican heritage. He had come to America to try his hand in the mines; he was looking forward to making his fortune. Unfortunately, his brother-in-law had been a coward, and that changed Joaquin's life forever. Tipped off that "the minions of the mob" were coming "to lay heavy hand upon him, he was gone." Joaquin Murieta was not going to sit around and wait for the Anglos to hang him.

In Los Angeles as well as in all of California, rustling was a hanging offense. According to Bell, "From that day until the day of his death, Joaquin Murieta was an outlaw and the terror of the southern counties. Until that [Reyes] confession, he stood in this community with as good a character as any other Mexican of his class."

Like Victor Hugo's Jean Valjean (whom Murieta may very well have inspired in the author's *Les Misérable*), Murieta became a fugitive on the run. He escaped to northern California, where he made the acquaintance of A. D. Hobson. Born in Yadkin County on the Yadkin River in East Bend, North Carolina in 1825, A. D. Hobson was of English and Welsh ancestry that went back to pre-Revolutionary times.

"In the spring of May 25, 1850, A. D. Hobson and Stephen Hobson in the company of five other young men, including David Hobson, brother of A. D. Hobson, Robert Spainhauer, and Stephen Potter, outfitted with mule teams and light wagons to join the Gold Rush to California," A. D.'s son James Cornelius Hobson, later wrote.

"On reaching Salt Lake City, the Hobson party who

were becoming short of means, decided to stop and work for a while in the Mormon town, where they disposed of their equipment. Alfred D. Hobson did some brick work for the wife of Brigham Young, while other members of the party found various other employment in the embryo city.

"Father said that the people in the city treated them very kindly. When preparing to leave Salt Lake City, the party equipped themselves with saddle horses and pack mules in order to travel lighter and make better time on their way to California.

"One man in the Hobson party had previously made the overland trip across the Plains to California. This man was chosen captain of the company on account of his familiarity with the route over which they traveled. When the party reached the edge of an 80 mile desert, the Humboldt Sink in Nevada, the captain of the party advised all members to cut a supply of grass and carry it along as fodder for the animals and to supply themselves with canteens of water as they were to start across the desert at nightfall. They would make a forced march, endeavoring to make the trip in one day and night, which was done.

"My Father having a brother, George Hobson, living in San Jose who had preceded him to Californian, went directly there to visit his brother. While there he provisioned and with his cousins, Stephen and Jesse Hobson who lived in San Jose, went to the southern mines locating a mining claim near Shaws Flat on the Tuolumne River. There, they were very successful in mining."

The mining camps were nothing more than canvas tents and shacks against the elements. With no sewage system, with men using the same groundwater for drinking as well as for defecating and urinating, cholera ran rampant. It was one great muddy sore of a hole in the ground, sitting on top of what looked like the biggest cache of gold in history.

"The mining claims adjoining that of the Hobson claims were owned and operated by a young Spaniard by the name of Joaquin Murieta, a fine looking affable fellow who often paid a pleasant visit to the Hobson cabin. Murieta had a very well paying claim," James Hobson continued.

Murieta established his claim after fleeing north from Los Angeles. But before too long, the Foreign Miners License Tax was imposed on Murieta. That plus the governor's first "dibs" edict forced Murieta off his claim. Whether Murieta was married at this point is unclear. Some versions of his life have Murieta married, his wife raped by the gringos, his claim stolen, and him beaten up. Married or not, beaten or not, subsequent events make it very clear that Murieta, to put it mildly, had had enough.

Horace Bell takes up the story.

"In the spring of 1853, Murieta commenced a succession of bold and successful operations [robberies] in the southern mines, beginning at San Andres in Calaveras County. His acts were so bold and daring, and attended with such remarkable success, that he drew to him all the Mexican outlaws, cut-throats and thieves that infested the country extending from San Diego to Stockton.

"No one will deny the assertion that Joaquin in his

organizations, and the successful ramifications of his various bands, his eluding capture, the secret intelligence conveyed from points remote from each other, manifested a degree of executive ability and genius that well fitted him for a more honorable position than that of chief of a band of robbers."

On about March 1, Murieta commenced his raids in Calaveras County, by the murder and robbery of teamsters and traveling miners. Emboldened by success, in April, trading posts and mining camps were raided and robbed. Stages were captured, the passengers robbed and murdered. Murieta even managed to pirate a ship on the San Joaquin River, capturing and stripping it, "in open daylight. He raided up and down the coast, slicing the throats of anyone with a hint of gold dust in their satchel or anything else of value.

"By the middle of May, the whole country from Stockton and San Jose to Los Angeles, a distance of 500 miles, was in arms. Murder and rapine were the order of the day. The bandits seemed to be everywhere, and to strike when and where least expected."

Murieta also traveled the road between Truckee, California, and Lake Tahoe. He would stop at Clinkenbeard's Road House for food and drink, where Clinkenbeard's young son would wait on him. It was like that all over wherever he rode—people *liked* Joaquin Murieta. That was the essential element of his popularity. Though barely twenty-three years old, Murieta had already become so famous that others were imitating his depredations.

Rallying to Murieta's banner came four other men; all

were bandits, and all had the first name of Joaquin. They, too, commenced raiding the southern mines. But none seems to have had Murieta's panache; his ability to appear and disappear at whim; and his intelligence network, which helped him consistently avoid capture and remain one step ahead of pursuing posses.

Finally, newly elected civilian governor John W. Bigler had had enough. Showing how ruthless the state could be in stopping violence without taking into ethical consideration the means employed, Bigler got the state legislature to commission $1,500 to hire gunfighter Harry Love, a former Texas Ranger, to raise a posse and bring in, dead or alive, the "party or gang of robbers commanded by the five Joaquins: Joaquin Botellier, Joaquin Carrillo, Joaquin Murieta, Joaquin Ocomorenia, and Joaquin Valenzuela."

These men were believed to be responsible for the majority of all cattle rustling, robberies, and murders perpetrated in the mother lode region since 1850. While all five engaged in cattle rustling, robberies, and murders, Murieta was the principal target because it was he who inspired the Mexicans, Spanish and Californios.

Love and his group of gunfighters were perhaps the first group of licensed American mercenaries assembled to kill men on American soil. They called themselves the California Rangers. It sounded better than hired guns or hired assassins. Showing a nascent public relations propensity, Love penned weekly columns on the rangers and their unrelenting search for Murieta, making them out to be the lawful scourge of the California frontier.

Love would later claim that in 1853, he and his rangers tangled with a group of Mexicans near Panoche Pass in San Benito County. The pass is more than a hundred miles from the mother lode region, which immediately cast doubt on Love's story. He said that during his standoff with the Mexicans, the rangers managed to kill two of them. The rangers then cut off the head of one and the hand of the other, placing these body parts in jars filled with alcohol.

When they got back to Sacramento, Love claimed it was the head of Joaquin Murieta and the hand of Murieta's equally famous lieutenant, "Three-Fingered Jack." There was no positive identification, and subsequent examination of the head by people who knew Murieta led all of them to claim it wasn't Murieta at all.

To the governor and the legislature, it made no difference. They had a head, they had a hand, the matter was settled; Joaquin Murieta was dead and so was Three-Fingered Jack. Not only did Love and his posse get the $1,500 as promised, but also the state legislature voted them another $5,000 in grateful appreciation of their services. Soon after, the deprivations of the Five Joaquins ceased, leading most to assume that Murieta's head was pickling in that alcohol jar.

Within a year, the truth of Murieta's life was irrevocably distorted. In 1854, a fictionalized version of Murieta's life was published that most took as fact. Horace Bell, though, sized up Murieta's place in California history quite accurately:

"In any country in America except the United States,

the bold defiance of the power of the government, a half year's successful resistance, a continuous conflict with the military and civil authorities and the armed populace, in any other country in America other than the United States, the operations of Joaquin Murieta would have been dignified by the title of revolution, and the leader with that of rebel chief.

"For there is little doubt that Joaquin's aims were higher than that of mere revenge and pillage. Educated in the school of revolution in his own country, where the line of demarkation [sic] between rebel and robber, pillager and patriot was dimly defined, it is easy to perceive that Joaquin felt himself to be more the champion of his countrymen than an outlaw and an enemy to the human race."

Murieta was the first of a true American archetype, but because of his Mexican and Spanish ancestry, he received his due only among his own people. He was a true rebel, an angry young man with a cause. His nearest successor in the next decade would be Jesse James.

The Mexicans had Murieta, the Chinese had unions, the Indians had. . . . no one.

Indians were discriminated against all over the United States, usually by forcing them off valuable lands that they owned by native right, onto reservations where they were herded and fed like pent-up cattle. In California, it was worse.

Organized civilian campaigns, sometimes with the support of the military, were organized against the Indians. Massacres and murders of Indians without impunity, were common events during the Gold Rush years. Miners regularly attacked Indians for the simple reason that they were Indians.

Prior to 1848, Indians outnumbered whites and Hispanics in California. There were approximately 150,000 Indians in the state. By the early 1850s, the white man was in the majority. By 1870, the former number had dwindled to 30,000. It would later be estimated that between 1848 and 1880, whites killed, conservatively, 100,000 Indians. The rest were felled by disease, starvation, and being worked to death.

After the discovery of gold by Marshall, there weren't enough people to work the diggings. The miners adopted a modified version of the Spanish/Mexican practice of peonage. Slavery may have been outlawed, but forced labor wasn't. The state legislature gave it the imprimatur of law.

In 1850 it passed the "Act for the Government and Protection of the Indians." It was actually a law that allowed any American to indenture an Indian for work. Indians were forced into work as indentured servants in the mines and on the ranchos.

Fall and winter, when it was hardest to get miners, that's when the white miners liked to conduct their Indian hunts. They were hunted down by the miners and taken forcibly, under the law, to the diggings, where they were put to work. They did not receive wages, they did not receive clothing, only food and a damp blanket to sleep on at night.

A favorite technique for getting the most work out of them was to hold back on the food, a carrot-and-stick approach. The harder the Indian worked, the less food he received, all the time thinking he would get more. Finally, many just keeled over from starvation, overwork, exhaustion. It seemed that everyone, north or south, east or west, rich or poor, Protestant or Catholic, everyone hated the Indian.

It didn't help that the gold miners never gave much thought to polluting the rivers they were sifting through. They never thought about how they might be affecting the salmon runs by their mining. Nor did they think that indiscriminate killing of game for food would hurt the Indians' main source of food supply. It wouldn't have made any difference. Cut off their food supply, starve them to death. The idea was to kill the Indians, wasn't it?

Indians would occasionally mount raids against the white settlements mostly for food, sometimes out of sheer frustration and hate. But they had neither the weaponry nor sophisticated military tactics that their Plains cousins the Sioux and the Cheyenne would later employ successfully against the U.S. military. By the 1860s, things got even worse.

Whites raided Indian villages, kidnapped men, women, and children, and sold them as slaves to ranchers and farmers. Californians looked the other way as the legislature determined that Indian peonage could be turned into Indian slavery without the passage of another law. By the end of the century, the Indian hunts and the peonage took their toll.

Most of California's Indians had been wiped out forever.

12.

ONE STAYED BEHIND

Robert James had read carefully in the *Liberty Tribune* a transcript of President Polk's speech of December 5, 1848. The president had described the discovery as "of such an extraordinary character as would scarcely command belief were they not corroborated by the authentic reports of officers in the public service."

All the local papers in Clay County as well as the rest of the country began to publish stories of local boys who got rich quick in the gold camps. The *Liberty Tribune* ran a story in January 1849 of Joseph H. Cutting, a local man; he had gone to the diggings and in little more than a month, amassed $1,500 in gold! That amounted to almost $40 per day, more than half Robert James's profit from his entire year's hemp harvest. That kind of money you didn't sneeze at.

Later in the year, the *Tribune* printed the story of another local man, Peter H. Burnett, who sent a dispatch back to the paper. In the article, Burnett claimed, "Men here [in the gold fields] are nearly crazy with the riches suddenly forced into their pockets. The accounts you have seen of the gold region are not over colored. The gold is positively inexhaustible."

Inexhaustible and entrancing, even to a man of the cloth. Finally, Robert James could stay home no longer. No matter his family, no matter his responsibilities, no matter his God—he had to try his hand in the gold fields. Along with a group of like-minded men from Clay County, he prepared to leave in the spring of 1850. Like all those other men, he was taking a tremendous chance.

Among cholera, dysentery, smallpox, not to mention injuries and an occasional murder, there was a 25 percent mortality rate in the camps. Of those who went to California in the Gold Rush, one in four never made it back. Multiply that by the three hundred thousand people who flocked to the gold fields in first years of the Gold Rush and that added up to seventy-five thousand dead. Those deaths had a ripple effect on the families of the survivors, as Robert James well knew.

In preaching to his congregation, Robert James had seen boys who lost their father come to no good. If he died, who would be there to counsel his sons Frank and Jesse and lead them on the path of righteousness? Zerelda was a strong woman, but boys needed their father. What man would raise his children? Nothing substituted for a father's presence and guidance, not to mention the financial burden that would be on Zerelda if something happened to him.

These were questions every man who left for the Gold Rush had to ask himself and answer in his own way. For the most part, it was the men who went and the women who stayed home to tend the families and the farms that the men left behind.

On April 14, 1850, Robert James preached his farewell sermon at New Hope, Missouri. Those who were there said later that he seemed very much taken with the emotion of the moment. He told his congregation that he was not going to California for gold but to minister spiritually to the miners. Most of his congregants nodded their heads and took his assertion at face value. One congregant that day, Jane Gill, did not believe him and later wrote down her response to James's sermon.

"Aaron made a golden calf to worship whilst Moses was on the mount. And priests and ministers with their members may do the same in this day and have done it no doubt."

This was a roundabout way of saying that once James was in the gold fields, he would abandon his preaching for what every man wanted, the lure of the yellow nuggets and dust. Whether Robert James really believed he was going to preach is hard to say, but no one who knew him as a farmer and businessman would doubt that he would at least try his hand at gold mining. How could he not, with everyone around him seemingly getting rich? Robert James packed his things.

Fully cognizant that his father was leaving, though he

didn't know for how long, his 2 1/2-year-old son Jesse cried uncontrollably. In halting though plain language, Jesse begged his father to stay. He must have felt like he was being abandoned, but the child's pleas fell on deaf ears.

Departing on a wagon train from St. Joseph, Robert James soon became a prolific letter writer. As the wagon train commanded by Major Seth Adams went west, James wrote and mailed his letters along the way.

In one, he wrote Zerelda: "Train up your children in the nurture and admonition of the Lord and live a Christian life yourself. . . . Give my love to all inquiring friends, and take a portion of it to yourself and kiss Jesse for me and tell Franklyn to be a good boy and learn fast." In subsequent letters he sounded depressed, the privations of his trek clearly getting into his thoughts and then his words.

Sometime in the summer of 1850, Robert James finally came to the Gold Rush town of Rough and Ready. The camp had been there for only one year, its existence pure accident.

Hearing the news of Marshall's discovery, a group from Shellsburg, Wisconsin, had saddled up to cross the Plains in covered wagons and make their fortune. Their leader was Captain A. A. Townsend. He had been an officer under General Taylor's command in the late war, and had acquitted himself bravely. It was he who coined the name for their outfit, the Rough and Ready Mining Company, in honor of his former commander. The camp they established north of Coloma acquired the same name.

The Wisconsin miners had been at their work for a

few months, showing very little for their labors when in September 1849 a hunter in their employ named Cheyenne Bodie stopped for a drink of water in a shallow stream near their diggings. Bending down, Bodie thrust his hand into the cool, clean water, but before the water touched his lips, something made him stop. His eyes were seeing something he had never seen before. There, in the shallow water, right near his hand, was something glittering. The color was bright yellow. He grabbed for it. The nugget was . . . gold!

Bodie was so excited, he didn't know what to do except go back to camp and tell the rest of the men about his find. That was enough. Word soon got out, and Rough and Ready became another boomtown. It turned out that Bodie had found something quite large; anyone who dug in Rough and Ready or sluiced the water hit pay dirt quickly.

To this end Captain Townsend returned to Wisconsin to recruit miners for their claim. The deal was that Townsend would pay their expenses out, and in return, they would agree to work for him for one year, sharing the gold they pulled out of the water and the ground fifty-fifty. Forty men took Townsend up on his offer and returned with him on the long trek to California.

Townsend was back in Wisconsin when, on April 7, 1850, Rough and Ready had a town meeting to decide its future. Its citizens were angry and frustrated. They paid taxes to a state that had not provided them with any sort of law and order. The solution, the townsfolk decided, was to become the first town in the United States to secede from the Union.

Constitutionally, of course, this was illegal. To do so was a federal crime, though the federal government had never had to enforce this provision of the Constitution. As for the government of the state of California, they watched and did nothing as the miners formed the Great Republic of Rough and Ready. To make things nice and legal, a Constitution was drafted that provided for a president, who was then elected.

As their first and soon to be only president, the miners chose E. F. Brundage. Brundage then appointed his own secretary of state and marshal. In other towns, the latter office would be known as "town marshal." In Rough and Ready it became "republic marshal." That office, like the other two, was doomed.

On June 28, 1850, the Great Republic of Rough and Ready faced its first big test when a fire raged through the town, destroying nearly every tent, shanty, and lean-to that got in the path of the flames. The republic sprang back, building shacks and shanties and erecting new tents. The place was just too rich to let go because of something as small as a fire.

The Great Republic of Rough and Ready was barely three months old as July 4 approached. When they were still just a town, Rough and Ready would, like the neighboring towns, be getting ready for a grand celebration in honor of the nation's birthday. Parades, speeches, all kinds of festivities usually marked the occasion. But that was in the past, when Rough and Ready was part of the United States. Now it was its own republic.

The citizens of Rough and Ready felt kind of lonely.

More than a few had had cause to regret their initial decision to declare independence from the Union. They had been patriotic American citizens, and then suddenly, they were no longer. They felt displaced in their own republic. And they wanted to celebrate the Fourth just like they always had. The solution was apparent.

A second town meeting was called. With Brundage, his secretary of state, and republic marshal all tendering their resignations, the town voted overwhelmingly to stop being a republic and go back to being part of the United States of America. That done, the July 4 celebration could proceed.

When Townsend got back to Rough and Ready early that fall, he was told of the goings on while he had been away. He had, indeed, missed a lot. The camp had grown and now included a miner/preacher named Robert James, who hailed from Clay County, Missouri. Townsend couldn't be sure how much mining he did, considering that every spare inch of ground was staked out for miles around and everyone always seemed to be working. A man needed to establish a claim just to have a plot of ground where he could put his head at night. Hundreds were already working every square inch that was to be had.

Robert James heard of a miner who had recently found an eighteen-pound nugget of gold. Captain Townsend and his brothers, who had accompanied him from Wisconsin, made more than $40,000 in just a few months of work. How much Robert James made digging for gold is hard to say, because no records were kept. Whatever it was, it couldn't have been much.

James had always had a strong constitution, but it could not withstand the diseases in Rough and Ready. Dysentery, cholera, smallpox, jaundice, syphilis, gonorrhea, take your pick, they all were lethal. Sometime during September 1850, Robert James took to bed with a severe illness. As he had no money, a fellow Missourian, Daniel H. Wright, stood his expenses. For two weeks, Dr. Josiah Newman attended him until finally, in the middle of the month, Robert James finally expired.

There was no funeral with a minister such as himself praising Robert James's life and extolling his virtues. His wife and family were far away and knew nothing about what had happened. In that, they were no different from the families of the thousands of others who died during the Gold Rush. Robert James's body was placed in a shallow grave. Whether anyone even said a few words of Scripture over the grave is open for dispute.

When Zerelda finally got a letter in October 1850 from Daniel H. Wright informing her of her husband's death, it contained Wright's bill for the money he had loaned Robert James during his illness. He had already gotten what was owed him by taking the last $10 from his wallet and by selling the dead man's mule, belongings, and boots.

Zerelda wasn't the first Gold Rush widow in the county, and she wouldn't be the last. Most widows in such a condition moved in with relatives or friends. Not Zerelda. James had made sure to have a white man help to work his farm while he was gone, so at least for a while she could stay there.

On October 25, 1850, the *Liberty Tribune* carried an obituary with the headline "Death of Rev Robert James." It said, "As a Revivalist, he had but few equals in this country," and went onto to describe the prosperity of the Baptist Church in Clay County when it was under his leadership.

That should have been it. Had Robert James been just any other ordinary preacher turned miner, it would have been. But James had miscalculated. He hadn't taken care of his family, except in the short term.

Robert's sons Frank and Jesse had to make due without their father's love and guidance. By all contemporary accounts, it made them angry as they grew up. It didn't help that both had vivid memories of the time shortly after their father's death.

On November 21, 1850, Zerelda sat down for the reading of Robert's will, except there was none. Robert hadn't bothered. His estate therefore went into probate. Zerelda soon discovered that under the law of the state, her sons inherited everything and she nothing because she was a woman. Because the boys were underage, the court appointed an officer of the court to liquidate the estate and pay off James's hometown creditors.

January 4, 1851, saw the twenty-six-year old widow, her eight-year-old son Frank—he preferred "Frank" to the more formal "Franklyn"—and three-year-old Jesse standing on the porch as the auctioneer shouted out for bids on Zerelda's property. Among that crowd of strangers were many friends and neighbors. How humiliating it must have been. Zerelda had enough cash to buy back some of her property, including some beds, a sow, books about baptism that belonged to Robert, and some of his other small possessions. But everything of value went, including Robert's rifle, the most significant gift a father could leave his son.

In seeking to help out the widow of their beloved preacher, James's congregation took up a collection for the widow and her children, "He was the humble instrument of God. He saw the awful condition we were in and helped us to see it too as we should have done during his pastoral charge of New Hope Church for seven years. We hereby agree and bind ourselves to relieve his heirs." They meant, of course, only part of his debt. After that it was a hand-to-mouth existence for Zerelda and her children.

On September 12, 1855, Zerelda remarried, to Dr. Reuben Samuels, in personality the direct opposite of Robert. Where Robert was strong, authoritative, and loving, Samuels was weak, meek, and cold, hardly the sort of personality to father children on the frontier.

The next crucial point where Robert would have made a difference came in 1861. With the Civil War already under way, Samuels stood by tacitly as his eighteen-year-old stepson joined up with William Quantrill. No matter Robert James's Southern sympathies, he would have died first before allowing Frank to join up with such a scoundrel. Quantrill had defied all of the Ten Commandments before he was twenty-one.

William C. Quantrill was born in Ohio on July 31,

1837. He became a schoolteacher in Ohio and Illinois. That makes him, perhaps, American history's only mass murderer with such a benign and educated background. Like many a pioneer from the East, his profession did not offer enough challenge, enough adventure, and so Quantrill went west in 1857. The following year came the charge that he was a horse-stealer, a hanging offense in any frontier town. Quantrill quickly found employment as a trail hand on a wagon train traveling west to Salt Lake City.

Quantrill would subsequently be involved in a number of murders and thefts in Utah, and later in 1860 he fled a Utah arrest warrant, taking up residence in Lawrence, Kansas. There, the Southern sympathizer joined a group of abolitionists for the sole purpose of setting them up. The latter had plans to go across the border to Missouri to free some slaves. But Quantrill was working an angle.

Secretly, Quantrill let his proslavery brethren know they were coming. When they got to the Missouri farm to free those slaves, the Southerners opened fire from their places of concealment in the brush surrounding the farm. In a hail of bullets, the abolitionists were cut down by the proslavers. Quantrill—who, of course, survived— smiled when the massacre was over.

In 1861, when Fort Sumter was attacked and the Civil War began, punitive raids by the Kansas-based Jay- hawkers began. A guerrilla band, they rode into Missouri to kill slaveowners. Quantrill decided to emulate their tactics, only his Confederate sympathies served as a thin veneer for what he really was: a cold-blooded murderer who liked killing. He enlisted to his banner men of similar disposition, every out-of-work thief and murderer he could find. His lieutenant was seventeen-year-old cherub-faced Archie Clements, who would scalp an enemy's head and give it to Quantrill as a souvenir.

It was into this band of misfits who showed depraved indifference to human life that Frank James decided to ally himself. If Robert James were still alive, he would never allowed it to happen, but if it did, he would have gotten the rest of his family out of harm's way. Instead, Zerelda and Jesse stayed put.

That wasn't too good an idea.

Missouri was considered a "border" state—that is, neutral on slavery. Of course the state wasn't, and had many proslavery counties besides Clay. Union soldiers stationed in Missouri were under orders from Washington to ferret out Confederate sympathizers, which meant regular raids on the homes of people who had relatives allied with Quantrill. Since Quantrill operated independently except for a brief period when the Confederates mistakenly gave him a captainship and shortly thereafter came to their senses and kicked him out, he was considered an outlaw.

In 1863, a detachment of Union Army soldiers rode out to the James farm. It was still called that despite Reuben Samuels' residence. The officer in charge, Lieutenant Rip Masters, asked for Frank, to which Zerelda replied that she knew nothing and Samuels shrugged. Jesse, fifteen years old, sassed the Northern soldier and leaped to the attack.

Masters's response was to punch Jesse senseless; he was then stomped by the soldiers who were in the process of burning the farm to the ground. Robert James, a man of peace, would have counseled patience, and Christ's dying words "Forgive them, Father, for they know not what they do."

Crap. That's what the James family had left after the soldiers got finished with their farm. Over time, it would be rebuilt. But Jesse's heart had been broken when his father went to the Gold Rush, stomped on when his mother remarried, and now it had been shredded by the bluecoats' beating. It doesn't take a genius to figure out that Robert James's death was the beginning of a downward spiral for Jesse James that became a problem for many.

Soon after that beating, Jesse sought out Quantrill, and at age sixteen in 1864, joined up and was assigned to Bloody Bill Andersen's detachment. Andersen was another one of Quantrill's "lieutenants." He wasn't called "Bloody" Bill for nothing; he liked to kill and mutilate. Jesse's first "engagement" was in September 1864. At Centralia, Kansas, Andersen's detachment, which included Frank and Jesse James and their cousins Cole and Bob Younger, rode hell-bent into the abolitionist town.

Andersen allowed his men to rape the women. Surprising a squad of twenty-six Union soldiers in transit, Andersen and his men cornered them at the town's railroad station. As Jesse watched, Andersen lined them up side by side and then went down the line of twenty-six, carefully shooting each man in the back of the head. Jesse drank it all in.

In April 1865, with the war finally at an end, blanket amnesty was offered to those who fought for the Southern cause, including the survivors of Quantrill's band. Quantrill himself, as well as Andersen and Clements, were all dead. To get amnesty, it was necessary for the former "soldiers" to take an oath of allegiance to the United States of America, and to do that, Missourians had to travel to their county seat.

This is the only moment in their lives of the James boys after their father died, where he would have counseled them to do what they did—ride into Liberty, swear the oath, and put the killing behind them. Unfortunately, the James boys happened to be traveling into Liberty during the week of April 14, 1865.

By the time they got to the outskirts of Liberty, news of President Lincoln's assassination by the actor John Wilkes Booth had been telegraphed. In anger, the Union garrison stationed there decided to shoot any rebels who had the audacity to come into town expecting to swear amnesty.

Ambushed on the trail into Liberty by Union soldiers, Jesse took a .36-caliber bullet to the rib cage, perilously close to his heart. Frank and Cole Younger got him to the safety of a relative's home in Nebraska. There, Dr. Reuben Samuels finally proved himself as an excellent surgeon. He had read of Pasteur's germ theory and so washed his hands before operating, which probably saved Jesse's life. Infection did not prove to be any obstacle in Jesse's recuperation.

After his recovery, Jesse James revolutionized robbery.

Organizing the prototype for the modern-day "gang," Jesse recruited experienced guerrillas such as the Youngers. For the next sixteen years, the James/Younger gang cut a swatch across the Midwest, murdering innocent bystanders in cold-blooded rage as they robbed banks; stagecoaches; and for the first time, trains. It was Jesse James who bears the dubious distinction of having been the first to rob a train.

But what gets lost in the retelling of the James legend is what effect Robert James could have had on his youngest boy had he not perished in the Gold Rush. If Robert had been alive to instill ethics and morality into his son's character, how many of the Union soldiers killed at Centralia would be alive today if Jesse had intervened?

How many of the James gang's twenty-odd known victims, and their ancestors, would be alive today if either of the brothers had not set foot down the criminal path because of their father's positive influence? Surely there were other factors in the mix, least of which was the racial tension of the time, adding to their murdering brew. But other guerrillas went on to lead normal lives, whereas Frank and Jesse clearly did not.

Consider that approximately twenty-five thousand died during the California Gold Rush. Robert James's death is but one example of how a Gold Rush death ripples through time to affect people to the present day.

13.

MORE GOLD RUSHES

B etween 1848 and 1852, the peak years of the Gold Rush, California's full-time population reached two hundred thousand. More than three hundred thousand had trekked across the continent in search of gold, and tens of thousands more arrived by ship.

Few of the miners who came did so with any intention of staying. Many did, and their relatives live in California today. What grew out of Marshall's discovery is, arguably, the most culturally diverse population in the country.

It should be enough to say that the Gold Rush ended in the 1850s as the gold ran out. It didn't. Not really. There were many gold rushes to come before the century ended. With every one, America and the world would look upon each through the California prism. There was always the chance that a discovery could equal or surpass Marshall's. That belief, *get rich quick*, fueled itself. Foreigners in Austria and Germany, France, England, China, Japan, all over the world, their eyes turned toward the United States.

California gold had changed the nation's character. It was not so much that the nation had shed its en masse belief that hard work and a strong spirit of God in their lives lead to rewards in the next. It was just no longer enough. Men like Samuel O'Neil had discovered that through speculation on their future, they could change their lot in life.

For the next fifty years, that belief was played out in boomtown after boomtown. Amazing reports of mineral wealth discovered in various parts of the United States would lure hundreds of thousands more to America. Known by the derisive term "greenhorn" to citizens born here, the immigrants gave up sedate lives to take a chance on America. Their ancestors in the United States today number in the tens of millions.

The country the greenhorns found when they got here was going through what a later generation would call the Industrial Revolution. Americans began to rely on machines to do the work of everything from humans to mules. Voices could suddenly be made to travel over wires, light to be born from an "electric" bulb.

Machines made life better and easier, but they also replaced human beings. No one was going to immigrate to America simply because they had better machines than anyone else. Besides, how could you even afford the machines when you had nothing? Immigrants put their life savings into expensive transoceanic fares. The one thing that kept immigrants coming until the century's end was the lure of the gold and what it could do for their lives.

These *were not* the people who came to America and settled in the slums of the dense Eastern cities, hoping to patiently work themselves up a little higher on the economic ladder to give their kids and grandkids a leg up. These *were* the people who were willing to forgo the civilized East and travel west into a vast wilderness where fortunes could be made quickly. It was these immigrants who subsequently settled the western part of the United States, including Idaho, California, Nevada, New Mexico, and Arizona.

Not coincidentally, all these places had their gold rushes that sparked that new American belief of *get rich quick*. Unfortunately, the gold was in a rather hostile environment of wild animals, dense tree growth that sometimes made it impassable, and hot, dry plains and deserts, places that hadn't seen regular habitation by anyone, including Indians, since the late Stone Age.

There was nothing late Stone Age about the Indian tribes on the Plains and deserts the white Europeans and their American counterparts encountered in their search for gold. The Sioux and the Cheyenne, arguably the strongest militarily, had a strong patriarchal society with defined tribal boundaries They were pragmatic enough to be willing to negotiate with the foreigners for the mineral rights, which meant nothing to them, in return for peace.

The California prism would be brought to bear on the Indians. This time, in the national limelight, the government would not be able to put a bounty on the Indian scalps, as the California legislature had. Instead, to allow the cavalry to go after them, they would have to show that the Indians were in some way violating federal law.

The search for another California Gold Rush would soon provoke American history's most celebrated battle between the army and the Indian nations, and it would create a legend of a man that defined the American character of the late nineteenth century that survives to this day.

James Marshall never seemed to have any luck. By 1850, the mill had been completely abandoned because of management problems that entangled the mill in legal difficulties. It was better for Sutter and Marshall to just let it go.

Marshall spent the first few years of the 1850s searching for gold himself, with little success. He was a millwright, not a miner, but his services were becoming outmoded as steam engines threatened to replace horses, thereby making a man with the talent of manufacturing wooden wheels obsolete.

In 1857, James Marshall bought fifteen acres of land in Coloma for $15. He built a cabin near the Catholic church. He decided to become a vintner. Investing in new and exotic varieties of grapevines, Marshall planted a vineyard on the hillside above the town cemetery. He dug a cellar in his cabin and began making wine.

By 1860, his vines were doing so well that his entry in the county fair received an award. But his drinking, which continued his whole life, finally wore him down as his liver slowly deteriorated and with it his financial and physical health. Marshall took to prospecting again and became part owner of a quartz mine near Kelsey, California.

Maybe, at last, he'd strike it rich.

By the end of the 1850s, the California Gold Rush boomtowns were in sharp decline in direct proportion to the placer gold that was running out in the American and Feather Rivers.

Huge mining combines had come in to get at the ore beneath the earth. Gradually, the prospectors were being pushed out in favor of actual miners, who traveled deep into the earth to get the gold ore that would later be distilled. Out-of-work prospectors soon found themselves turning their collective heads to the east. Some of them climbed over the Sierra Nevada into Nevada, where they began mining gold on the eastern slope.

By that time, the Mexicans and the Chinese, with their more sophisticated mining techniques, were long gone, frozen out by xenophobic laws. The white California miners on the eastern slope of the Sierra Nevada in 1859 were literally throwing away pounds of silver every day because they were looking for gold. It took a while for two guys to get smart and realize that there was something special in the blue mud they were throwing away. They decided to take a sample to be assayed in Virginia City.

Just as they were leaving, Frank Comstock confronted them. A loafer who would give Washington's legendary Beau Hickman a run for his money in the loafing department, Comstock also had a dishonest streak. The two guys who had the blue mud in hand were told by Comstock that it was his land they had been working on. Instead of fighting it out with fists or guns, the two guys compromised and cut Comstock in as a full partner.

Thus, when the blue mud was assayed as being full of silver, the discovery became known worldwide as the Comstock Lode. It was a vein of silver that ran half a mile wide and seventy miles long. During the next twelve years it would be mined two thousand feet into the earth, where the temperature rose to 130 degrees Fahrenheit.

The California prospectors set off, en masse, to Virginia City. Mining the Comstock Lode for all it was worth, nearby Virginia City became the largest city between Denver and San Francisco, thus helping to settle the surrounding country. Unfortunately, the Comstock Lode required sophisticated machinery to mine. The California prospectors discovered that the kind of "mining" they had done was small potatoes compared to what was necessary here: huge reserves of capital and industrial skills were necessary to get to the silver ore deep in the earth. That was way beyond the capability of the average prospector, immigrant or otherwise.

Still the belief was there, and men streamed into Virginia City looking to strike it rich. In 1861, with the Comstock Lode still going strong, albeit controlled by mining combines of American big business, the country's attention turned to a more immediate problem. The country was at war, with itself.

❀ ❀ ❀

The United States found itself embroiled in a civil war. While one meaning of the word "civil" is being friendly with another, the Civil War was anything but civil. Hundreds of thousands of Americans died on the Confederate and Union sides. The man who turned the tide, who cut the Confederacy in half and thus ended the war, was a survivor of the Gold Rush, William Tecumseh "Cump" Sherman.

In 1850, Cump had married his foster sister Eleanor, Thomas Ewing's daughter. Resigning his army commission in 1853, Cump became a partner in a San Francisco banking establishment, Lucas, Turner, & Co. He oversaw the construction of the new bank building, which opened on July 11, 1854, at 800 Montgomery Street. It still stands, and is today known as Sherman's Bank.

Cump grew restless. Since he couldn't go west, into the Pacific Ocean, he showed the contrariness that would serve him well in Georgia years later, by turning east, and traveled in the opposite direction of the pioneers. He settled for a year in Leavenworth, Kansas, where he practiced law between 1858 and 1859. Then the military bug hit him again. He took the job of superintendent of the Louisiana State Military Academy at Alexandria, Louisiana.

A Northerner by birth and temperament, he resigned from the military academy in January 1861. When the Civil War started the same year, Cump joined the Union Army as a colonel. He commanded a brigade in the First Battle of Bull Run in July 1861. By August he had been made a brigadier general of volunteers and reassigned to

Kentucky. No sooner had he taken command of the army's Department of the Cumberland in October than he was reassigned to the Department of the Missouri.

A heroic division commander at the bloody Battle of Shiloh in April 1862, he was promoted to major general in May. In subsequent battles at Corinth, Vicksburg, and Arkansas Post, he continued to distinguish himself in battle as an intelligent, able soldier. In July 1863 he was made a brigadier general in the regular army.

Sherman's experiences during the Gold Rush period had seasoned him into a hard, competent man who understood that victory was surviving. No wonder, then, that Colonel Mason's adjutant went onto become, to the present day, the most reviled man in the southern United States.

Had Sherman's subsequent actions not shortened the war, it would certainly have gone on longer and affected the silver rush to come. That he could be so brilliant against one enemy, however, and so ignorant of the other says a lot about the man's willingness, at least, to put it all on the line for what he felt was right.

Sherman had seen in the California gold fields how important a man's spirit was. Without it, he'd fail at the backbreaking work of gold prospecting every time. He had to *believe* to get it done. In the same way, he knew that if the South were to be beaten, the sooner he vanquished the rebellious spirit of its civilians, the sooner the war would be over.

In September 1864 he applied the same careful thought to how to defeat the enemy as he had years before on Sutter's request to own the land on which gold had been discovered. Sitting in his Atlanta headquarters, Cump tried to decide where to move his army next. The March to the Sea was conceived as the final psychological blow to the Confederacy, one that would make it fall to its knees.

Looking at census records, he tried to determine which route across Georgia would supply his men with food and forage for their animals. A skeptical President Lincoln was presented with Cump's report that he could march across Georgia, to the ocean, and thereby cut the Confederacy in half. The point wasn't so much to engage the enemy but to show the civilians that the Union could do it with impunity.

The president waited until his November 1864 reelection before giving Cump the go-ahead. By that time, most of Georgia had been cleared of Confederate forces. For his march to the sea from Atlanta to Savannah, Cump divided his men into two wings. He gave them strict orders to forage as much as they needed, though not to use force against the civilian population unless it was used against them. In that case, they were to proceed to level the town where such an incident occurred and move on.

Meeting little military resistance, Cump and his men took Savannah. In their wake, they left burned-out hulks that had once been homes and towns to the guerrillas who fired upon the Union troops. As for crops, any in the army's path had been totally gone over by Cump's men.

On December 21, Cump telegraphed President

Lincoln that Savannah was now under Union Army control, offering the city and twenty-five thousand bales of cotton as Christmas presents. In his wake, Cump left more destruction than any military campaign, before or since, on the continent. But Cump knew that the kind of ruthlessness he showed in war would shorten it.

He was right. As a result of his March to the Sea, Cump had split the Confederacy into two parts, depriving each "side" of supplies without which they would be forced to surrender or perish.

After the war, Sherman stayed in the regular army, with a commission of lieutenant general. He would soon have a hand, once again, in a major gold discovery.

On April 9, 1865, the war ended when General Lee presented his sword to General Grant at Virginia's Appomattox Courthouse. Five days later, President Lincoln was assassinated by John Wilkes Booth during a performance of *Our American Cousin* at Washington's Ford's Theater.

It was on that day, when the nation lost its greatest president, that John Sutter once again showed his penchant for poor timing. He chose to petition the U.S. Congress for the "loss" of his land to the Gold Rush on the day Lincoln died. To say the least, the Congress was preoccupied with other matters.

Booth's plan that night had not been just to assassinate Lincoln. Coconspirator David Herold was supposed to kill Vice President Johnson but "chickened" out. But coconspirator Lewis Paine did attack and attempt to kill the third in line to presidential succession, Secretary of State William Seward. Were it not for the riding accident Seward had recently been in, leaving him wearing a leather brace around his back, Paine would have succeeded. But the brace served to stop the blade of Paine's knife from sinking into his throat. Instead, Paine slashed him across the face, a wound from which the secretary would recover.

Had Booth succeeded in killing all three, the federal government would have fallen into ruin because the next in line to head the executive branch was the president pro tempore of the Senate, a political nonentity named Lafayette Sabine. But Booth hadn't succeeded.

When things began to get back to normal in late May, the last thing Congress or anyone else wanted to deal with were the grievances of a sixty-three-year-old man who once had visions of a grand empire in his youth. Showing the stubbornness that had characterized his ability to build his fort in the wilderness, and finance the building of the sawmill where gold was discovered, Sutter decided to stay in the East and pursue his claim to his last breath.

By 1868, the country had recovered its collective breath and was ready to move forward. Once again, the seed of the new American Dream, planted by Marshall and Sutter, was about to blossom. There was an expectation now that prosperity was just around the corner.

While most of the nation's attention was focused on Washington, where President Johnson was being impeached by a reactionary Congress, and his trial in the Senate was about to begin, the country's economic interests were being negotiated in Laramie, Wyoming.

That's where Cump Sherman, now a full general, went to represent the interests of the U.S. government.

Cump knew that if the hostile Indians were not pacified, they would be wiped out by force. He knew war, and he didn't want to see it again. Instead, he wanted the western tribes to give up their ancestral lands and live on reservations, where the government would provision them. If he could succeed in doing that, then the land they controlled would come under the aegis of the federal government, which would do everything possible to promote its growth in accord with the government's avowed policy of "Manifest Destiny."

Under the Treaty of 1868, the Great Sioux Reservation in Dakota Territory was established, on which the Sioux— Brule, Ogallala, Miniconjou, Yanktonai, Hunkpapa, Blackfeet, Cuthead, Two Kettle, Sans Arcs, Sante, and Arapaho—would settle. In so doing, the federal government reaffirmed the Sioux hunting rights on land the Sioux controlled, including the Black Hills of what is now South Dakota.

But by 1871, rumors were already circulating on the frontier that the Black Hills were full of riches. President Grant had to rethink his administration's policy of containment and contentment of the Sioux balanced by the country's push for more prosperity, more money.

Meanwhile, in Lititz, Pennsylvania, Captain John Sutter of the Swiss Guard took up residence in a Moravian community to which one of his children belonged. Once again, Sutter set to work on petitioning Congress, only this time he decided to see about getting some congressmen to cosponsor a bill on the House floor to pay him for the loss of his lands during the Gold Rush. Having served in California's first legislature, he was well aware of the practice of petitioning elected representatives and planned to take full advantage of it in coming years, as long as his health held out.

By the end of the 1860s, James Marshall was back to speculating, hoping to raise funds to develop a mine. He went on a lecture tour, only to find himself penniless, stranded in Kansas City, Missouri.

Leland Stanford, one of the "Big Four" who built California's Central Pacific Railroad, stepped in to pay Marshall's train fare back to his hometown in New Jersey, where he was able to visit his mother and sister, whom he hadn't seen in years. A few months later, he returned to Kelsey and moved into the Union Hotel.

In 1872 the California state legislature passed a bill awarding Marshall a pension of $200 a month. He used it to pay off some debts and equip a blacksmith shop in Kelsey. The state subsequently reduced the pension to $100 per month, and capped it at six years. Marshall's frequent public inebriation seems to account, this time, for the legislature's actions.

Back in Washington, President Grant's secretary of the interior, Columbus Delano, decided to take a second, more formal look at the fragmented reports coming out of the Black Hills about its potential mineral wealth.

On March 28, 1872, he wrote:

> I am inclined to think that the occupation of this region of the country is not necessary to the happiness and prosperity of the Indians, and as it is supposed to be rich in minerals and lumber it is deemed important to have it freed as early as possible from Indian occupancy.
>
> I shall, therefore, not oppose any policy which looks first to a careful examination of the subject. . . . If such an examination leads to the conclusion that country is not necessary or useful to Indians, I should then deem it advisable . . . to extinguish the claim of the Indians and open the territory to the occupation of the whites.

Of course, Delano was abrogating the terms of the treaty without giving the Sioux a chance to renegotiate. He couldn't do that anyway. It could take years to get them to the table again and besides, they wouldn't believe anything the government said from that point onward.

No, the best way now to find out what was really in the Black Hills was for the government to send an expedition to find out what was there. This would be no ordinary military expedition, nor would it be commanded by an ordinary man.

14.

THE BELIEF LIVES ON

George Armstrong Custer. The very name struck fear into Cump Sherman's heart.

When his old friend and commander Ulysses S. Grant was elected president, he promoted Cump to the grade of full general and gave him overall command of the U.S. Army. Cump's second in command was General Philip "Little Phil" Sheridan, whose protégé was Custer.

Custer had made his reputation in foolish Union charges during the Civil War that despite leading to great loss of life, were successful in beating back the Confederates. Custer became the youngest brevet general (a wartime rank) in U.S. history. After the war he was commissioned a lieutenant colonel and given command of the 7th Cavalry on the western frontier.

Cump never had much use for Custer. He put up with

him because of Sheridan. That plus the fact that Custer had just taken command of Fort Abraham Lincoln in the Dakota Territory, close to the Black Hills, meant that he was likely to get the assignment to explore the Black Hills.

He did.

In the summer of 1874 Custer led a thousand-man expedition into the Black Hills. Being the vain, stupid, and courageous man that he was, Custer brought along the 7th Cavalry's band to play the regimental theme song, "The Gary Owen," at particularly dramatic moments along the way. These included gathering examples of extraordinary flora and fauna to be analyzed later. The expedition did, however, have a resident geologist, Horatio Ross. His job was to inspect and gather specimens of any valuable minerals, especially gold and silver.

In mid-July, Custer and his men camped near the present town in South Dakota that is named after him. Ross was inspecting the bed of nearby French Creek when he spotted gold. Being the publicity hound that he was, Custer immediately dispatched his favorite scout, Charley Reynolds, to bring the news to the outside world.

Reynolds took four nights to make the 115-mile ride to Fort Laramie, avoiding Sioux along the way who looked at his ride as an incursion. From Fort Laramie, word of the gold discovery was telegraphed to Cump. Custer's thirty-five-hundred-word dispatch described the Black Hills in detail. Yet the meat of it is only a small paragraph in the middle:

Gold has been found at several places, and it is the belief of those who are giving their attention to this subject that it will be found in paying quantities. I have on my table forty or fifty small particles of pure gold . . . most of it obtained today from one panful of earth.

Custer had found himself in the same situation as Marshall and Sutter before him, having to figure out what to tell the rest of the world about a gold discovery. Like the latter two men, Custer chose to downplay the find, but even in doing so, it was clear that a bonanza was in the offing.

By the last week in July 1874, newspapers in the United States and worldwide were giving the discovery front-page coverage. Meanwhile, Horatio Ross was not about to let any moss grow under him. Along with a few other partners, Ross staked his claim to District No. 1, the area in which he had discovered the gold. He called his company Custer Mining.

Finishing up, the expedition traveled through the central and northern Black Hills, and then left the area near Bear Butte. Arriving back at Fort Lincoln on August 30, 1974, Custer had covered twelve hundred miles in sixty days. By the time he returned to the fort, prospectors had already taken the field.

It made no difference that the Sioux had legal right to the Black Hills; the rush was on, and the government would do everything it could to promote it. At first, miners gathered in the southern Black Hills, but the diggings there proved meager. Prospectors began traveling through the hills looking for better spots.

There had been earlier "gold rushes" that turned out to be false alarms when the area in which an initial strike was made did not pan out. For a few years, it looked like the Black Hills would fall into this category. Things changed, however, when some peripatetic miners discovered Deadwood and Whitewood Creeks in the northern Black Hills. In those locations, each shovelful of dirt revealed a gold bonanza to those who staked their claims first.

Fueled by the mining fever, the town of Deadwood sprang up literally overnight. It was a claptrap affair of wooden shacks and canvas tents. The best place in town was the Gem saloon run by Al Swerengen, who controlled the town's rackets. There was no law, so men such as Swerengen were free to do as they pleased to make money.

The faded lawman Wild Bill Hickok came to town to try his hand at prospecting, but spent more time at the poker tables instead, where he made the mistake of incurring the wrath of a coward named "Broken Nose" Jack McCall. McCall shot him in the back of the head. That prompted shopkeeper Seth Bullock to become the town's first sheriff, a political ascendancy that would lead Bullock to eventually become an advisor to President Theodore Roosevelt.

As for Hickok's murder, it made no difference to the prospectors. They took murder in stride. Like California, death and disease of all kinds were rampant. In and around Deadwood, every piece of available land was quickly claimed by prospectors once again lured by the promise of *get rich quick*.

The Black Hills gold was placer gold. The same as the California discovery, placer gold was loose gold pieces mixed with the rocks and dirt around streams. Prospectors knew that gold occurred naturally in quartz rock. The trick was to find the rock formation or formations from which the placer gold had leached after being subjected to millions of years of erosion.

On April 9, 1876, prospectors Fred and Moses Manuel, Hank and Frank Harney, and Alex Engh discovered a gold-laden rocky outcropping near present-day Lead. They staked a claim, naming their new mine the Homestake. It would later be deduced that Deadwood Creek's placer gold flowed from this vein.

More than that, what these men had unwittingly discovered was the richest gold vein in U.S. history. The Homestake would produce 10 percent of the world's gold supply over the next century and a quarter. This kind of production needed investors who could bring in the proper mining equipment. No surprise then that the Homestake wound up in the hands of three wealthy Californians who had made their money in the California Gold Rush: William Hearst, J. B. Haggin, and Lloyd Tevis. They would go on to make another fortune from the Homestake.

The Homestake's quartz rock was brittle enough to be easily crushed, thus releasing the gold inside. Mercury would then be applied to the rock to separate the gold. Elsewhere in the Black Hills, the gold was not so easily extracted from the rock and was quite difficult to get at without more complicated, and expensive, chemical processes. That didn't stop the miners from flooding in, nor did it stop the Indians, many of whom left the reservation precisely because the government had abrogated the Treaty of 1868.

Custer's annihilation at the hands of a superior force of Sioux and Cheyenne warriors on June 25, 1976, on the Little Big Horn River was a direct result of the Indians' dissatisfaction with the United States, once again breaking an Indian treaty. Gold was gold; it was worth a person's life to find it as long as that life was someone else's. As for Custer, Sheridan was quick to shed himself of his protégé's memory: "Had the 7th Cavalry been held together [Custer divided his force into three parts before attacking] it would have been able to handle the Indians on the Little Big Horn."

Sheridan was too polite. He neglected to point out that the impetuous boy general had attacked the largest group of Indian warriors ever gathered in one place on the North American continent in modern times. It was Custer who had led the miners into the Black Hills, though the Indians did not know Custer was commanding the 7th until the Battle of the Little Big Horn was over. Later estimates place the hostile force as high as ten thousand warriors, though five thousand seem more likely.

In Washington, President Ulysses Grant agreed with his former colleague Sheridan, telling the *New York Herald*, "I regard Custer's Massacre as a sacrifice of troops, brought on by Custer himself that was wholly unnecessary."

After the massacre, the Indians fled, splitting up, with some, under the leadership of Sitting Bull, going to

Canada. That left the miners free to explore the Black Hills and retain their scalps at the same time. Unfortunately, as it always does, the placer gold ran out. And while everyone else hoped to find a bonanza like the Homestake, it didn't happen, at least not immediately.

Chemical processes invented in the 1890s would make gold extraction from nonbrittle rock easier. But even later Black Hills mines, including those at Carbonate, Bald Mountain, and Galena, could not hold a candle to the Homestake, which didn't close down its operations until 2001.

On June 16, 1880, Congress adjourned before passing a bill that would have given Sutter what he had been seeking: financial restitution for the Gold Rush, to the tune of $50,000. Two days later, John Augustus Sutter died. He was returned to Lititz and buried in the Moravian Brotherhood's cemetery.

Back in 1849, Samuel McNeil, on his way home, had run into Sutter at Monterey and penned this account as part of his book:

"At the appointed time we started in the *Panama.* Raising steam and firing a farewell gun, we were on our glorious way [from San Francisco] with 300 passengers on board. Among them was the world-renowned Capt. Suter [sic], being a delegate to the convention held at Monterey to form a state government. Him and I conversed considerably together. He again spoke of Col. Frémont, again relating the grievances I before mentioned, that is, how Frémont stole his property.

" 'Freemont is a tyrant and a blackguard,' Capt. Suter [sic] said but spoke very highly of Col. Kearney who superseded Frémont on that military station.

" 'Before the discovery of the gold,' he told me, 'the inhabitants slaughtered the cattle only for the hide and tallow, but now they slaughter them for the meat and throw the hide and tallow away.' Sutter also related to me how he first emigrated to that wild region.

"Once he kept a store in Louisville, Kentucky. There he foolishly went bail for a friend (or enemy), and through the imprudence of the person he bailed he was ruined or almost. From there he went to New Orleans. Thence to Fort Independence and across the Plains and Rocky Mountains to the Columbia River in Oregon. From there to the Sandwich Islands. The government of those islands furnished him with ten servants to act as life guards, and, accompanied by them, he went to Santa Barbara on the Pacific Coast."

More likely, Marshall bought some slaves and took them with him as indentured laborers to California.

"There the government, for the proper settlement of the country, granted him the region in which most of the gold mines are. I then asked him, to tell me the worth of his property at this time. He supposed about $500,000. He has an amiable son in California, and a wife and two daughters in Germany, adding that he had sent for the latter, and they would soon be in California. The Capt. is a German, sixty years old, and much of a gentleman."

The captain was also a liar and a visionary, a quintessentially American mix. As for Mrs. Sutter, she died the following January. The notice of her passing appeared in, among other papers, the *Tombstone Epitaph*, which served the mining boomtown of Tombstone, Arizona.

Despite being part of the United States since the Treaty of Guadalupe-Hidalgo ended the Mexican-War, Arizona was still a sparsely settled territory, filled with hostile Indian tribes led by the likes of the brilliant Apache warriors Geronimo and Cochise.

Ed Schieffelin, though just thirty years old in 1877, was one of those who had bought into the Gold Rush dream. He had been prospecting for more than a decade and had never struck it rich. That spring, when Ed left Camp Huachuca, his fellow though less hardy miners told him that he'd find his tombstone rather than silver.

Moving into the hills, he found a wash, and scattered all along it were pieces of silver. Ed wasn't an experienced prospector for nothing. He knew enough to follow the wash, up to a red and black ledge of what looked at first sight to be silver ore. Getting right up to it, Schieffelin figured the vein to be fifty feet long and twelve inches wide.

Climbing onto the ledge, he stuck his pick into the rough surface of the rock and pried out a few pieces. Turning them over in his hand slowly, he saw that the rock was caked dark. It was pure silver. Schieffelin had finally gotten his strike. He thought of his fellow miners words of warning: "All you'll find out there will be your tombstone."

A man with a great sense of humor, Schieffelin named

his claim the Tombstone. The name stuck and was then used to describe the settlement that grew around the Tombstone Mine and other mines discovered in what became known as the Tombstone Hills. The really smart businessmen, of course, started businesses that soon thrived in a mining community fueled by what seemed to be an inexhaustive supply of silver in the nearby hills.

Within two years the town had grown to five thousand full-time residents. Miners flocked to Tombstone from all over the world to see if they, too, could strike it rich. Lawlessness, of course, thrived in Tombstone like any boomtown, only this one had a marshal named Virgil Earp. Along with the brothers he deputized, Wyatt and Morgan, they were known throughout the western towns they worked in as the Fighting Earps.

The way it worked was that Wyatt would come in and get a job in a saloon as a bouncer or faro dealer with a piece of the take. Brothers Virgil and Morgan would become lawmen, while brother James was the bartender who sold whiskey and girls to the miners. Sometimes parts were reversed, with Wyatt the head lawman and Virgil and Morgan his deputies.

It made no difference who played what part. It was a pretty good racket. The Earps gave people what they wanted for a price, and were protected by their own kin. Unfortunately, the Clanton/McLaury gang ruled the roost in Tombstone.

The gang were "ranchers" who got most of their beef, it was suspected, by rustling from Mexican ranchers across the border. Some locals who fell afoul of them also found themselves missing beef. Many in Tombstone, including the Earps, believed the Clantons and the McLaurys to be holdup artists who murdered to reach their nefarious goals.

The Clantons and the McLaurys formed an instant dislike to the starchy, uptight Earps, who would not tolerate anyone or anything who adversely affected business. After the former physically threatened the latter many times, the stage was set for the most famous gunfight in American history, the gunfight at the O.K. Corral on November 21, 1881.

After the shooting was over, the only man left standing without a scratch was Wyatt Earp. At that moment, the legend of the tall stalwart, taciturn American who faced down an overwhelming foe in pursuit of righteous justice was born. No matter that it bore little relation to reality. Wyatt Earp sold well then and sells well now. More importantly, the image of the American man he fostered would find its way into every facet of American society.

Earp would also have a hand in the next big gold rush, in Alaska, which began in 1897, when gold was discovered in the Klondike in Canada's Yukon Territory. Once again lured by the California get-rich-quick ideal, thousands of prospectors flocked to Alaska. By 1898, the best gold fields had already been claimed. Miners began searching other parts of Alaska.

A major strike in Nome in 1898 brought Wyatt Earp and his wife, Josie, to the town, where they ran a saloon. They made money, but most of the miners did not get rich. Many stayed, however, helping to settle the territory of Alaska, which eventually became the forty-ninth state.

As a new century dawned in 1900, the Gold Rushes were over. Well, sort of.

After all his other business ventures had failed, James Marshall had gone back to his smithy's shop, where he continued to shoe horses and mules until the time of his death at age seventy-five in 1885.

The man who dug his grave was Andrew Monroe, a man who knew something about busting a few chains. He realized what an honor it was to serve someone who had, very directly, helped his mother, Nancy Gooch, buy his freedom. As for Nancy, she died in 1901.

General William Tecumseh "Cump" Sherman retired in 1883 and subsequently lived in New York City, where he died on February 14, 1891. He is buried in Calvary Cemetery, St. Louis, Missouri.

During the twentieth century, the same kind of get-rich-quick mentality that had become a part of the American character during the California Gold Rush found a new outlet and fueled two stock market crashes and the dot com boom of the 1990s. But the more far-reaching effect of the Gold Rushes in the western United States, and especially California, was to accelerate the country's growth by light-years.

Railroads and roads were built to link the continent together to these outposts of civilization that rose to become great cities. Out of this growth came new territories, new states, new technology, new money, and more than anything else, a new worldwide belief that in the United States, anyone can make his fortune by the sweat of his brow and a little bit of luck. Clearly, more than a few people had in California.

How much money did the California Gold Rush diggings yield in total? No one knows for sure, but best estimates are 125 million ounces combined, from 1848 to 1900. In 2005 dollars, with gold selling for $425 an ounce in early 2005, that would be $53.125 billion.

Today, anyone who has ever believed in even the minutest facet of the American Dream is being affected by the same emotions as Cump Sherman, James Marshall, Captain John Sutter of the Swiss Guards, and all the rest of the dreamers, including the shoemaker from Lancaster, Ohio, Samuel McNeil.

What happened to Samuel McNeil? Once again, the shoemaker deserves the last word:

"On the 12th of October, 1849, I landed in Cincinnati. There I took the cars for Xenia, and from that place the coach to Columbus—and the coach like wise from Columbus to Lancaster. Here I met my Ellen at the gate, the happiest hour I ever experienced, reminding me of the fact that it was my most sorrowful hour when I went out of that gate to start for California. I acquired gold in California, and more than gold was acquired at home in my absence. I presented her plenty of the gold, and in return she presented to me a lovely son.

"Robinson Peters, John D. Martin, and James Pratt, furnished me with $400 to go to California on the halves. I went, acted honorably, gave them the half, and, impelled by gratitude, I honor them, and hope and pray that they, their children, and their children's children, may enjoy every necessary earthly blessing, and die happily, feeling convinced that they had performed their duty towards God and man as their predecessors had done.

"The shoemaker is convinced that California in time will become a glorious State, or States, of this glorious Union, and that thousands, in future years, will be emigrating from the States to it. Wishing it and them the greatest prosperity and highest happiness, to present to them the following song, hoping that they will sing it as they are journeying to that land which gives as well as promises, wealth and happiness to the honorable and industrious:

The California Emigrant's Song

Far onward towards the setting sun,
We are bound upon our way,
Nor till each ling'ring day is done
Our toilsome march we stay:
We're trav'ling on, a pilgrim band,
Another home to find,
Remote from that dear native land
We now have left behind!

The clime we seek is rich and fair,
As blessed isles of yore,
And lovelier prospects open there
Than e'er was seen before!
Vast plains spread out on ev'ry side,

Stretch to the sloping skies:
Broad rivers roll in tranquil pride,
And tow'ring forests rise!

There mines of California gold
Their shining treasures show,
Which coming years shall yet unfold
To glad the bold and true!
That treasure we shall joyful find
With labor's sweetest smile,
To help the State, in purse and mind,
And bless ourselves the while!

There smiling uplands catch the beams
Of pearly morn serene,
Gay verdant meadows fringe the streams
That silvery wind between!
Of ev'ry hue and sweet perfume,
Wild flowers luxuriant spring,
While birds, with varied note and plume,
'Mid bowers of Nature sing!
But cherish'd home! 'tis painful still
To quit thy much loved shore,
For fears our sorrowing bosoms fill,
We ne'er may see thee more!

Yet thy green hills and sunny vales,
Those scenes of childhood all,
How oft 'till recollection fails,
Fond memory shall recall!

For there are faithful ones endear'd
By Nature's tend'rest ties,
Whose cordial smiles so oft have cheer'd
Life's burdening miseries!
Comrades, whom first in youth we knew,
In that bright region dwell:
Friends, whom we prov'd in perils true,
We bid them all farewell!

The joy must fade which most delights
The fond enraptur'd heart,
And souls, that friendship's chain unites,
Must still be torn apart!
From home departing, doom'd by fate,
Like wand'rers o'er the main,
From dearest friends we separate,
Never to meet again!

Farewell! farewell! but not forever:
We yet shall meet again
Beyond the reach of absence here,
Beyond the reach of pain!
There is on high a brighter land
Than California's shore,
Where rich and poor, not one behind,
Shall meet forevermore!

EPILOGUE

This account rests in the Monterey County Historical Society in California. It is contained in the unpublished diary of Daniel Martin. In the autumn of 1877, Daniel Martin was working as a vaquero on the Laurel Ranch, in the Carmel Valley.

One morning, as Martin was about to depart on his daily duties, his boss, Sam Clinkenbeard, hailed him and said to wait for a while. There was an old man who had stayed there all night. He would be down to saddle his horse in a moment.

Martin picks up the story in this passage from his unpublished diary:

Clinkenbeard wanted me to hear or witness the conversation. Then, the old man approached.
The old man put his hand in his pocket.

"How much do I owe you for staying here last night?' he asked Clinkenbeard.

"Nothing, we are of the old California style but I would like to ask you some questions," Clinkenbeard replied. "Were you ever in the Sierra Nevada Mountains?"

"Yes, a long time ago."

"Did you ever stop at Clinkenbeard's Road House between Lake Tahoe and Truckee and buy provisions and sometimes stay with your party all night there?"

"Yes, but how did you know?"

"I am Clinkenbeard's son who used to wait on you at times. Aren't you Joaquin Murieta?"

"Yes."

"Don't you know you are supposed to have been killed?"

"I hear so, but I got away and went to Mexico, the Americans were getting too *valiente* [desperate]."

"What are you doing back here now?"

"I came after some treasures that I had hidden in the Big Canon above here—the Chipinos (Indian) and I came down here last night thinking I would find the Boronda family still here."

"Are you going to stay in California?"

"No, I am going right back to Mexico, I like it better there among my people."

Joaquin Murietta saddled up his beautiful mare with the silver bridle and rode off into the sunset, perhaps the biggest Gold Rush winner of all.

Afterword

COLOMA, 2005

Samuel McNeil would not recognize the place. Sutter's Fort had been made of stucco. This, the reconstructed Sutter's Fort in the twenty-first century, had a white brick foundation with an atypical California chichi red stucco roof.

No longer was Sutter's Fort five miles outside Sacramento City. The city had crept out all five miles and beyond. You could see the freeway in the distance. What was left of Sutter's land was the reconstructed fort set into a park smack dab in the middle of the city. Instead of the voices of settlers, today children's voices rise high above the din from the freeway traffic. The children come from area schools, as far away as Los Angeles, to be educated in their state's history. Some of those children had ancestors who mined in the Gold Rush and decided to stay.

To get to Coloma, it's back into the car and out onto the freeway, north into the foothills of the Sierra Nevada. As I drove, for some reason I thought of Roy Earle, Humphrey's Bogart's killer with a heart in *High Sierra*, which took place where I was driving. The Sierras had a brooding quality, between the interminable fast-food stands and the gray clouds coming in over the mountains.

To get to Coloma, you take a left at Hangtown and keep going. It's rural country, over rolling hills. Suddenly, the foliage on the right side that seemed to cover the roadway gave way to a grand view of the Sierra Nevada misting up in the gray twilight. Positively terrifying, considering that the drop-off looked to be more than a hundred feet, and Governor Schwarzenegger, no matter how much I like him, had failed to put in any shoulders.

When I was sixteen, I was sent to California to live with my Uncle Harry for a month. It was my idea. I *had* to see California. I did the whole tourist route—Disneyland, Knott's Berry Farm, and Universal Studios—and when I finally went home, I knew I had to go back. I did, the next year, and it was awful.

Somehow, what pleased me at sixteen didn't quite work at seventeen, when I had already learned to drive and was not content to sit around in my uncle's house and wait for him to take me someplace. I went home in two weeks flat. The next time I was in California, I knew that wherever I went, the place would always be with me.

When I was twenty-two, I found myself traveling through the Feather River Valley on a bus. Someone in the front seat began playing "500 Miles," the old Civil War standard Peter, Paul, and Mary brought back to a new generation. Looking out the window, it wasn't hard to see the place in Gold Rush times; it looked the same. The next year I went to film school at the University of Southern California in Los Angeles. At first I thought California was heaven, the El Dorado of legend, with its opportunity to become a big shot in the film business. I had bought into the dream. The reality was more like the line in Larry Gatlin's song "All the Gold in California": "All the gold in California is in a bank in the middle of Beverly Hills in somebody else's name."

Now I was twenty-five years in the future, traveling to where the dream had started. Except for the reconstruction of the sawmill, I might have kept going without realizing exactly where I was. Only a few brick buildings were left of what had been a thriving settlement. The Gooch-Monroe family had eventually bought the actual site where Marshall discovered gold and had given it over to the state, which had made a park of it.

The state has made a concerted attempt for the past century to keep the town the way it was. That means that the path I was walking on, down by the American River, was the same one Marshall took that morning in January 1848. My boots crunched on the gravel as his must have, though it is possible it was just a well-worn, muddy-grass path then.

Most of the trees that surrounded the tailrace in Marshall's time are still there. The tailrace itself, dammed up a little downriver, has brackish waters. Despite the algae growth, you could clearly see to the bottom. I looked; I didn't see any gold. The reeds had overgrown the sections along the banks Marshall and the Mormons had cut out.

I listened. All I could hear, like Marshall, was the river splashing against the stones in its path. All that was missing was the gold.

The next day, I came back and took the path to the reconstruction of Marshall and Sutter's sawmill. The actual sawmill fell victim to the elements and eventually collapsed during various floods. But some of the timbers have been recovered and repose in a plain glass and log storage shed next to the reconstructed mill.

The mill itself must have been a marvel of mid-nineteenth-century ingenuity. The reconstruction stood about fifty feet above the river, leaning out into it, as the original must have, with the tailrace behind it leading the water through the channel to the waiting paddlewheel that would power the sawmill. Looking around, I saw that Marshall had picked a good spot. He had never counted on anything being more valuable than the timber he was cutting.

Marshall's cabin is up in the hills above Coloma. It looks like it has weathered the 150 years since its origins remarkably well, except that a picture taken in the 1930s by the Work Projects Administration shows it to be rather dilapidated. No matter. Marshall's clear lines and excellent carpentry are clear even in the earlier photograph.

Above the cabin is a monument the state placed in Marshall's memory. It looks unwieldy, like it's about to topple at any moment, probably like Marshall himself in his later years.

There was only one thing left to do in Coloma now: go panning for gold. You can still do it. There's an area directly across the river from where Marshall made his discovery where anyone can come in and pan for gold. *I was too close. I had to do it.*

I bought a pan in the souvenir shop, the same kind of tin pan the miners used, and drove over a narrow, barely one-lane bridge, over what looked like a cold American River. It was about 11:00 A.M.; I had waited as long as I could. It was October and the weather was mild, though I still wore a sweatshirt that had previously staved off the morning chill.

Walking down the sand dunes to the riverbank, I stopped when I got to the river's edge and looked at the river flowing by me. Again, except for a passing truck, the water was the only sound. But it wasn't then. Then it was noisy, with men screaming when they hit pay dirt, others crying out in frustration, and still others murmuring to themselves as they went about the very difficult labor of panning for gold.

The water was surprisingly warm around my bare toes. Intently, for the next hour, I panned for gold in the American River. My heart didn't miss any beats as I got to the end, with the black sand to sift through, but I was excited.

Whatever happened, I had made it to El Dorado and so, in a way, had my father.

Coloma,
October 15, 2004

Appendix I

THE TREATIES

There were two treaties which led to California's independence from Mexico and its surrender to the United States.

The first was the Treaty of Cahuenga. It was signed in Los Angeles on January 13, 1847. The second was the Treaty of Guadalupe-Hidalgo, which formalized the end of the Mexican-American War and laid out the terms of peace for both sides. While copies of the second treaty still exist, none of the first are known to have survived.

The text of the Treaty of Cahuenga that follows was taken from Colonel John C. Frémont's memoirs. While there is no question that he profited when California became a state—the land he had bought in the Sacramento/Coloma area was gold-rich—there is no reason to believe that Frémont's recollection of the treaty is anything other than true.

To All Who These Presents Shall Come, Greeting: Know Ye, that in consequence of propositions of peace, or cessation of hostilities, being submitted to me, as Commandant of the California Battalion of the United States forces, which have so far been acceded to by me as to cause me to appoint a board of commissioners to confer with a similar board appointed by the Californians, and it requiring a little time to close the negotiations; it is agreed upon and ordered by me that an entire cessation of hostilities shall take place until to-morrow after-noon (January 13), and that the said Californians be permitted to bring in their wounded to the mission of San Fernando, where, also, if they choose, they can move their camp to facilitate said negotiations.

Given under my hand and seal this 12th day of January, 1847.

J. C. Frémont,
Lieutenant-Colonel U.S.A.,
and Military Commandant of California.

ARTICLES OF CAPITULATION made and entered into at the Rancho of Couenga, this thirteenth day of Jan-uary, Anno Domini, eighteen hundred and forty-seven, between P. B. Reading, Major; Louis Mclane, Jr., Commanding Artillery; Wm. H. Russell, Ord-nance Officer; commissioners appointed by J. C. Frémont, Lieutenant-Colonel United States Army and Military Commandant of the territory of Cali-fornia; and José Antonio Carrillo, Commandante de

Esquadron, Agustin Olivera, Diputado, commissioners appointed by Don Andres Pico, Commander-in-Chief of the California forces under the Mexican flag.

ARTICLE I.—The Commissioners on the part of the Californians agree that their entire force shall, on presentation of themselves to Lieutenant-Colonel Frémont, deliver up their artillery and public arms, and they shall return peaceably to their homes, conforming to the laws and regulations of the United States, and not again take up arms during the war between the United States and Mexico, but will assist in placing the country in a state of peace and tranquillity.

ARTICLE II.—The Commissioners on the part of Lieutenant-Colonel Frémont agree to and bind themselves on the fulfillment of the first article by the Californians, that they shall be guaranteed protection of life and property, whether on parole or otherwise.

ARTICLE III.—That until a treaty of peace be made and signed between the United States of North American and the Republic of Mexico, no Californian or other Mexican citizen shall be bound to take the oath of allegiance.

ARTICLE IV.—That any Californian or other citizen of Mexico desiring, is permitted by this capitulation to leave the country without let or hindrance.

ARTICLE **V.**—That in virtue of the aforesaid articles, equal rights and privileges are vouchsafed to every citizen of California as are enjoyed by the citizens of the United States of North America.

ARTICLE **VI.**—All officers, citizens, foreigners or others shall receive the protection guaranteed by the second article.

ARTICLE **VII.**—This capitulation is intended to be no bar in effecting such arrangements as may in future be in justice required by both parties.

P. B. READING
Major California Battalion
JOSÉ ANTONIO CARRILLO
Commandante de Esquadron
WM. H. RUSSELL
Ordnance Officer California Battalion
AGUSTIN OLVERA
Diputado
LOUIS MCLANE, JR.
Commanding Artillery, California
Battalion

Approved.	*Approbado.*
JOHN C. FRÉMONT	ANDRES PICO
Lieutenant-Colonel U.S.A.	*Commandante de Esquadron*
and Military Commandant of California	*y en Gife de las*
	Guerzas Nationales en
	California

ADDITIONAL ARTICLE.

That the paroles of all officers, citizens and others of the United States, and of naturalized citizens of Mexico, are by this foregoing capitulation cancelled; and every condition of said paroles from and after this date are of no further force and effect; and all prisoners of both parties are hereby released.

(Signed as above.)

CIUDAD DE LOS ANGELES, January 16, 1847

TREATY OF PEACE, FRIENDSHIP, LIMITS, AND SET-TLEMENT BETWEEN
THE UNITED STATES OF AMERICA AND THE UNITED MEXICAN STATES
CONCLUDED AT GUADALUPE HIDALGO, FEBRUARY 2, 1848

RATIFICATION ADVISED BY SENATE, WITH AMEND-MENTS, MARCH 10,
1848; RATIFIED BY PRESIDENT, MARCH 16, 1848; RATIFICATIONS
EXCHANGED AT QUERETARO, MAY 30, 1848; PRO-CLAIMED, JULY 4, 1848.
IN THE NAME OF ALMIGHTY GOD

The United States of America and the United Mexican States animated by a sincere desire to put an end to the calamities of the war which unhappily exists between the two Republics and to establish upon a solid basis relations of peace and friendship, which shall confer reciprocal benefits upon the citizens of both, and assure the concord, harmony, and mutual confidence wherein the two people should live, as good neighbors have for that purpose appointed their respective plenipotentiaries, that is to say: The President of the United States has appointed Nicholas P. Trist, a citizen of the United States, and the President of the Mexican Republic has appointed Don Luis Gonzaga Cuevas, Don Bernardo Couto, and Don Miguel Atristain, citizens of the said Republic; Who, after a reciprocal communication of their respective full powers, have, under the protection of Almighty God, the author of peace, arranged, agreed upon, and signed the following: Treaty of Peace, Friendship, Limits, and Settlement between the United States of America and the Mexican Republic.

ARTICLE I.—There shall be firm and universal peace between the United States of America and the Mexican Republic, and between their respective countries, territories, cities, towns, and people, without exception of places or persons.

ARTICLE II.—Immediately upon the signature of this treaty, a convention shall be entered into between a commissioner or commissioners appointed by the General-in-chief of the forces of the United States, and such as may be appointed by the Mexican Government, to the end that a provisional suspension of hostilities shall take place, and that, in the places occupied by the said forces, constitutional order may be reestablished, as regards the political, administrative, and judicial branches, so far as this shall be permitted by the circumstances of military occupation.

ARTICLE III.—Immediately upon the ratification of the present treaty by the Government of the United States, orders shall be transmitted to the commanders of their land and naval forces, requiring the latter (provided this treaty shall then have been ratified by the Government of the Mexican Republic, and the ratifications exchanged) immediately to desist from blockading any Mexican ports and requiring the former (under the same condition) to commence, at the earliest moment practicable, withdrawing all troops of the United States then in the interior of the Mexican Republic, to points that shall be selected by common agreement, at a distance from the seaports not exceeding thirty leagues; and such evacuation of the interior of the Republic shall be completed with the least possible delay; the Mexican Government hereby binding itself to afford every facility in its power for rendering the same convenient to the troops, on their march and in their new positions, and for promoting a good understanding between them and the inhabitants. In like manner orders shall be despatched to the persons in charge of the custom houses at all ports occupied by the forces of the

United States, requiring them (under the same condition) immediately to deliver possession of the same to the persons authorized by the Mexican Government to receive it, together with all bonds and evidences of debt for duties on importations and on exportations, not yet fallen due. Moreover, a faithful and exact account shall be made out, showing the entire amount of all duties on imports and on exports, collected at such custom-houses, or elsewhere in Mexico, by authority of the United States, from and after the day of ratification of this treaty by the Government of the Mexican Republic; and also an account of the cost of collection; and such entire amount, deducting only the cost of collection, shall be delivered to the Mexican Government, at the city of Mexico, within three months after the exchange of ratifications.

The evacuation of the capital of the Mexican Republic by the troops of the United States, in virtue of the above stipulation, shall be completed in one month after the orders there stipulated for shall have been received by the commander of said troops, or sooner if possible.

ARTICLE **IV.**—Immediately after the exchange of ratifications of the present treaty all castles, forts, territories, places, and possessions, which have been taken or occupied by the forces of the United States during the present war, within the limits of the Mexican Republic, as about to be established by the following article, shall be definitely restored to the said Republic, together with all the artillery, arms, apparatus of war, munitions, and other public property, which were in the said castles and forts when captured, and which shall remain there at the time when this treaty shall be duly ratified by the Government of the Mexican Republic. To this end, immediately upon the signature of this treaty, orders shall be despatched to the American officers commanding such castles and forts, securing against the removal or destruction of any such artillery, arms, apparatus of war, munitions, or other public property. The city of Mexico, within the inner line of intrenchments surrounding the said city, is comprehended in the above stipulation, as regards the restoration of artillery, apparatus of war, & c.

The final evacuation of the territory of the Mexican Republic, by the forces of the United States, shall be completed in three months from the said exchange of ratifications, or sooner if possible; the Mexican Government hereby engaging, as in the foregoing article to use all means in its power for facilitating such evacuation, and rendering it convenient to the troops, and for promoting a good understanding between them and the inhabitants.

If, however, the ratification of this treaty by both parties should not take place in time to allow the embarcation of the troops of the United States to be completed before the commencement of the sickly season, at the Mexican ports on the Gulf of

Mexico, in such case a friendly arrangement shall be entered into between the General-in-Chief of the said troops and the Mexican Government, whereby healthy and otherwise suitable places, at a distance from the ports not exceeding thirty leagues, shall be designated for the residence of such troops as may not yet have embarked, until the return of the healthy season. And the space of time here referred to as, comprehending the sickly season shall be understood to extend from the first day of May to the first day of November.

All prisoners of war taken on either side, on land or on sea, shall be restored as soon as practicable after the exchange of ratifications of this treaty. It is also agreed that if any Mexicans should now be held as captives by any savage tribe within the limits of the United States, as about to be established by the following article, the Government of the said United States will exact the release of such captives and cause them to be restored to their country.

ARTICLE V.—The boundary line between the two Republics shall commence in the Gulf of Mexico, three leagues from land, opposite the mouth of the Rio Grande, otherwise called Rio Bravo del Norte, or Opposite the mouth of its deepest branch, if it should have more than one branch emptying directly into the sea; from thence up the middle of that river, following the deepest channel, where it has more than one, to the point where it strikes the southern boundary of New Mexico; thence, west-wardly, along the whole southern boundary of New Mexico (which runs north of the town called Paso) to its western termination; thence, northward, along the western line of New Mexico, until it intersects the first branch of the river Gila; (or if it should not intersect any branch of that river, then to the point on the said line nearest to such branch, and thence in a direct line to the same); thence down the middle of the said branch and of the said river, until it empties into the Rio Colorado; thence across the Rio Colorado, following the division line between Upper and Lower California, to the Pacific Ocean.

The southern and western limits of New Mexico, mentioned in the article, are those laid down in the map entitled "Map of the United Mexican States, as organized and defined by various acts of the Congress of said republic, and constructed according to the best authorities. Revised edition. Published at New York, in 1847, by J. Disturnell," of which map a copy is added to this treaty, bearing the signatures and seals of the undersigned Plenipotentiaries. And, in order to preclude all difficulty in tracing upon the ground the limit separating Upper from Lower California, it is agreed that the said limit shall consist of a straight line drawn from the middle of the Rio Gila, where it unites with the Colorado, to a point on the coast of the Pacific Ocean, distant one marine league due south of the southernmost point of the port of San Diego, according to the plan of said port made in the year 1782 by Don Juan Pantoja, second sailing-master of the Spanish fleet, and published at Madrid in the year 1802, in the atlas to the voyage of the schooners Sutil and Mexicana; of which plan a copy is hereunto added, signed and sealed by the respective Plenipotentiaries.

In order to designate the boundary line with due precision, upon authoritative maps, and to establish upon the ground land-marks which shall show the limits of both republics, as described in the present article, the two Governments shall each appoint a commissioner and a surveyor, who, before the expiration of one year from the date of the exchange of ratifications of this treaty, shall meet at the port of San Diego, and proceed to run and mark the said boundary in its whole course to the mouth of the Rio Bravo del Norte. They shall keep journals and make out plans of their operations; and the result agreed upon by them shall be deemed a part of this treaty, and shall have the same force as if it were inserted therein. The two Governments will amicably agree regarding what may be necessary to these persons, and also as to their respective escorts, should such be necessary.

The boundary line established by this article shall be religiously respected by each of the two republics, and no change shall ever be made therein, except by the express and free consent of both nations, lawfully given by the General Government of each, in conformity with its own constitution.

ARTICLE **VI.**—The vessels and citizens of the United States shall, in all time, have a free and uninterrupted passage by the Gulf of California, and by the river Colorado below its confluence with the Gila, to and from their possessions situated north of the boundary line defined in the preceding article; it being understood that this passage is to be by navigating the Gulf of California and the river Colorado, and not by land, without the express consent of the Mexican Government.

If, by the examinations which may be made, it should be ascertained to be practicable and advantageous to construct a road, canal, or railway, which should in whole or in part run upon the river Gila, or upon its right or its left bank, within the space of one marine league from either margin of the river, the Governments of both republics will form an agreement regarding its construction, in order that it may serve equally for the use and advantage of both countries.

ARTICLE **VII.**—The river Gila, and the part of the Rio Bravo del Norte lying below the southern boundary of New Mexico, being, agreeably to the fifth article, divided in the middle between the two republics, the navigation of the Gila and of the Bravo below said boundary shall be free and common to the vessels and citizens of both countries; and neither shall, without the consent of the other, construct any work that may impede or interrupt, in whole or in part, the exercise of this right; not even for the purpose of favoring new methods of navigation. Nor shall any tax or contribution, under any denomination or title, be levied upon vessels or persons navigating the same or upon merchandise or effects transported thereon, except in the case of landing upon one of their shores. If, for the purpose of making the said rivers navigable, or for maintaining them in such state, it should be necessary or advantageous to establish any tax or contribution, this shall not be done without the consent of both Governments.

The stipulations contained in the present article shall not impair the territorial rights of either republic within its established limits.

ARTICLE VIII.—Mexicans now established in territories previously belonging to Mexico, and which remain for the future within the limits of the United States, as defined by the present treaty, shall be free to continue where they now reside, or to remove at any time to the Mexican Republic, retaining the property which they possess in the said territories, or disposing thereof, and removing the proceeds wherever they please, without their being subjected, on this account, to any contribution, tax, or charge whatever.

Those who shall prefer to remain in the said territories may either retain the title and rights of

Mexican citizens, or acquire those of citizens of the United States. But they shall be under the obligation to make their election within one year from the date of the exchange of ratifications of this treaty; and those who shall remain in the said territories after the expiration of that year, without having declared their intention to retain the character of Mexicans, shall be considered to have elected to become citizens of the United States.

In the said territories, property of every kind, now belonging to Mexicans not established there, shall be inviolably respected. The present owners, the heirs of these, and all Mexicans who may hereafter acquire said property by contract, shall enjoy with respect to it guarantees equally ample as if the same belonged to citizens of the United States.

ARTICLE **IX.**—The Mexicans who, in the territories aforesaid, shall not preserve the character of citizens of the Mexican Republic, conformably with what is stipulated in the preceding article, shall be incorporated into the Union of the United States. and be admitted at the proper time (to be judged of by the Congress of the United States) to the enjoyment of all the rights of citizens of the United States, according to the principles of the Constitution; and in the mean time, shall be maintained and protected in the free enjoyment of their liberty and property, and secured in the free exercise of their religion without; restriction.

ARTICLE **X.**—[Stricken out]

ARTICLE **XI.**—Considering that a great part of the territories, which, by the present treaty, are to be comprehended for the future within the limits of the United States, is now occupied by savage tribes, who will hereafter be under the exclusive control of the Government of the United States, and whose incursions within the territory of Mexico would be prejudicial in the extreme, it is solemnly agreed that all such incursions shall be forcibly restrained by the Government of the United States whensoever this may be necessary; and that when they cannot be prevented, they shall be punished by the said Government, and satisfaction for the same shall be exacted all in the same way, and with equal diligence and energy, as if the same incursions were meditated or committed within its own territory, against its own citizens.

It shall not be lawful, under any pretext whatever, for any inhabitant of the United States to purchase or acquire any Mexican, or any foreigner residing in Mexico, who may have been captured by Indians inhabiting the territory of either of the two republics; nor to purchase or acquire horses, mules, cattle, or property of any kind, stolen within Mexican territory by such Indians.

And in the event of any person or persons, captured within Mexican territory by Indians, being carried into the territory of the United States, the

Government of the latter engages and binds itself, in the most solemn manner, so soon as it shall know of such captives being within its territory, and shall be able so to do, through the faithful exercise of its influence and power, to rescue them and return them to their country. or deliver them to the agent or representative of the Mexican Government. The Mexican authorities will, as far as practicable, give to the Government of the United States notice of such captures; and its agents shall pay the expenses incurred in the maintenance and transmission of the rescued captives; who, in the mean time, shall be treated with the utmost hospitality by the American authorities at the place where they may be. But if the Government of the United States, before receiving such notice from Mexico, should obtain intelligence, through any other channel, of the existence of Mexican captives within its territory, it will proceed forthwith to effect their release and delivery to the Mexican agent, as above stipulated.

For the purpose of giving to these stipulations the fullest possible efficacy, thereby affording the security and redress demanded by their true spirit and intent, the Government of the United States will now and hereafter pass, without unnecessary delay, and always vigilantly enforce, such laws as the nature of the subject may require. And, finally, the sacredness of this obligation shall never be lost sight of by the said Government, when providing for the removal of the Indians from any portion of the said territories, or for its being settled by citizens of the United States; but, on the contrary, special care shall then be taken not to place its Indian occupants under the necessity of seeking new homes, by committing those invasions which the United States have solemnly obliged themselves to restrain.

ARTICLE **XII.**—In consideration of the extension acquired by the boundaries of the United States, as defined in the fifth article of the present treaty, the Government of the United States engages to pay to that of the Mexican Republic the sum of fifteen millions of dollars. Immediately after the treaty shall have been duly ratified by the Government of the Mexican Republic, the sum of three millions of dollars shall be paid to the said Government by that of the United States, at the city of Mexico, in the gold or silver coin of Mexico The remaining twelve millions of dollars shall be paid at the same place, and in the same coin, in annual installments of three millions of dollars each, together with interest on the same at the rate of six per centum per annum. This interest shall begin to run upon the whole sum of twelve millions from the day of the ratification of the present treaty by—the Mexican Government, and the first of the installments shall be paid-at the expiration of one year from the same day. Together with each annual installment, as it falls due, the whole interest accruing on such installment from the beginning shall also be paid.

ARTICLE **XIII.**—The United States engage, moreover, to assume and pay to the claimants all the amounts now due them, and those hereafter to become due, by reason of the claims already liquidated and decided against the Mexican Republic, under the conventions between the two republics severally concluded on the eleventh day of April, eighteen hundred and thirty-nine, and on the thirtieth day of January, eighteen hundred and forty-three; so that the Mexican Republic shall be absolutely exempt, for the future, from all expense whatever on account of the said claims.

ARTICLE **XIV.**—The United States do furthermore discharge the Mexican Republic from all claims of citizens of the United States, not heretofore decided against the Mexican Government, which may have arisen previously to the date of the signature of this treaty; which discharge shall be final and perpetual, whether the said claims be rejected or be allowed by the board of commissioners provided for in the following article, and whatever shall be the total amount of those allowed.

ARTICLE **XV.**—The United States, exonerating Mexico from all demands on account of the claims of their citizens mentioned in the preceding article, and considering them entirely and forever canceled, whatever their amount may be, undertake to make satisfaction for the same, to an amount not exceeding three and one-quarter millions of dollars. To ascertain the validity and amount of those claims, a board of commissioners shall be established by the Government of the United States, whose awards shall be final and conclusive; provided that, in deciding upon the validity of each claim, the boa shall be guided and governed by the principles and rules of decision prescribed by the first and fifth articles of the unratified convention, concluded at the city of Mexico on the twentieth day of November, one thousand eight hundred and forty-three; and in no case shall an award be made in favour of any claim not embraced by these principles and rules.

If, in the opinion of the said board of commissioners or of the claimants, any books, records, or documents, in the possession or power of the Government of the Mexican Republic, shall be deemed necessary to the just decision of any claim, the commissioners, or the claimants through them, shall, within such period as Congress may designate, make an application in writing for the same, addressed to the Mexican Minister of Foreign Affairs, to be transmitted by the Secretary of State of the United States; and the Mexican Government engages, at the earliest possible moment after the receipt of such demand, to cause any of the books, records, or documents so specified, which shall be in their possession or power (or authenticated copies or extracts of the same), to be transmitted to the said Secretary of State, who shall immediately deliver them over to the said board of commissioners; provided that no such application shall be made by or at the instance of any claimant, until the facts which it is expected to prove by such books, records, or documents, shall have been stated under oath or affirmation.

ARTICLE **XVI.**—Each of the contracting parties reserves to itself the entire right to fortify whatever point within its territory it may judge proper so to fortify for its security.

ARTICLE **XVII.**—The treaty of amity, commerce, and navigation, concluded at the city of Mexico, on the fifth day of April, A.D. 1831, between the United States of America and the United Mexican States, except the additional article, and except so far as the stipulations of the said treaty may be incompatible with any stipulation contained in the present treaty, is hereby revived for the period of eight years from the day of the exchange of ratifications of this treaty, with the same force and virtue as if incorporated therein; it being understood that each of the contracting parties reserves to itself the right, at any time after the said period of eight years shall have expired, to terminate the same by giving one year's notice of such intention to the other party.

ARTICLE **XVIII.**—All supplies whatever for troops

of the United States in Mexico, arriving at ports in the occupation of such troops previous to the final evacuation thereof, although subsequently to the restoration of the custom-houses at such ports, shall be entirely exempt from duties and charges of any kind; the Government of the United States hereby engaging and pledging its faith to establish and vigilantly to enforce, all possible guards for securing the revenue of Mexico, by preventing the importation, under cover of this stipulation, of any articles other than such, both in kind and in quantity, as shall really be wanted for the use and consumption of the forces of the United States during the time they may remain in Mexico. To this end it shall be the duty of all officers and agents of the United States to denounce to the Mexican authorities at the respective ports any attempts at a fraudulent abuse of this stipulation, which they may know of, or may have reason to suspect, and to give to such authorities all the aid in their power with regard thereto; and every such attempt, when duly proved and established by sentence of a competent tribunal, They shall be punished by the confiscation of the property so attempted to be fraudulently introduced.

ARTICLE **XIX.**—With respect to all merchandise, effects, and property whatsoever, imported into ports of Mexico, whilst in the occupation of the forces of the United States, whether by citizens of either republic, or by citizens or subjects of any neutral nation, the following rules shall be observed:

1. All such merchandise, effects, and property, if imported previously to the restoration of the custom-houses to the Mexican authorities, as stipulated for in the third article of this treaty, shall be exempt from confiscation, although the importation of the same be prohibited by the Mexican tariff.

2. The same perfect exemption shall be enjoyed by all such merchandise, effects, and property, imported subsequently to the restoration of the custom-houses, and previously to the sixty days fixed in the following article for the coming into force of the Mexican tariff at such ports respectively; the said merchandise, effects, and property being, however, at the time of their importation, subject to the payment of duties, as provided for in the said following article.

3. All merchandise, effects, and property described in the two rules foregoing shall, during their continuance at the place of importation, and upon their leaving such place for the interior, be exempt from all duty, tax, or imposts of every kind, under whatsoever title or denomination. Nor shall they be there subject to any charge whatsoever upon the sale thereof.

4. All merchandise, effects, and property, described in the first and second rules, which shall have been removed to any place in the interior,

whilst such place was in the occupation of the forces of the United States, shall, during their continuance therein, be exempt from all tax upon the sale or consumption thereof, and from every kind of impost or contribution, under whatsoever title or denomination.

5. But if any merchandise, effects, or property, described in the first and second rules, shall be removed to any place not occupied at the time by the forces of the United States, they shall, upon their introduction into such place, or upon their sale or consumption there, be subject to the same duties which, under the Mexican laws, they would be required to pay in such cases if they had been imported in time of peace, through the maritime custom-houses, and had there paid the duties conformably with the Mexican tariff.

6. The owners of all merchandise, effects, or property, described in the first and second rules, and existing in any port of Mexico, shall have the right to reship the same, exempt from all tax, impost, or contribution whatever.

With respect to the metals, or other property, exported from any Mexican port whilst in the occupation of the forces of the United States, and previously to the restoration of the custom-house at such port, no person shall be required by the Mexican authorities, whether general or state, to pay any tax, duty, or contribution upon any such exportation, or in any manner to account for the same to the said authorities.

ARTICLE **XX.**—Through consideration for the interests of commerce generally, it is agreed, that if less than sixty days should elapse between the date of the signature of this treaty and the restoration of the custom houses, conformably with the stipulation in the third article, in such case all merchandise, effects and property whatsoever, arriving at the Mexican ports after the restoration of the said custom-houses, and previously to the expiration of sixty days after the day of signature of this treaty, shall be admitted to entry; and no other duties shall be levied thereon than the duties established by the tariff found in force at such custom-houses at the time of the restoration of the same. And to all such merchandise, effects, and property, the rules established by the preceding article shall apply.

ARTICLE **XXI.**—If unhappily any disagreement should hereafter arise between the Governments of the two republics, whether with respect to the interpretation of any stipulation in this treaty, or with respect to any other particular concerning the political or commercial relations of the two nations, the said Governments, in the name of those nations, do promise to each other that they will endeavour, in the most sincere and earnest manner, to settle the differences so arising, and to preserve the state of peace and friendship in which the two countries are now placing themselves, using, for this end, mutual representations and pacific negotiations. And if, by these means, they should not be enabled to come to an agreement, a resort shall not, on this account, be had to reprisals, aggression, or hostility of any kind, by the one republic against the other, until the Government of that which deems itself aggrieved shall have maturely considered, in the spirit of peace and good neighbourship, whether it would not be better that such difference should be settled by the arbitration of commissioners appointed on each side, or by that of a friendly nation. And should such course be proposed by either party, it shall be acceded to by the other, unless deemed by it altogether incompatible with the nature of the difference, or the circumstances of the case.

ARTICLE **XXII.**—If (which is not to be expected, and which God forbid) war should unhappily break out between the two republics, they do now, with a view to such calamity, solemnly pledge themselves to each other and to the world to observe the following rules; absolutely where the nature of the subject permits, and as closely as possible in all cases where such absolute observance shall be impossible:

I.   The merchants of either republic then residing in the other shall be allowed to remain twelve months (for those dwelling in the interior), and six months (for those dwelling at the seaports) to collect their debts and settle their affairs; during which periods they shall enjoy the same protection, and be on the same footing, in all respects, as the citizens or subjects of the most friendly nations; and, at the expiration thereof, or at any time before, they shall have full liberty to depart, carrying off all their effects without molestation or hindrance, conforming therein to the same laws which the citizens or subjects of the most friendly nations are required to conform to. Upon the entrance of the armies of either nation into the territories of the other, women and children, ecclesiastics, scholars of every faculty, cultivators of the earth, merchants, artisans, manufacturers, and fishermen, unarmed and inhabiting unfortified towns, villages, or places, and in general all persons whose occupations are for the common subsistence and benefit of mankind, shall be allowed to continue their respective employments, unmolested in their persons. Nor shall their houses or goods be burnt or otherwise destroyed, nor their cattle taken, nor their fields wasted, by the armed force into whose power, by the events of war, they may happen to fall; but if the necessity arise to take anything from them for the use of such armed force, the same shall be paid for at an equitable price. All churches, hospitals, schools, colleges, libraries, and other establishments for charitable and beneficent purposes, shall be respected, and all persons connected with the same protected in the discharge of their duties, and the pursuit of their vocations.

2. In order that the fate of prisoners of war may be alleviated all such practices as those of sending them into distant, inclement or unwholesome districts, or crowding them into close and noxious places, shall be studiously avoided. They shall not be confined in dungeons, prison ships, or prisons; nor be put in irons, or bound or otherwise restrained in the use of their limbs. The officers shall enjoy liberty on their paroles, within convenient districts, and have comfortable quarters; and the common soldiers shall be dispose(in cantonments, open and extensive enough for air and exercise and lodged in barracks as roomy and good as are provided by the party in whose power they are for its own troops. But if any office shall break his parole by leaving the district so assigned him, o any other prisoner shall escape from the limits of his cantonment after they shall have been designated to him, such individual, officer, or other prisoner, shall forfeit so much of the benefit of this article as provides for his liberty on parole or in cantonment. And if any officer so breaking his parole or any common soldier so escaping from the limits assigned him, shall afterwards be found in arms previously to his being regularly exchanged, the person so offending shall be dealt with according to the established laws of war. The officers shall be daily furnished, by the party in whose power they

are, with as many rations, and of the same articles, as
are allowed either in kind or by commutation, to
officers of equal rank in its own army; and all others
shall be daily furnished with such ration as is allowed
to a common soldier in its own service; the value of
all which supplies shall, at the close of the war, or at
periods to be agreed upon between the respective
commanders, be paid by the other party, on a
mutual adjustment of accounts for the subsistence
of prisoners; and such accounts shall not be mingled with or set off against any others, nor the balance due on them withheld, as a compensation or
reprisal for any cause whatever, real or pretended
Each party shall be allowed to keep a commissary of
prisoners, appointed by itself, with every cantonment of prisoners, in possession of the other; which
commissary shall see the prisoners as often a he
pleases; shall be allowed to receive, exempt from all
duties a taxes, and to distribute, whatever comforts
may be sent to them by their friends; and shall be
free to transmit his reports in open letters to the
party by whom he is employed. And it is declared
that neither the pretense that war dissolves all
treaties, nor any other whatever, shall be considered
as annulling or suspending the solemn covenant
contained in this article. On the contrary, the state
of war is precisely that for which it is provided; and,
during which, its stipulations are to be as sacredly
observed as the most acknowledged obligations
under the law of nature or nations.

ARTICLE **XXIII.**—This treaty shall be ratified by the President of the United States of America, by and with the advice and consent of the Senate thereof; and by the President of the Mexican Republic, with the previous approbation of its general Congress; and the ratifications shall be exchanged in the City of Washington, or at the seat of Government of Mexico, in four months from the date of the signature hereof, or sooner if practicable. In faith whereof we, the respective Plenipotentiaries, have signed this treaty of peace, friendship, limits, and settlement, and have hereunto affixed our seals respectively. Done in quintuplicate, at the city of Guadalupe Hidalgo, on the second day of February, in the year of our Lord one thousand eight hundred and forty-eight.

> N. P. TRIST
> LUIS P. CUEVAS
> BERNARDO COUTO
> MIGL. ATRISTAIN

Appendix II

ADVICE TO MINERS

by Samuel McNeil

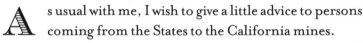

A s usual with me, I wish to give a little advice to persons coming from the States to the California mines.

Let each person have only 2 good flannel shirts, and the suit of clothes he usually wears, the gold he intends spending in a belt fastened around his body;—1 good six-shooter Colt pistol—good butcher knife instead of a bowie knife, as with the former, one can eat, but not with the latter—a good rifle. These are all the necessary articles he should have.

If a man comes through the Isthmus, with a huge trunk full of clothes and the mining implements, he is obliged to pay to $16 per 100 lbs. for their conveyance, $20 per hundred from San Francisco to Sacramento City, and $20 per hundred from Sacramento City to the mines. Then he has paid more for those articles than the prices at which they may be obtained in California.

If a trunk is stored in San Francisco or in Sacramento City, he has to pay $3 per month. I had twenty trunks stored in my possession at that price, I placed them under a tree outside the tent. People in the States may talk about conveniences, but after a person is obliged to lug a cradle, two blankets, pick, shovel, crowbar, and a week's provision, on his back, walking fifteen miles per day through the hot sun, up and down the mountains, he has no use for a trunk full of clothes and a tent.

The person who digs gold lives like the wild man, deprived of every comfort of life and society. I believe that there is enough of gold in California region to supply the world, but the difficulty in obtaining it has never been so great in any other region, and yet has it never been gathered so plentifully in the same length of time. You cannot show me any other spot on earth where a laboring man can make $16 per day by hard work [about $400 in 2005], yet I would not advise any person to come to this country.

But reader, judge for yourselves, for I have told you the truth. I am willing that any person who has worked in the mines should read my work, and, he, from personal experience, will discover that I have not varied from the truth.

Appendix III

PRESIDENT POLK'S 1848 STATE OF THE UNION ADDRESS

The President shall from time to time give to the Congress Information of the State of the Union, and recommend to their Consideration such Measures as he shall judge necessary and expedient.

—U.S. Constitution Article II, Section 3

P resident Polk's State of the Union Address in December 1848 was the one historical document that set the Gold Rush in motion by confirming for the world Marshall's discovery.

This is a considerably abridged version, highlighting the president's comments regarding the California gold. The world that Polk spoke about is also of specific note to those interested in current events of the nineteenth century.

His words echo through the centuries.

Fellow-Citizens of the Senate and of the House of Representatives:

In reviewing the great events of the past year and contrasting the agitated and disturbed state of other countries with our own tranquil and happy condition, we may congratulate ourselves that we are the most favored people on the face of the earth. While the people of other countries are struggling to establish free institutions, under which man may govern himself, we are in the actual enjoyment of them—a rich inheritance from our fathers. While enlightened nations of Europe are convulsed and distracted by civil war or intestine strife, we settle all our political controversies by the peaceful exercise of the rights of freemen at the ballot box.

I am happy to inform you that our relations with all nations are friendly and pacific. Advantageous treaties of commerce have been concluded within the last four years with New Granada, Peru, the Two Sicilies, Belgium, Hanover, Oldenburg, and Mecklenburg-Schwerin. Pursuing our example, the restrictive system of Great Britain, our principal foreign customer, has been relaxed, a more liberal commercial policy has been adopted by other enlightened nations, and our trade has been greatly enlarged and extended. Our country stands higher in the respect of the world than at any former period. To continue to occupy this proud position, it is only necessary to preserve peace and faithfully adhere to the great and fundamental principle of our foreign policy of noninterference in the domestic concerns of other nations. We recognize in all nations the right which we enjoy ourselves, to change and reform their political institutions according to their own will and pleasure. Hence we do not look behind existing governments capable of maintaining their own authority. We recognize all such actual governments, not only from the dictates of true policy, but from a sacred regard for the independence of nations.

While this is our settled policy, it does not follow that we can ever be indifferent spectators of the progress of liberal principles. The Government and people of the United States hailed with enthusiasm and delight the establishment of the French Republic, as we now hail the efforts in progress to unite the States of Germany in a confederation similar in many respects to our own Federal Union. If the great and enlightened German States, occupying, as they do, a central and commanding position in Europe, shall succeed in establishing such a confederated government, securing at the same time to the citizens of each State local governments adapted to the peculiar condition of each, with unrestricted trade and intercourse with each other, it will be an important era in the history of human events. Whilst it will consolidate and strengthen the power of Germany, it must essentially promote the cause of peace, commerce, civilization, and constitutional liberty throughout the world.

Since the exchange of ratifications of the treaty of peace with Mexico our intercourse with the Government of that Republic has been of the most friendly character. The envoy extraordinary and minister plenipotentiary of the United States to Mexico has been received and accredited, and a diplomatic representative from Mexico of similar rank has been received and accredited by this Government. The amicable relations between the two countries, which had been suspended, have been happily restored, and are destined, I trust, to be long preserved. The two Republics, both situated on this continent, and with coterminous territories, have every motive of sympathy and of interest to bind them together in perpetual amity.

It has been my constant aim and desire to cultivate peace and commerce with all nations. Tranquility at home and peaceful relations abroad constitute the true permanent policy of our country. War, the scourge of nations, sometimes becomes inevitable, but is always to be avoided when it can be done consistently with the rights and honor of a nation.

One of the most important results of the war into which we were recently forced with a neighboring nation is the demonstration it has afforded of the military strength of our country. Before the late war with Mexico European and other foreign powers entertained imperfect and erroneous views of our physical strength as a nation and of our ability to prosecute war, and especially a war waged out of out own country. They saw that our standing Army on the peace establishment did not exceed 10,000 men.

Accustomed themselves to maintain in peace large standing armies for the protection of thrones against their own subjects, as well as against foreign enemies, they had not conceived that it was possible for a nation without such an army, well disciplined and of long service, to wage war successfully. They held in low repute our militia, and were far from regarding them as an effective force, unless it might be for temporary defensive operations when invaded on our own soil. The events of the late war with Mexico have not only undeceived them, but have removed erroneous impressions which prevailed to some extent even among a portion of our own countrymen.

That war has demonstrated that upon the breaking out of hostilities not anticipated, and for which no previous preparation had been made, a volunteer army of citizen soldiers equal to veteran troops, and in numbers equal to any emergency, can in a short period be brought into the field. Unlike what would have occurred in any other country, we were under no necessity of resorting to drafts or conscriptions. On the contrary, such was the number of volunteers who patriotically tendered their services that the chief difficulty was in making selections and determining who should be disappointed and compelled to remain at home.

Our citizen soldiers are unlike those drawn from the population of any other country. They are composed indiscriminately of all professions and pursuits—of farmers, lawyers, physicians, merchants, manufacturers, mechanics, and laborers—and this not only among the officers, but the private soldiers in the ranks. Our citizen soldiers are unlike those of any other country in other respects. They are armed, and have been accustomed from their youth up to handle and use firearms, and a large proportion of them, especially in the Western and more newly settled States, are expert marksmen. They are men who have a reputation to maintain at home by their good conduct in the field. They are intelligent, and there is an individuality of character which is found in the ranks of no other army. In battle each private man, as well as every officer, rights not only for his country, but for glory and distinction among his fellow-citizens when he shall return to civil life.

The war with Mexico has demonstrated not only the ability of the Government to organize a numerous army upon a sudden call, but also to provide it with all the munitions and necessary supplies with dispatch, convenience, and ease, and to direct its operations with efficiency. The strength of our institutions has not only been displayed in the valor and skill of our troops engaged in active service in the field, but in the organization of those executive branches which were charged with the general direction and conduct of the war. While too great praise can not be bestowed upon the officers and men who fought our battles, it would be unjust to withhold from those officers necessarily stationed at home, who were charged with the duty of furnishing the Army in proper time and at proper places with all the munitions of war and other supplies so necessary to make it efficient, the commendation to which they are entitled.

The credit due to this class of our officers is the greater when it is considered that no army in ancient or modern times was even better appointed or provided than our Army in Mexico. Operating in an enemy's country, removed 2,000 miles from the seat of the Federal Government, its different corps spread over a vast extent of territory, hundreds and even thousands of miles apart from each other, nothing short of the untiring vigilance and extraordinary energy of these officers could have enabled them to provide the Army at all points and in proper season with all that was required for the most efficient service.

It is but an act of justice to declare that the officers in charge of the several executive bureaus, all under the immediate eye and supervision of the Secretary of War, performed their respective duties with ability, energy, and efficiency. They have reaped less of the glory of the war, not having been personally exposed to its perils in battle, than their companions in arms; but without their forecast, efficient aid, and cooperation those in the field would not have been provided with the ample means they possessed of achieving for themselves and their country the unfading honors which they have won for both.

The war with Mexico has developed most strikingly and conspicuously another feature in our institutions. It is that without cost to the Government or danger to our liberties we have in the bosom of our society of freemen, available in a just and necessary war, virtually a standing army of 2,000,000 armed citizen soldiers, such as fought the battles of Mexico. But our military strength does not consist alone in our capacity for extended and successful operations on land. The Navy is an important arm of the national defense. If the services of the Navy were not so brilliant as those of the Army in the late war with Mexico, it was because they had no enemy to meet on their own element. For the able and gallant services of the officers and men of the Navy, acting independently as well as in cooperation with our troops, in the conquest of the Californias, the capture of Vera Cruz, and the seizure and occupation of other important positions on the Gulf and Pacific Coasts, the highest praise is due. Their vigilance, energy, and skill rendered the most effective service in excluding munitions of war and other supplies from the enemy, while they secured a safe entrance for abundant supplies for our own Army. Our extended commerce was nowhere interrupted, and for this immunity from the evils of war the country is indebted to the Navy.

Occupying, as we do, a more commanding position among nations than at any former period, our duties and our responsibilities to ourselves and to posterity are correspondingly increased. This will be the more obvious when we consider the vast additions which have been recently made to our territorial possessions and their great importance and value.

Within less than four years the annexation of Texas to the Union has been consummated; all conflicting title to the Oregon Territory south of the forty-ninth degree of north latitude, being all that was insisted on by any of my predecessors, has been adjusted, and New Mexico and Upper California have been acquired by treaty. The area of these several Territories, according to a report carefully prepared by the Commissioner of the General Land

Office from the most authentic information in his possession, and which is herewith transmitted, contains 1,193,061 square miles, or 763,559,040 acres; while the area of the remaining twenty-nine States and the territory not yet organized into States east of the Rocky Mountains contains 2,059,513 square miles, or 1,318,126,058 acres. These estimates show that the territories recently acquired, and over which our exclusive jurisdiction and dominion have been extended, constitute a country more than half as large as all that which was held by the United States before their acquisition. If Oregon be excluded from the estimate, there will still remain within the limits of Texas, New Mexico, and California 851,598 square miles, or 545,012,720 acres, being an addition equal to more than one-third of all the territory owned by the United States before their acquisition, and, including Oregon, nearly as great an extent of territory as the whole of Europe, Russia only excepted.

The Mississippi, so lately the frontier of our country, is now only its center. With the addition of the late acquisitions, the United States are now estimated to be nearly as large as the whole of Europe.

It would be difficult to calculate the value of these immense additions to our territorial possessions. Texas, lying contiguous to the western boundary of Louisiana, embracing within its limits a part of the navigable tributary waters of the Mississippi and an extensive seacoast, could not long have remained in the hands of a foreign power without endangering the peace of our southwestern frontier. Her products in the vicinity of the tributaries of the

Mississippi must have sought a market through these streams, running into and through our territory, and the danger of irritation and collision of interests between Texas as a foreign state and ourselves would have been imminent, while the embarrassments in the commercial intercourse between them must have been constant and unavoidable.

New Mexico, though situated in the interior and without a seacoast, is known to contain much fertile land, to abound in rich mines of the precious metals, and to be capable of sustaining a large population. From its position it is the intermediate and connecting territory between our settlements and our possessions in Texas and those on the Pacific Coast.

Upper California, irrespective of the vast mineral wealth recently developed there, holds at this day, in point of value and importance, to the rest of the Union the same relation that Louisiana did when that fine territory was acquired from France forty-five years ago. Extending nearly ten degrees of latitude along the Pacific, and embracing the only safe and commodious harbors on that coast for many hundred miles, with a temperate climate and an extensive interior of fertile lands, it is scarcely possible to estimate its wealth until it shall be brought under the government of our laws and its resources fully developed. From its position it must command the rich commerce of China, of Asia, of the islands of the Pacific, of western Mexico, of Central America, the South American States, and of the Russian possessions bordering on that ocean. A great emporium will doubtless speedily arise on the Californian coast which may be destined to rival in importance New Orleans itself. The depot of the vast commerce which must exist on the Pacific will probably be at some point on the Bay of San Francisco, and will occupy the same relation to the whole western coast of that ocean as New Orleans does to the valley of the Mississippi and the Gulf of Mexico.

To this depot our numerous whale ships will resort with their cargoes to trade, refit, and obtain supplies. This of itself will largely contribute to build up a city, which would soon become the center of a great and rapidly increasing commerce. Situated on a safe harbor, sufficiently capacious for all the navies as well as the marine of the world, and convenient to excellent timber for shipbuilding, owned by the United States, it must become our great Western naval depot.

It was known that mines of the precious metals existed to a considerable extent in California at the time of its acquisition. Recent discoveries render it probable that these mines are more extensive and valuable than was anticipated. The accounts of the abundance of gold in that territory are of such an extraordinary character as would scarcely command belief were they not corroborated by the authentic reports of officers in the public service who have visited the mineral district and derived the facts which they detail from personal observation.

Reluctant to credit the reports in general circulation as to the quantity of gold, the officer commanding our forces in California visited the mineral district in July last for the purpose of obtaining accurate information on the subject. His report to the War Department of the result of his examination and the facts obtained on the spot is herewith laid before Congress.

When he visited the country there were about 4,000 persons engaged in collecting gold. There is every reason to believe that the number of persons so employed has since been augmented. The explorations already made warrant the belief that the supply is very large and that gold is found at various places in an extensive district of country.

Information received from officers of the Navy and other sources, though not so full and minute, confirms the accounts of the commander of our military force in California. It appears also from these reports that mines of quicksilver are found in the vicinity of the gold region. One of them is now being worked, and is believed to be among the most productive in the world.

The effects produced by the discovery of these rich mineral deposits and the success which has attended the labors of those who have resorted to them have produced a surprising change in the state of affairs in California. Labor commands a most exorbitant price, and all other pursuits but that of searching for the precious metals are abandoned. Nearly the whole of the male population of the country have gone to the gold districts. Ships arriving on the coast are deserted by their crews and their voyages suspended for want of sailors. Our commanding officer there entertains apprehensions that soldiers can not be kept in the public service without a large increase of pay. Desertions in his command have become frequent, and he recommends that those who shall withstand the strong temptation and remain faithful should be rewarded.

This abundance of gold and the all-engrossing pursuit of it have already caused in California an unprecedented rise in the price of all the necessaries of life. That we may the more speedily and fully avail ourselves of the undeveloped wealth of these mines, it is deemed of vast importance that a branch of the Mint of the United States be authorized to be established at your present session in California.

Among other signal advantages which would result from such an establishment would be that of raising the gold to its par value in that territory. A branch mint of the United States at the great commercial depot on the West Coast would convert into our own coin not only the gold derived from our own rich mines, but also the bullion and specie which our commerce may bring from the whole west coast of Central and South America.

The West Coast of America and the adjacent interior embrace the richest and best mines of Mexico, New Granada, Central America, Chili, and Peru. The bullion and specie drawn from these countries, and especially from those of western Mexico and Peru, to an amount in value of many millions of dollars, are now annually diverted and carried by the ships of Great Britain to her own ports, to be recoined or used to sustain her national bank, and thus contribute to increase her ability to command so much of the commerce of the world.

If a branch mint be established at the great commercial point upon that coast, a vast amount of bullion and specie would flow thither to be recoined, and pass thence to New Orleans, New York, and other Atlantic cities. The amount of our constitutional currency at home would be greatly increased, while its circulation abroad would be promoted. It is well known to our merchants trading to China and the West Coast of America that great inconvenience and loss are experienced from the fact that our coins are not current at their par value in those countries.

The powers of Europe, far removed from the West Coast of America by the Atlantic Ocean, which inter- venes, and by a tedious and dangerous navigation around the southern cape of the continent of America, can never successfully compete with the United States in the rich and extensive commerce which is opened to us at so much less cost by the acquisition of California.

The vast importance and commercial advantages of California have heretofore remained undeveloped by the Government of the country of which it constituted a part. Now that this fine province is a part of our country, all the States of the Union, some more immediately and directly than others, are deeply interested in the speedy development of its wealth and resources. No section of our country is more interested or will be more benefited than the commercial, navigating, and manufacturing interests of the Eastern States. Our planting and farming interests in every part of the Union will Be greatly benefited by it. As our commerce and navigation are enlarged and extended, our exports of agricultural products and of manufactures will be increased, and in the new markets thus opened they can not fail to command remunerating and profitable prices.

Invoking the blessings of the Almighty upon your deliberations at your present important session, my ardent hope is that in a spirit of harmony and concord you may be guided to wise results, and such as may redound to the happiness, the honor, and the glory of our beloved country.

BIBLIOGRAPHY

Bell, Horace. *Reminiscences of a ranger; or, Early times in Southern California*. California: Yarnell, Caystile, & Mathes, 1881.

Connell, S. Evan. *Son of the Morning Star*. San Francisco: North Point Press, 1984.

Delano, Alonzo. *Life on the Plains and among the diggings; being scenes and adventures of an overland journey to California: with particular incidents of the route, mistakes and sufferings of the emigrants, the Indian tribes, the present and future of the great West*. New York: Miller, Orton, 1857.

Hansen, Ron. *The Assassination of Jesse James by the Coward Robert Ford*. New York: Ballantine Books, 1983.

Hobson, Jay. *The Hobson Family Lineage*. North Carolina: Ohio: Lofthouse, 1994.

Koeppel, Elliot H. *The California Gold Country: Highway 49 Revisited*. California: Malakoff, 1999.

Lake, Stuart. *Wyatt Earp: Frontier Marshal*. Boston: Houghton Mifflin, 1931.

McNeil, Samuel. *McNeil's travels in 1849, to, through and from the gold regions, in California*. Columbus, Ohio: Scott & Bascom, 1850.

Simpson, Henry. *The Emigrant's Guide to the Gold Mines*. United Kingdom: Headframe, 1848.

Stiles, T. J. *Jesse James: Last Rebel of the Civil War*. New York: Alfred A. Knopf, 2002.

INDEX

Acapulco route to California, 97, 99
Act for the Government and Protection of
    the Indians (1850), 204, 205
agriculture in Southern California, 29–30
Alaska, 9, 247–48
Alcaldes, 85
"All the Gold in California" (Gatlin), 257
Alta California (newspaper), 178–79
Alvarado, Juan, 9
American Dream, 249
American Fur Co., 5
American History (Muzzey), 17
American Indians. *See* Native Americans
American River (California)
    Larkin's description of, 79–83
    mining camps on, 150–51
    panning for gold, 74–77
    state park at sawmill site, 257–59
    Sutter's sawmill, 31–37, 38, 65,
        68–69, 257–58
Americans. *See also* racism and class dis-
        tinctions
    get rich quick attitude, 224–25, 240,
        247, 248
    post-gold rush character, 224
    pre-gold rush character, 73, 106–7
    pursuit of wealth en masse, 106, 107–8
Andersen, "Bloody Bill," 219
Anderson, Samuel, 160
Appotomax Courthouse, VA, 232
Arabian Nights, California compared to, 101
Arizona, 245–47
Armour, John, 108
arson in San Francisco, 175

Baden, Germany, 3
Baja Peninsula, 42–43
Baton Rouge, LA, 122
Battle of Fallen Timbers (1794), xxii
Battle of the Little Big Horn, 242
the Bear Flag Revolt, 20
Bell, Horace, 194–99, 199–200, 201–2
Bennet (Sutter's messenger to Mason), 62,
    63, 65
Bigler, Henry W., 38–39, 40, 58–60

Bigler, John W., 201
Black Hills gold rush
    Americans' excuse for breaking treaty,
        235–36
    Custer and, 238–39, 242
    Deadwood camp, 240
    Homestake mine, 241, 243
    Treaty of 1868 with Sioux, 234
Bodie, Cheyenne, 211
Book of Mormon (Smith), 52
Booth, John Wilkes, 232–33
Bowie knife vs. butcher knife, 291
Brannan, Sam, 65, 89–90
Brazos, TX, 125–26
Breen, Patrick, 28
Britain, 102–4, 108–9, 170–71, 175–76, 294
Brundage, E. F., 212, 213
Buchanan, James, 72
bullfight in Mexico, 138–39
Burnett, Peter H., 208
butcher knife vs. Bowie knife, 291

California. *See also* crime in California; *spe-
        cific cities*
    antislavery stand of, 188, 189
    the Bear Flag Revolt, 20
    Mexican American War, 18–19, 20–21,
        29–31
    Polk's State of the Union speech
        about, 105–6, 207, 303–7
    racism in, 189–91, 191–94
    slavery of Indians, 203–5
    state courts, Chinese and, 190
    statehood, 43, 172
    tourist attractions, 256
"The California Emigrant's Song, 249–52
California Gold Rush. *See also entries beginning
        with "gold"*
    American Indians and, 203–5
    beginning of, 112–13
    crime rate, 148–49, 169–71, 173–76
    effect of deaths during, 221
    effect on Indians, 138
    as hope for family's future, 107, 111,
        118–19